"I wish we had a book like this 30 years ago... Our generation of game writers and developers (whose sanity barely survived the late 80's thru early 90's) had to learn to do it on our own - on the fly - no drivers' manual or safety net. So how amazing is it to find this wealth of practical knowledge, proven experience and genuine inspiration for upcoming game writers today? Very clearly, Brian and Diandra have poured their passion, creativity and many, many experiences into this book. You wanna write games? Good. Start here." - **Chris Metzen**, Executive Creative Director, *Warcraft*

"*The Definitive Game Narrative Guide offers* clear insight to what's needed to succeed as a writer in the game industry. It's a quest giver that can prep you for the adventures ahead!" - **James Waugh**, Senior Vice President Franchise Story and Creative Strategy, *Lucasfilm*

"*The Definitive Game Narrative Guide* is an invaluable guide to the fundamental building blocks of storytelling in games. A must read for any writer interested in a career in the video game industry." - **Drew Karpyshyn**, lead writer: *Star Wars: Knights of the Old Republic, Mass Effect, Mass Effect 2*. Narrative director: *Exodus*

W0018499

The Definitive Game Narrative Guide

The Definitive Game Narrative Guide is the ultimate start and end point for storytelling in video games. Whether you're an aspiring writer or a seasoned game developer, this book offers an in-depth, comprehensive look at the entire narrative process.

Written by two industry veterans with experience across some of the biggest AAA franchises, this guide covers the basics to the advanced, including the "why" for each topic as much as the "how."

This book explores the nuances of world building, character development, interactive storytelling, and the technical challenges unique to game narrative. With real-world examples, practical insights, and expert advice, it provides a look into how game stories come together, from the smallest indie project to massive AAA teams.

The Definitive Game Narrative Guide is more than a how-to book, as it also serves as an industry insider's perspective on what makes game storytelling truly great. It discusses techniques to navigate the creative workplace, working as a creative, and most importantly, collaborating with other creatives and disciplines, such as art and design.

An essential tool for anyone looking to level up their understanding of game narrative. This book will help you bring unforgettable stories to life in an interactive form.

Brian Kindregan is a veteran of BioWare, Blizzard, Epic Games, Ubisoft, NetEase, and Tencent. Brian has been a creative director, a narrative director, a lead writer, and a senior writer. In a previous life, he was a storyboard artist and animator in the film business and directed two seasons of a CG television series. He's also taught at a number of universities and lectured on game narrative at Harvard's Graduate School of Design. You can find him on Substack at @briankindregan.

Diandra Anne Lasrado is a veteran of BioWare, Blizzard, Riot Games, Carbine, Activision, Aniplex, and more. Diandra has been a lead narrative designer, senior narrative designer, and senior editor. She's worked on *World of Warcraft*, *League of Legends*, *Wildstar*, *Diablo*, and more. She has mentored a number of young developers and lectured at Harvard's Graduate School of Design. You can find her on BlueSky at @mesaanasedai and Substack at @mesaanasedai.

The Definitive Game Narrative Guide

Brian Kindregan and
Diandra Anne Lasrado

CRC Press
Taylor & Francis Group
Boca Raton London New York

CRC Press is an imprint of the
Taylor & Francis Group, an **informa** business

Designed cover image: Ellen Jin

First edition published 2026
by CRC Press
2385 NW Executive Center Drive, Suite 320, Boca Raton FL 33431

and by CRC Press
4 Park Square, Milton Park, Abingdon, Oxon, OX14 4RN

CRC Press is an imprint of Taylor & Francis Group, LLC

© 2026 Brian Kindregan and Diandra Anne Lasrado

ISBN: 9781041036913 (hbk)
ISBN: 9781041036890 (pbk)
ISBN: 9781003624882 (ebk)

DOI: 10.1201/9781003624882

Typeset in Times
by codeMantra

Contents

SECTION 1   Storytelling

SECTION 2   Game Storytelling

SECTION 3   *Characters*

SECTION 4 Dialogue and Voice Over

SECTION 5   Cutscenes

SECTION 6   Intellectual Property

SECTION 7   Game Narrative Professional

Foreword

Congratulations, you've just bought a ticket for the express to the heart of game writing.

What you are about to read is a pure shot of the good stuff. It's deeply comprehensive, amazingly accessible, and brilliantly actionable. If you've ever had a question about how to tackle any sort of game writing task, you'll find the answer in these pages. It's honest, it's sharp, and it's 100% accurate. This is a book that gets straight to the point and gives you everything you need to do good work in that craziest of writing media, video games.

Diandra and Brian have been through the wars. They've been asked to do damn near anything imaginable as it relates to game writing over the years, and they've done it with style, skill, and grace that we lesser mortals can only envy. The fact that they finally took the time to distill their experience down to its essence, in a way that's welcoming and immediately useful, is a gift to everyone who ever even dreamed of writing for games. There is a vast body of knowledge out there about game writing that has accumulated over the decades, but what they have managed to do is boil it down to the utter truths and present them to you.

In a way, I envy you the journey of discovery ahead of you. You're getting the good stuff that took so many of the rest of us so long—and so many missteps—to discover; you're getting it wonderfully written; and you're getting it all in one place. This is the book I wish I'd had when I was starting out on my game writing journey. May it be the guiding light for yours.

—Richard Dansky, Game Writer, Designer, and Narrative Director

Acknowledgments

We'd like to acknowledge the invaluable help, encouragement, and feedback of Drew Karpyshyn, James Waugh, Chris Metzen, and Richard Dansky. We'd like to express our special thanks to Ellen Jin, whose artistic brilliance took our half-baked idea and made it beautiful; Jess Cheng, for her invaluable aid with graphics; and Eric Elliot, for moving heaven and earth to let us use Blizzard images. We would also like to acknowledge Cassandra Khaw and Alyssa Wong, both tireless storytellers who have inspired and helped us greatly. Finally, this book would not have been possible without the support of the game narrative community.

Skip This Introduction

How-to Books are often packed full of fluff. This book is pretty long, but we have tried to only focus on what is necessary.

It's aimed at people in different stages of their career, so some parts may not be relevant to you right now. But many parts should be! Feel free to skip and skim to find what you need.

This book is structured to build on earlier sections, so reading all of it may be useful. But you get to decide that.

So, why are you still reading this introduction? Let's talk about writing!

WHO ARE WE?

When it comes to game narrative, there are a lot of genuine pros, some self-appointed experts, and a few grifters too. Just because we've published a book doesn't mean we know what we're talking about. You may have some questions!

If you want to get to the game narrative stuff, skip ahead. But if you're wondering, "Who the heck are you, and why should I listen to you?" then this section will answer your questions.

BRIAN KINDREGAN

Growing up, I knew that I would do something involving storytelling and drawing. I got my first shot at that in high school, when I discovered that there was a claymation animation studio in Boston called "Olive Jar." I thought animation was something that happened far away in sunny California, so I jumped at the chance to work in claymation. I interned at Olive Jar for a while, which just meant showing up after school and working for free for a few hours. But it was a great experience, as I got to work on a video for the band Dokken, and several interstitials for ABC that played on their Saturday morning cartoon lineup for decades. If you're of a certain age, you grew up seeing them over and over.

I majored in Character Animation at California Institute of the Arts. I'd become interested in animation because I wanted to be a storyboard artist, combining my loves of storytelling and drawing. After graduation, I worked as a cleanup artist, an animator, and eventually got my break as a storyboard artist.

I was probably the worst artist on any given team I was on, but my main focus was trying to convey my ideas for story and character through drawing. Over the years I storyboarded on animated movies like *Space Jam* and *The Iron Giant*, live action movies like *Chasing Liberty*, and television shows like *Johnny Bravo* and *The Grim Adventures of Billy & Mandy*. In 2001, I storyboarded and did character

DOI: 10.1201/9781003624882-1

design on a short at Sony Imageworks called *The Chubb Chubbs!*, which went on to win the Oscar for best animated short.

I'd always played video games, starting on my dad's monochrome IBM PC, playing Infocom text adventures. During my years in film, I converted to Mac, and was only able to play the titles ported to that platform, so I played a lot of Blizzard, BioWare, and MicroProse games. In retrospect, it makes sense that I'd go on to work for two of those three companies.

In the early 2000s, I was disenchanted with film and storyboard work, and saw that BioWare was looking for writers. I'd loved *Baldur's Gate 1 & 2*, and jumped at the chance to work for them. It required creating a mod in *Neverwinter Nights*, which meant going out and buying a PC, as NWN was not available on MAC at the time.

I dove into the mod, and fell in love with interactive storytelling. It wasn't just a chance to write and tell stories. When I realized I could script interactions through artificial intelligence (AI), and make changes in the world based on the player's actions, a light bulb went off over my head, which still shines to this day.

At BioWare I wrote on *Jade Empire*, and loved it. The film industry briefly sucked me back down to LA to direct two seasons of an animated show *The Zula Patrol*. But after a few years, BioWare released a new game called *Mass Effect*. The lead writer, Drew Karpyshyn, asked me to return to work on the sequel, and I happily obliged. Leaving games for film had been a mistake, and this was my chance to fix it.

I wrote on *Mass Effect 2*, and toward the end of that game, I wanted to return to southern California, but to stay in the games industry. I was lucky to find a senior writer role at Blizzard Entertainment, on *StarCraft 2: Wings of Liberty*.

A few months into that job, they made me lead writer. I went on to lead the writing on *StarCraft II: Heart of the Swarm*. When that shipped, I jumped over to the *Diablo III* team. They had just shipped their base game, and were starting up on the first expansion. They needed someone to lead the writing, so I came over for *Reaper of Souls*.

After that, I moved on to Epic games as narrative director on *Paragon* and *Robo Recall*. Then I went to Ubisoft to work on an unannounced open world game, which was sadly canceled, but would have been awesome. After Ubisoft, I joined NetEase as Creative Director, and shipped *Naraka: Bladepoint*, also working on *FragPunk*. Finally, I went to Tencent as Creative Director, on an unannounced multiplayer game.

What I Know about Game Narrative

I've had a wide range of experiences, good and bad. I've worked on big hits and canceled titles. On teams with healthy cultures, and teams with toxic cultures. I've made a lot of mistakes, and even occasionally gotten a thing or two right.

Diandra and I share a goal with this book of helping get everyone off to a solid start, creating a strong foundation, and maybe even helping you avoid some of the worst mistakes.

Diandra Anne Lasrado

When I was young I had no idea what I really wanted to do when I "grew up." I had a wide range of interests from the sciences to the arts. In high school I thought about going into genetic engineering as a way to help humanity, but as I worked toward that goal I realized I had no deep passion for it. The thing I had loved the most at the time was working in the library of the town I grew up in, and honestly that's all that I thought I would do. It wasn't until I met Brian playing *City of Heroes* and we went on an adventure that took us across the world that I was able to take a moment and analyze what I truly loved about the library, and come to the realization that it was the unlimited access to stories and knowledge.

I had always loved video games, but growing up in my small town, the idea of working for a game studio seemed like something out of a fairy tale. But traveling across the world to live in an unfamiliar country gives you a new perspective, and suddenly when the opportunity for a position at BioWare arose, it seemed that maybe SOME fairy tales could come true.

Though I started off as Technical Editor, my jobs across the industry have ranged from Localization Editor, Marketing Writer, Localization Manager, Narrative Designer, and Lead Narrative Designer. My love of the industry and the discipline of storytelling inspired me to always take on new and interesting positions that supported writing in every aspect. I've worked all across the industry, not only at BioWare but at Riot Games, Snail Games, Carbine Games, Aniplex of America, Blizzard Entertainment, and Crystal Dynamics.

The multiple layers that go into storytelling have always been my passion, especially those that reach wide audiences.

What I Know about Game Narrative

Having worked on games for nearly two decades with a sharp focus on anything narrative or narrative adjacent, I have experience looking at game story through the lens of the wider goal of the game itself.

Sometimes you have to find the little things that add meaning and texture to your world if you're working on a game that does not have a dedicated story. Narrative supports everything and everything supports narrative, which is what we are trying to show in this book.

Brian and I believe that going back to basics is what keeps you strong as a storyteller. So if you are just starting out or have been in it awhile, we believe there is something for everyone here.

WHY WE WROTE THIS BOOK

Game narrative is still a new artform, and a powerful one. There are many more questions than answers out there. It's time for game narrative to develop a consensus and canon of best practices. There is probably no single work that will do that. Rather, it requires a number of seminal or influential works. We have the humility to know our book can't do that by itself, but the cockiness to think that our book can be one of those works.

We've learned many lessons, usually the hard way, and this book is meant to pass those lessons along to you, minus all the pain and humiliation that we went through to learn them.

You may find over time that you disagree with some of our points, and that's perfectly okay, but everything here serves as a strong basis for developing yourself and your career as a game narrative professional.

SECTIONS

The Definitive Game Narrative Guide is broken down into seven sections. Narrative is a big, unwieldy topic that flows into every part of game development, and lots of other topics as well. So any attempt to impose a structure will have some weird bits.

But we're pretty happy with how this worked out!

SECTION 1: STORYTELLING

This section presents a review of the basics for storytelling in general, in order to establish a foundation that we can use to talk about narrative in games. It is not as deep or comprehensive as other volumes that deal solely with storytelling in general, but will give us a good baseline to build on.

SECTION 2: GAME STORYTELLING

Building off our discussion of the foundations of storytelling, we move into storytelling in games specifically.

SECTION 3: CHARACTERS

Once we have a handle on storytelling in games, it's time to discuss the most important aspect of any storytelling: Characters. This section comes later in this book because it builds on what has come before.

SECTION 4: DIALOGUE AND VOICE OVER

Writing dialogue for Voice Over, and shepherding your writing through the VO process, are two of the most important and ubiquitous tasks a game narrative professional engages in during the early and middle parts of their career. It truly pays off to understand this stuff.

SECTION 5: CUTSCENES

Cutscenes seem like a small part of a game's overall narrative, yet they are a huge topic because they are used as marketing, are often the player's first look at the game, characters, and narrative, and are the most expensive narrative asset produced for the game.

Section 6: Intellectual Property

Making a story that can become an Intellectual Property is one of the most important parts of game narrative. Having a cohesive universe that can spawn an array of stories means that you have made something that can touch multiple generations over the years.

Section 7: Game Narrative Professional

The final section is about being a game narrative professional. Perhaps the most unique part of being a storyteller in games is that you work as part of a team, whether you are Indie or AAA. That changes how you tell stories. This section covers the collaborative nature of a game narrative person. It also touches on a subject aimed more at beginners and students: being a professional in a creative field.

SIDEBAR: THE RIGHT WAY TO USE A HOW-TO BOOK

There are a few places in this book where we grapple with the raw, intuitive · side of creativity. In most places, however, we focus on a more analytical approach, establishing rules that work, giving examples and use cases, and adding context on why.

This is true of most or all how-to books, podcasts, video streaming channels, and university classes. There's a great reason for this: rules, context, exceptions, and analyses can all be conveyed in a linear, straightforward fashion. Most importantly, in an objective fashion.

The raw, disordered creative process that we all start with defies easy analysis, or even summary. A lot of it has to do with you—what's important to you? What do you think about when your mind is adrift? When you overhear people talking, what do you notice? How do you process feelings—your own and those of other people? We do elaborate on some ways to harness those questions in a few places, but it makes for some pretty unsatisfying reading.

The straightforward analysis of rules and paradigms, on the other hand, is something you can take notes about, and apply to your work two minutes later.

But you should always keep two things in mind: first, the analytical stuff is most useful for revising your work, for identifying and fixing problems you can't quite put your finger on, for explaining what you're trying to do to teammates, and for hewing your work closely to the standards of a project. And second, you should always start with the more subjective, less structured side of things: your own thoughts and feelings.

This book can be immensely valuable to you, if you keep those two points in mind.

Section 1

Storytelling

A review of the basics for storytelling in general, in order to establish a foundation that we can use to talk about narrative in games. It is not as deep or comprehensive as other volumes that deal solely with storytelling, but will give us a good baseline to build on.

DOI: 10.1201/9781003624882-2

1 The Basics

IN THIS CHAPTER

- Introduce the building blocks of story
- Talk about what makes an interesting story
- Learn how to resolve a story

There are countless volumes dealing with the philosophies of storytelling, principles, values, best practices, genres, media, tips and tricks, and more. We're focused on game narrative, but it is worthwhile to touch on some basics. However, we will not be able to do a deep dive when the topic is so vast.

Narrative in games gives the player context, adding meaning and dimension to actions that the player takes. However, helping the player make sense of the game experience is not all that narrative is or does. It's merely the basic requirement.

Narrative is so much more.

We would recommend seeking out prominent works that deal with the basic philosophy of storytelling. For more practical, hands-on works, screenplay writing offers many interesting options because screenplays are constrained by many outside factors, and so "how to" books on the subject tend to be more mechanical. In this way, they are similar to game narrative.

BREAKDOWN OF THE BASICS

The basic elements of a narrative go something like this:

An interesting and sympathetic character(s) has a compelling problem. Their efforts to solve the problem bring them into conflict with another character or faction. In the end, the problem is resolved or definitively unresolved.

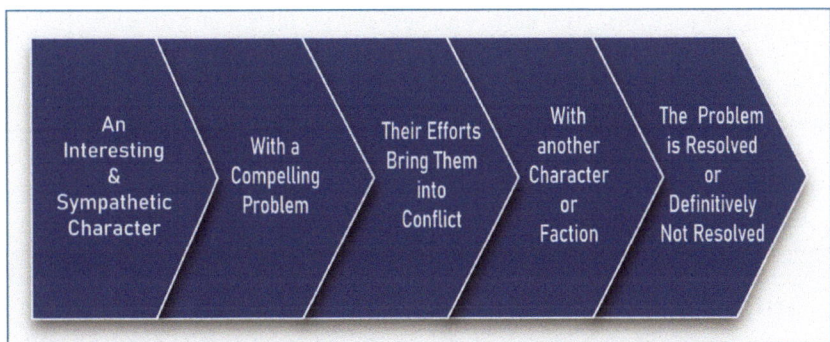

DOI: 10.1201/9781003624882-3

INTERESTING AND SYMPATHETIC CHARACTER(S)

We want to watch interesting characters and know more about them. However, this does not mean we must like them. We can be intensely interested in characters we despise. The only important thing is that these characters have some quality that makes us want to watch.

When we say a character is sympathetic, this does not mean they must be likable. By "sympathetic" we mean that we can in some way identify with them. There is some quality to the character and their problems that we recognize. That's it.

EXAMPLES: SYMPATHETIC AND UNSYMPATHETIC

AN UNSYMPATHETIC EXAMPLE

In the television show *The Good Place*, the demon Shawn is an unlikable and unsympathetic character. He enjoys torturing humans and punishing his own subordinates. He is petty, spiteful, childish, and a liar. There is nothing redeeming about him—but to be sympathetic, a character does not need to be redeemable. They simply need some quality or something in their backstory that we can connect to. But Shawn has no such quality or backstory.

It's impossible to see inside him, so we only look at him from the outside.

In a normal scenario, this would make a thin, uninteresting villain. In the case of Shawn, it is by design, since he is meant to look like the villain of the story, but we soon realize that he is not, he's just a pawn in a broken system. The writers of *The Good Place* knew what they were doing by making him this way.

But in general, you would not want a character who is important to your story to be so shallow.

A SYMPATHETIC EXAMPLE

In *Warcraft 3: Reign of Chaos*, Crown Prince Arthas encounters a plague that turns humans into undead. He decides to purge the town of Stratholme, killing all residents, even those who have not yet turned into undead.

Everyone around him warns him not to do this: he should look for another way, and not jump straight to massacring civilians. But he charges ahead and does it anyway.

Arthas is not a likable character. At least, we hope you're not in favor of massacring innocent civilians. But he is a sympathetic one, in that he had to make a hard choice, and he made the one he thought was right. That does not excuse his decision, but it means that we look at him and wonder what we would do in his shoes. Or we remember a time we had to make a hard decision, and we chose poorly.

That moment, where you put yourself in a character's shoes, or relate a character's situation to one in your own past, makes a character sympathetic. We can hate them, or distrust them, or want to defeat them, but we still have some kind of connection to them.

This is what we mean by sympathetic.

A COMPELLING PROBLEM

We are immediately drawn to a character with a problem. How will they solve it? Can they solve it? What happens if they don't? The character can have the problem when we meet them, or we can be with them when they encounter the problem.

- A woman who has just been fired and doesn't know how she'll feed her family.
- A man who picked up a suitcase in the park and is now being chased by homicidal criminals.
- A starship captain whose ship was ambushed and badly damaged, is trying to hold her command together long enough to escape her pursuers.
- A sorcerer who must hold back the forces of evil, but whose brother has been kidnapped by those same forces.
- A starving mouse who can see a nice piece of cheese—but it's resting near the mouth of a sleeping cat.

These are problems great and small, with all kinds of characters, but when we hear about them, some part of our mind engages and asks "What happens next? What will they do?"

THEIR EFFORTS TO SOLVE THEIR PROBLEM GENERATES CONFLICT WITH ANOTHER CHARACTER OR FACTION

This other character is the antagonist. In this context, "another character" can mean a wide variety of entities.

The conflict can be with an institution—a lone environmentalist tries to stop a big oil company from drilling in the fields of his hometown.

It can be a philosophy or mindset—a rebel tries to rouse her people by fighting the "what can you do?" mentality that keeps them lethargic.

It can be nature—taming an area so your family can settle there.

It can even be inside the character themselves—fighting their own baser instincts.

The conflict in question can be symmetrical: the man with the suitcase wants to live, and the homicidal criminals chasing him want to kill him. Or it can be asymmetrical: the sorcerer wants to rescue her brother from the evil forces, and the evil forces want to rule the world. But their different motivations put them in opposition.

The antagonist is any entity or force that can be named and can in some way "fight back" against our protagonist. Usually, it is another living character. Either way, our interesting, sympathetic character has a compelling problem that brings them into conflict with another character/faction/force. When they take steps to solve their compelling problem, the other character takes countersteps that foil their plan, and changes the story.

Our starving mouse tries to quietly steal the cheese—but the cat wakes up and bats the cheese away. Now our mouse still does not have the cheese, and the problem has changed—now the mouse must survive/escape/outwit the cat. And it would be great if he could still grab the cheese along the way!

As the protagonist takes steps to solve the problem, the antagonist takes countersteps, causing the protagonist to take new steps, which causes the antagonist to take new countersteps. This is the essence of conflict.

Ideally, each new set of steps and countersteps should escalate the tension/pace/stakes, and overall feel of the situation.

The new steps and new countersteps will not necessarily be a straight line—i.e., sometimes a character, whether protagonist or antagonist, may set out in a new direction, or try something strange, different, or at least not obvious. The further along the conflict goes, the more likely this is.

SIDEBAR: PRO AND ANTAGONISTS

The words protagonist and antagonist are ubiquitous in story discussions, and most of us know basic meanings: "The hero and villain!" That's not quite accurate, but close enough for most situations.

A closer way to frame it would be that the protagonist is the main — character, while the antagonist is the character opposed to the protagonist. As we've seen in American prestige TV over the last few decades, the main character doesn't have to be "the hero." Walter White from *Breaking Bad* and Tony Soprano from the *Sopranos* are both point-of-view characters who drive the story forward, initiating action and responding to conflict. This makes them both "the main character," but both are the villain—or one among many villains—in their story.

Are they antiheroes? Not quite, as an antihero is atypical of established heroic qualities or traits. They may be unpredictable, mercurial, and morally gray, but they are not the villain, and fulfill the role of hero, even if they don't embody it. An easy example is Deadpool.

If the protagonist drives the story forward, but does not have to be the hero or antihero, then we can just describe them as the main character. This usually involves being the point-of-view character as well. When the feds are closing in on Tony Soprano, we have an instinctive desire for him to escape, even though the feds are the morally superior characters. This is because we see the world through Tony's eyes.

The most important thing about the terms protagonist and antagonist is that together, they indicate the basics we're discussing in this chapter.

"Prot" indicates the first or primary. "Ist" indicates an individual associated with a particular role. And "agon" is an ancient Greek word meaning "contest" or "competition." So the protagonist is the main character in the contest or conflict. "Ant" means against. So the antagonist is a character who is against the main character in the contest.

That's our interesting or sympathetic character, "pro" and "ist," with a compelling problem, which brings them into conflict "agon," with another character or faction "ant" and "ist."

The basics of storytelling are right there in the words!

UNTIL THE SITUATION IS RESOLVED OR DEFINITIVELY UNRESOLVED

The initial problem our protagonist faced may grow into a new problem. As their world gets bigger and their experiences get deeper, the initial problem they had may no longer be that important. If they do develop a new problem with greater stakes and greater risk, it will be thematically tied to their original problem.

EXAMPLE

In *Horizon Zero Dawn*, the protagonist Aloy sets out to find the cultists who attacked her tribe, with an implicit goal of exploring the wider world. But she quickly discovers that she was targeted by the cultists due to her resemblance to an ancient, important figure. This puts her on the trail of new and bigger goals which quickly absorb the original one. The original goal is still present, but now it's part of a larger context.

It is also possible that the initial problem remains as the central focus, and each new development is a further setback to block the protagonist from achieving that goal.

EXAMPLE

In the 2018 game *God of War*, Kratos and Atreus set out to scatter Faye's ashes from the highest peak in the nine realms. A rich, deep story follows, but that goal remains the same throughout. Every challenge and setback is another obstacle to the problem of reaching the highest peak in order to scatter the ashes. Everything that happens fits within the context of that original goal. In this example, we're using the word goal, but it is the same idea as a problem. You could say, "the problem is that Faye's dying wish was to have her ashes scattered from the highest peak, and Kratos wishes to honor that goal, but he is not currently on the highest peak." That would be a clunky way to describe it, but the concept is the same.

Whatever problem the protagonist has—whether the initial one, or a larger, "ultimate" one—it must be resolved in some way. Typically, the protagonist solves their problem—saves the kingdom, defeats the monster, rekindles their marriage, finds meaning for their life, and gets admitted to the school of their choice.

But they can also fail to solve their problem—so long as they fail definitively, in such a way that we know the resolution: this problem will never be solved. Perhaps the protagonist is killed, or their spouse leaves them, or the kingdom is lost. Even if the protagonist failed, the problem is resolved—it is no longer a problem. Now it is just reality.

A story with no resolution can be interesting and well crafted. But most people seek some sort of resolution to the matter at hand. Audiences are smarter than most people give them credit for, and are entirely willing to accept non-traditional outcomes, such as an ambiguous resolution. But no resolution at all does not resonate with most people. If there is no resolution, no sense that things drew to a close in some way—why bother with the whole endeavor?

GOOD ENDINGS

One phrase used to describe well-crafted endings is "surprising and inevitable." That is to say, you did not see it coming, or perhaps just the manner in which it plays out—but once it happens, it seems like the only way it could have happened.

One way in which a resolution can be meaningful and surprising is that it resolves the real problem, not the one that the audience assumed mattered. As this real problem emerges, or even as it gets solved, the audience realizes that this was what the story was really about all along.

EXAMPLE

The 1970s film *Rocky*. It's the story of a small-time Philadelphia boxer who has never accomplished anything. He's thrown out of his boxing club because he's a "bum," and he makes his living beating up people for a loan shark. It's clear that he will never accomplish anything.

And then, against all odds, he gets a shot at the world heavyweight title. A chance to go up against Apollo Creed, the best boxer in the world. He trains hard and becomes a local celebrity. He does everything right. And then he goes to the title match, fights 15 rounds against the champ. And loses on a split vote—1 judge votes for Rocky, the other 2 for Apollo Creed.

The story most of us have been trained to understand is that he will train hard in an uplifting montage, learn and grow, and then beat his enemy and win.

It is true, the problem of "Will Rocky win the world championship match?" is resolved—he doesn't. But that was not really the problem at hand, the problem that the story was truly about. The Champ, Apollo Creed, was never the antagonist that was keeping Rocky from solving his problem.

Rocky's problem was that he was a person of little account. He never accomplished anything, never went the distance. He always gave up, failed, and took the easy way out. The antagonist in this story was Rocky himself. And the problem at hand was not "Will Rocky win?" It was "Will Rocky go the distance? Will he stay in the fight all the way to the end, and never give up?"

When the match ends, Rocky is still standing. He never gave up, even when he was so badly beaten up that his trainers begged him to quit. The resolution to the problem of "Will Rocky give up?" is that he did not give up. Because of that, winning or losing the match was irrelevant.

When they are announcing the judge's votes, Rocky is desperately trying to find Adrian, his girlfriend, to whom he wishes to prove his willingness and ability to go the distance.

This is an example of an ending that is surprising and inevitable. Surprising, because we thought that Rocky was out to win the championship, and that winning the fight was what the story was about. Inevitable, because we watched Rocky make the journey from shock, through believing that he could never do this, to finding belief, to doing everything in his power to prepare, to showing up. Of course he went the distance—we just spent half the story watching him train. We didn't know that was the real problem at hand—but as soon as we discovered that, it felt right. Going the distance was far more important than winning a fight. The former is a lifelong achievement, the latter is transient. There will always be other fights. And there were plenty of other Rocky movies.

In games, it is harder to find the surprising but inevitable ending, because the player must participate in moving the story forward, which means that the signposts along the way must be clearer.

SIDEBAR: MAINSTREAM VS EXPERIMENTAL

The general story concepts we discuss here, as well as almost all storytelling concepts discussed in this book, are vulnerable to the charge: "This is not the only way to tell stories! You are ignoring many amazing innovative works!"

This is absolutely true. Avant Garde or experimental movements are constantly finding new ways to tell story. Many of them, if reduced to the basics, still fit the concepts we discuss in this book. But some do not. Some methods are blazing trails into new territory.

However, there is the important matter of proportion. The vast majority of stories told in the world will fit within the frameworks we cover, not just the most mainstream, formulaic stories. Experimental, atypical stories still operate the same way, under the surface.

A simple example is the 2000 film *Memento*. Told as two narratives, both sequential, but one in traditional sequence, and the other in reverse sequence. The film requires viewers to assemble the linear narrative progression in their head as they watch. It's a breathtaking narrative execution. But the narrative concepts under the surface, a character-driven tale of loss, revenge, and tragic regret, operate in just the same manner as any mainstream, classical Film Noir. And as viewers assemble the reverse sequence story in their head, it becomes even more traditional.

Our focus on mainstream narrative is not intended as a slight. Some of the experimental narratives will succeed and move the artform forward, and eventually be incorporated into mainstream storytelling. But it is more important for this book to cover that mainstream in depth than to thin itself out trying to cover the breadth of possible storytelling. Anyone interested in more experimental story will find interesting works and guides out in the world that can build upon the foundation in this book.

TWISTS

There are twists in game narrative—the twist in *BioShock* is legendary, as is the one in *Star Wars: Knights of the Old Republic*. But they both came in the middle of the story, letting the player absorb the twist and deal with the fallout of this unexpected development. A twist at the end of a game would rob the player of the ability to do anything about it.

But a twist is not the same thing as a surprising-and-inevitable ending. Surprising and inevitable have the emotional resonance that we described from *Rocky*. A twist, on the other hand, is more of an intellectual surprise layered into the story. There is certainly nothing wrong or trivial about that.

A twist in your story can be a great talking point—if it's done well, people will certainly talk about it. But it's not a foundational story building block.

Because twists are highly situational, the only advice we can give on them is that they only work when there is a plausible story without them. If the stakes have been set, and the conflict is in motion, and the player thinks, "this is what the story is about, I wonder how it will resolve?", then the twist drops, and it scrambles up everything, then that will be a successful twist.

Too often the story without the twist is somehow lacking because the storytellers have been so focused on the twist, and this ends up telegraphing the twist.

Bioshock's twist works because the player spends the first half of the game thinking that the player character, Jack, has ended up in the city of Rapture by chance—a plane crash. There is a dangerous enemy who will clearly be the final boss of the game: Ryan. All the pieces are in place for a good, competent game story.

Then we learn that nothing is what it seems, and Jack's entire identity gets upended in dramatic fashion. The character we thought would be the final boss is not the final boss. All of this works because the story made sense without the twist.

STORY IS ABOUT IDENTITY

All story is in some way about identity. Think about the shorthand we use to describe stories: coming-of-age, buddy story, romance. These all describe a kind of identity.

A person who was alone. Then they met someone and discovered something greater and more powerful than themselves, and became a person in love. That's a change to their identity.

Story is about who a character is in the world, what their identity is, and how that changes. At the start of Shakespeare's *Julius Caesar*, the character Brutus is known as one among the most noble and honest men in Rome. By the end, he is considered a murderous conspirator who must commit suicide. His identity has changed in the world, even if his own conception of himself has not.

EXAMPLE: *KNIGHTS OF THE OLD REPUBLIC*

The twist in this game is the discovery that you, the player character, are the villain of the story thus far. You were Darth Revan, and were captured by the Jedi. They brainwashed you into believing you had a different identity so that you would fight for their cause, against Darth Malak, your former apprentice.

Once you discover this, you have a choice—you can continue with your new identity, deciding that however you came by it, this is you. Or you can revert to your old personality. This is a great twist for two reasons—one is that it could only be done in a game. There is no movie, no book, where you could discover that you are the antagonist. But more pertinent to our current topic, it is entirely about identity. Who are you? How do others look at you? Does your past define your future? Your potential? What if you don't remember that past at all? Does discovering your past change who you are now?

These are deep questions for a story to grapple with.

CHAPTER SUMMARY

In this chapter, we discussed the following topics:

- Narrative offers context, meaning, and dimension to the events of the game. But it does far more than that—those are simply the basic requirement.
- The basic elements of a narrative are as follows:
  - An interesting and sympathetic character(s).
  - Has a compelling problem.

- Their efforts to solve it bring them into conflict with another character or faction.
    - In the end, the problem is resolved, or definitively unresolved.
- A good ending feels surprising and inevitable. You did not see it coming, but when it happens, it feels like the only way it could have played out.
- Twists can be exciting and worthwhile, but they are not a foundational building block of narrative. In games, they work better in the middle of the story rather than at the end.
- Story is about identity. Who a character is in the world.

2 Narrative Concepts

This chapter is devoted to high-level narrative concepts, and is a bit less "how to" and a bit more "food for thought." Nonetheless, these are vital concepts that any storyteller must get to know. While everything here applies to storytelling in general, we will be specific to games anytime that is possible.

TRUST

Storytelling is about trust between the storyteller and the audience. Trust is a murky resource, hard to quantify or even define. And it is constantly in flux. It's not a binary, on-off state; rather it comes and it goes. A smart storyteller is always thinking about trust on some level.

It's a crucial ingredient in both directions. If the storyteller does not trust their audience, or the audience does not trust the storyteller, everything begins to break down. We must examine it from two angles: how much trust does the storyteller have in their players? And, how much trust do the players have in the storyteller?

TRUST YOUR PLAYERS

The storyteller must trust that their audience is lively, curious, intuitive, and intelligent. The moment a storyteller begins to think "these savages will never get it unless I spell it out…," they and their story are doomed.

Audiences know when they are being talked down to. They know when the storyteller is overexplaining.

Here is an old joke:

There are two types of people in this world.

1. Those who can extrapolate from incomplete data.

The joke requires trust in the audience. If they are the second type of person, they won't get the joke, will not recognize that it is a joke, and may declare the

DOI: 10.1201/9781003624882-4

joke teller "stupid." Telling the joke at all means that you trust your audience is the first type, or that everyone in earshot is the first type. This is the essence of the discussion about trusting your players.

Here are some areas where it can be easy to lose trust in your players. We don't include intuition on this list because intuition is the ability to leap to the correct conclusion based on incomplete evidence, meaning it is the result of any of the following processes. Emotional intelligence can make one intuitive, just as life experience can.

Perception or Open-Mindedness

Will a player look beneath the surface? Are they capable of looking beneath the surface? When presented with incomplete or even contradictory facts, are they open-minded enough to consider what is really going on, rather than to immediately react negatively? A storyteller who does not trust that players are perceptive, or open-minded enough to consider that they don't have all the information, will make choices about how smart, fast, or witty the story can be.

EXAMPLE: SAMARA

In *Mass Effect 2*, the character of Samara was built around rigid self-control. She felt many emotions strongly, but kept such tight control of herself that there was little external sign. The few times she ever did reveal inner turmoil, she did so in a calm, cerebral manner. Often, she would apologize for revealing her inner feelings.

Yet, players could simply take what they knew of her backstory, add it to the code she was sworn to obey, listen to how she spoke about herself, and perceive a great depth to her. An entire story left unsaid. The evidence for it was there, but it would require players who were willing to look beneath the surface. The character herself was never going to reveal this.

If the storytellers had believed that players were simply not perceptive enough to catch on, they would have balked at creating a character with so much depth. They would have reduced Samara to a simpler character who would come right out and tell you about what she feels and what is going on under the surface.

Emotional Intelligence

This is the ability to understand emotions and how they differ from intellect. If the storyteller thinks their players are not very good at emotional intelligence, they may change their story to avoid deeper emotional issues, or add exposition to try and explain what a character is feeling or why.

EXAMPLE: *KILLING EVE*

This show tells the story of an MI5 agent and an international assassin who hunt each other, and have tried to kill each other. They also share a deep connection that borders on—and sometimes crosses into—a romantic relationship.

Most people reading this book can understand how two people can move back and forth from attempted murder to intimate closeness. But a storyteller who does not trust their audience will fear that players will be confused by the contradiction. "That's stupid!" these hypothetical players may declare. "How could you want to be close with someone who just tried to kill you, and put you in the hospital?" That storyteller will avoid emotional complexity of this sort, making the game's story that much less rich.

Or they will feel obligated to add a dreadful scene where one character explains why and how they could have such feelings.

Life Experience

If you were once friends with a self-destructive narcissist who used and abused everyone around them until they flamed out socially and disappeared, then you will recognize such traits in a fictional character. From there, you will either love the portrayal of that character for its realism or hate that character because they trigger you.

However, someone who has never known a person like that firsthand will find that character unlikely. "Who would manipulate everyone around them to the point that they become shunned? It's a predictable failure, and it's so unbelievable, no one would do that."

Life experience affects player's opinions in two ways. First, a player who has read widely, or knows people who have had a variety of experiences, or who have had a variety themselves, will be familiar with many concepts that might arise in a story. More importantly, having learned about the existence, indeed the frequency, of many things that they once thought impossible, players will have developed an open mind and even if they are not familiar with a particular concept, they will not rush to judgment.

EXAMPLE: REAL-LIFE STRANGENESS

Many people who are dying of hypothermia will rip off all their clothes, just before they freeze to death.

A storyteller who does not trust in the life experience of the player community may fear that players who don't know as much about the world and how it works will declare the story "stupid" or "lazy" if it includes such a beat. Instead they'll work around that beat, thus reducing the impact of the horrifying scene where the heroes discover a caravan that froze to death in a mountain pass. Or perhaps worse, they'll include a knowledgeable character who will explain to the hero—and players—about paradoxical undressing.

Media Literacy

Storytelling varies wildly between media, and often even within a single medium. Those who are literate in the style of a particular medium can take in information at a faster and deeper tempo than those who are not.

Imagine you watched a movie scene where the characters agree to go to the supermarket to buy frozen burritos. Then, the next scene is the characters standing in the frozen food aisle at the store, coming to grips with the lack of frozen burritos.

But wait! They were just in their living room, in their pajamas, discussing the planned trip. Now they are already at the store, fully dressed. How did this happen?

Everyone reading this is surely familiar with the way films simply cut out the predictable, boring, unnecessary continuity in a story. In fact, it's so common that you may doubt that anyone could be confused by it.

But if you go back in time to an era before film, and showed those two scenes to an audience, they would be deeply confused. Their context would be theater, where any change of location or time would involve a set change, requiring a brief pause, and very likely a narrator to tell them where and when the new scene is. Perhaps, at best, they could equate it to a novel where a similar jump may have happened, but that is unlikely.

Storytellers in games know that the player's media literacy affects how they absorb information, and so their trust in the media literacy of their players affects how they make decisions.

EXAMPLE

In a single-player role playing game, or RPG, it is a convention that NPCs in the hero's adventuring party will seek life advice or guidance from the hero. It's not mandatory, but happens quite often.

A storyteller creating a game aimed primarily at PvP players may fear that they will not understand this convention and be annoyed or confused by other characters asking for their help. Instead, they will cut that part of the game, making the role-play part of the experience that much shallower.

How Much to Trust?

There is a real difficulty in knowing how much to trust your audience because not all of your audience has the same level of perception, life experience, or other factors discussed above. You may have a character make an intuitive emotional leap that many players will understand and appreciate. But some others who have not experienced as many life events may think that leap is "convenient." They may think the character just guessed the truth because you, the storyteller, wanted them to. Other players who simply aren't as perceptive may not notice that there is a deeper emotional current in the scene, and just get confused.

If some players will get it, while others will think it's forced, and others still will get confused... What does it even mean to trust your audience?

In some ways, it is a question of percentages. Almost any idea will click with some players, and not with others. An idea that clicks with everyone is referred to as "the lowest common denominator," and is justly considered bad or weak. A lowest common denominator idea is so watered down that it has become inoffensive. Anyone can "get" it, but no one is excited by it or interested in it.

In the example earlier of Samara in *Mass Effect 2*, there were indeed a lot of players who found her boring or uninteresting. They cited her endless talk about her code, her overly formal manner, the fact that she never expressed emotion as reasons that she was boring.

Another percentage of players perceived that there was more under the surface, and that they were not going to get the real story—or at least it was not going to be told to them. They would have to extrapolate or intuit the truth. Oftentimes, an idea that requires more work or insight to "get" lands more powerfully with the players who do get it. And that was the case here: the players who felt a connection with Samara felt it strongly. But others did not. Fortunately, in the case of Samara, *Mass Effect 2* had a large cast of characters, so individual squad members could appeal to specific types of players.

That's why percentages matter. If your idea will land with 2% of players and be missed or disliked by 98%, you should probably rework it or find a new idea. It is fine to only appeal to a portion of your players. In fact, as mentioned earlier, trying to appeal to all of them is usually bad. But going too far in the other direction makes your ideas niche.

SIDEBAR: LOWEST COMMON DENOMINATOR? OR UNIVERSAL?

An idea that appeals to everyone is exciting to no one. All the rough edges have been sanded off of it, and it cannot offend anyone. Such a "lowest common denominator" is bland and dull, and a story made up of such ideas will be dreadful and forgettable. A better option is an idea that appeals to many, but which some do not like. Of course, implementing such an idea means sticking by it when teammates, or even studio heads, who don't like it come to you to complain about it.

However, the best ideas and concepts can be described as "universal," and they speak to everyone. Do you feel dizzy? It feels like we just changed directions very fast, but there is a difference between a lowest common denominator idea and a universal concept or theme.

A universal concept or theme is one that we all recognize because it exists within us. We all understand jealousy, affection, revenge, fairness, hate, love, and a range of other human drives. These are not simply emotions. Revenge, for instance, is not an emotion. It's a drive. It is fueled by emotions like anger and resentment.

A story should be built on universal themes. Everyone consuming the story will recognize those themes from their own life. They've felt all those feelings, and acted on those drives. It will help the story transcend culture, life experience, and identity.

The universal concept or theme is not an "idea" as such. It's the underlying foundation that the idea rests on. The idea itself, on the other hand, must be defined by specificity and fearlessness.

Example: A story about revenge has a powerful universal theme. Everybody on the team agrees it's a good direction. But after you start work on it, you get feedback like "Your protagonist can't seek revenge by doing X or Y, because that will lose the sympathy of too many players!" and "Be careful not to offend anyone!".

If you get to the point where your tale of revenge offends no one and everyone finds it "okay," you've managed to reduce your story to the lowest common denominator, and completely undermined that great universal theme.

Note that we are not suggesting you should set out to be offensive, or that being offensive is the measure of how good a story is. We are saying that any good idea will have rough edges that some people will find difficult to accept, and that you must learn to live with this fact. Seeking to make those people like the idea undermines the whole endeavor.

How Do You Know?

If you know your idea may not land with all your players, and you want to trust your player community, how do you judge whether to use an idea or not?

The best answer that we can give is that it's a sense you develop over time. You have your own boundaries and thresholds for what is intuitive, what is confusing, what makes sense, and what does not. In some ways, your instincts match that of most players. In other ways, not at all.

Over time, you will get feedback on where you are in sync with most players, and where you are not. Pay close attention to that, so you begin to understand when to trust your instincts and when to seek out feedback.

Eventually you will develop a sense about which ideas will land, how much support they need, and how important it is to get them in the game.

Another aspect is the particular community. Certain games and IPs attract a certain mentality of player. There is lots of variation within each community, so don't fall into the trap of generalizing too broadly, or putting too much stock in generalizations.

With that said, communities do begin to develop a personality of their own. Certain games attract very rational, logic-oriented players who have less emotional experience or intuition. Other communities attract players with extremely high emotional intelligence. So if you're writing for an IP with an existing community, get to know them. Lurk in the subreddit or other spaces. Do NOT interact with them. But get to know which leaps they make and which they don't. What are the concepts and story beats that you thought would be obvious that seem to go right over their heads?

The final part of knowing how to deal with this topic is to follow the name of this overall section: Trust Your Players. It can be easy to dismiss others as dense, stupid, or ignorant. But players are smart. They are perceptive, and trusting them always ends up being rewarding.

Do Your Players Trust You?

To tell the clearest story possible, you must set up ideas, introduce them, develop them, and finally pay them off, strictly in that order. You must answer any questions the player would have, before they have them.

If you do this, your story will be crystal clear, and incredibly boring. It will be unplayable. We will expand on this later in the "Don't be Boring" section. But for this section, the key thing to understand is: to tell a story well, you must be free to introduce some chaos to your story. You must be able to jump around, dazzle the player, and make them lean forward with curiosity, even intrigue.

But to do any of that, you need the player's trust.

If you introduce a story beat, a character, or a concept that makes no sense, there are two possible reactions players can have:

"Huh, that doesn't make any sense. I wonder what's going on? I'd better keep going, I'm sure the storyteller is going to pay this off later – should be exciting!"

Or

"That doesn't make any sense. This storyteller is dumb and disorganized. They don't know how to tell a story. Maybe I should quit and go play something else."

The player's reaction comes down to just one thing: trust. If they trust the storyteller, they will go along with what is happening, confident that it will all make sense—and be exciting—in the end.

If you have lost their trust, or never gained it, they will have to start considering whether or not it is worth their time to stick with this game. They're confused, and it is entirely possible that you are an unskilled storyteller who will waste their time. This may sound harsh, but put yourself in the player's shoes. They have given many a game or movie or novel a chance in the past, and often it ended up wasting their time.

At the start, they are looking for a way out. And if you gained their trust and then lost it, they are even more adamantly looking for a way out.

How Do You Gain Trust?

Players begin to trust the storyteller over time, through competence. They begin the experience with very little trust, unless they know your work from somewhere else or the game is a new title in an IP they already love.

Each time there is a story beat, cinematic, interaction that is handled well, they begin to trust a little more. If it is funny, witty, or especially impactful, they start to trust a lot more. Competence over time is the most effective thing you can do to build trust.

A specific act that can help is to introduce some element to a scene that does not make sense, but on a very small scale. Then pay off or reveal the truth at the end of the scene. If the player is saying "Oh come on!" in the middle of a scene, but then is surprised at the end, you have turned the tables on them in a way that makes them trust you more quickly. Yes, we are talking about player manipulation.

Case Study: *Knights of the Old Republic*

In this game there are several small story beats that seem inconsistent. They happen here and there in the story, and the game moves on. Most players will assume that these are storytelling mistakes or lapses.

When our character goes to the Jedi Council to request training, a member says that they don't normally accept adults for training, but this is a special case. Why? Because we are the player character?

In another moment, Bastila tells us that Jedi don't kill their prisoners. Yet we have seen Bastila capture the infamous Darth Revan in a flashback—so where is Revan today? Everyone talks about them like they no longer exist. Miscommunication on the writing team?

Another member of the Jedi Council warns that undertaking the main quest of the game could lead us down "an all too familiar path," clearly meaning the dark side of the force. Yet, our character's background has nothing to do with the force—dark or light side. We've only just discovered our aptitude for the force. Careless writing? Did the writer mean "familiar if you've watched or played other Star Wars products?"

Midway through the story, we learn the major twist of the game: that we are in fact Darth Revan. We were captured by the Jedi and brainwashed to have a new identity.

Suddenly all those little inconsistencies click into place, and our trust for the storytellers skyrockets. Everything makes sense, it was all carefully planned, and we are in awe.

Everything about this scenario is part of larger arcs and character stories in the game. But nestled in there is the moment where you made the player question if you knew what you were doing, and later answered: Yes, I do know what I'm doing. I was aware that everything was not adding up ... but then it did add up.

That kind of beat can be very important. The next time the player encounters something that is not immediately clear, they will give you the benefit of the doubt—for a little while. It's not a get-out-of-jail-free card, but it is a building block of trust.

How Do You Lose Trust?

It should be clear at this point that trust is lost the same way that it is gained: the level of skill and competence displayed by the storyteller. When you waste the player's time or confuse them unnecessarily, they lose trust. Eventually, there is no trust left, and they give up.

Take our earlier example from *Star Wars: Knights of the Old Republic*. The character Bastila told us that Jedi never kill their prisoners. Yet there seemed to be an inconsistency in that the story implied that the Jedi had killed Revan. An inconsistency wouldn't lose trust—it would make us a bit wary, and start to lose trust.

But if we'd had a scene where a character stated: "Yep, we killed Revan! No big deal for us!" Then players would lose trust in the storytellers altogether, since it seemed like different parts of the game were written by different people who weren't in communication with each other.

Another scenario that could lose trust would be if players encountered the reveal, learned that they are Revan, and later in the story someone broadly hinted at a secret having to do with their identity. Players would know the second beat was supposed to come first, but clumsy structuring allowed it to come too late.

Most professional storytellers are not wildly incompetent. They know that A comes before B, which comes before C. However, there are constant forces at work on a game story, gale force winds that rip and tear at the story's structure. Sometimes levels need to be moved around, or a nonlinear or branching structure is imposed on a previously well-constructed story. In the scramble of last-minute changes, some edges get ragged. Some beats slip through the cracks.

Most of the time when you've encountered a game narrative that was confusing or overly simplistic, it was not planned that way. Rather, late changes came in and scattered the story. In some cases, there was nothing the storyteller could do; it was too late and chaos would be the defining factor. In others, the storyteller reacted too slowly, or held on to an old idea too long, and they missed their chance to patch up the story.

Whatever scenario caused the rift, players don't know and don't care. They will gain or lose trust solely on the quality of the experience they are having.

It is important to remember that until you have lost all of the player's trust, you can still regain it. It's just hard work.

THE STAKES: WHAT IS LOST? WHAT IS GAINED?

One of the most important concepts in a story are the stakes. If the protagonists fail, what happens? What will be lost? If the protagonists win, what happens? What is gained?

This seems obvious, yet it is easy for storytellers to lose track of this over time. Perhaps you've established the stakes at the start of the process, but as the story has been developed further, it's been lost. Or the story has changed in a way that makes the original stakes irrelevant now. More often, the stakes just don't get reinforced.

Case Study: *Diablo III: Reaper of Souls*

At the game's start, we witness the Angel of Death, Malthael, seize the Black Soulstone, an artifact of immense power. He wishes to bring about the end of humanity, and now he has the power to do it.

So, the stakes are clear from the start. But this is an ARPG, meaning the player will not see the antagonist on screen very often, until the end, when you fight him. Most of your time as a player will be spent achieving short term goals, overcoming intermediate enemies, and progressing your build.

If we on the narrative team had assumed that we were all set because we established the stakes at the outset, and therefore we had not tried to reinforce them throughout the game, you could easily have lost track of the real threat. Perhaps you would be aware of it as some vague feeling that something bad was going to happen if you don't keep going, but that is always true, and it would lose all immediacy.

Thus, we were compelled to try and reinforce the stakes at every opportunity, to keep them relevant.

One key way that we did this was to make a mystery of how Malthael planned to use the Black Soulstone to wipe out humanity. While the player character tries to stop Malthael's minions from massacring the population of Westmarch, Tyrael, an NPC, uses a sliver of the Black Soulstone to try and deduce Malthael's plan. The combination of mystery and intrigue, with an artifact of the stone itself, and the understanding that Malthael plans to do something worse than the massacre we see unfolding in front of us, keeps the stakes reinforced.

Keep the Stakes Centered

In the previous section, we said you must keep bringing up the stakes to keep it in the forefront of the player's mind. But you must also find a way to work the stakes into all aspects of your story, in a thematic sense.

It is not enough to have characters mention the stakes. You must also work them into your plot and story beats.

Case Study: *Diablo III: Reaper of Souls*

During the course of the game, we encounter many situations that are tied to Malthael's possession of the Black Soulstone. A section in the middle of the game sees the player character hunt down their enemy Adria. The player has many reasons to want to kill Adria, but that is not enough, because those reasons are not tied to the stakes, that Malthael is going to use the Black Soulstone to wipe out humanity.

So we made Adria the sole character capable of divining the location of the Black Soulstone. This kept the Soulstone a relevant part of the story, and introduced a new tension: the player wants to kill this character, but needs something from her.

Another way to keep the Stakes centered is to show how the threat of the bad outcome affects the world. When people think the world is going to end (metaphorically or literally), they change their behaviors. Some go on crime sprees. Some join cults and worship anything they can. Some seek out loved ones to make amends. Some hoard toilet paper and sit at home with a shotgun.

In *Reaper of Souls*, the angel Imperius, no fan of humans, grudgingly helps the player character through a portion of a level. It is out of character for him to help a human at all, much less one whose ultimate goal is to kill a fellow angel. But he knows he must, because Malthael's possession of the Black Soulstone has increased the stakes beyond the tolerable. It's too dangerous.

All of these actions, taken by side or background characters, are manifestations of fear, fear of the bad outcome. This keeps the stakes centered. Reaper of Souls is an apocalyptic scenario, but the same points hold true for even the smallest story. The negative stakes and the positive stakes both can be reflected in the world around your story.

LET THE STAKES EVOLVE

The story will change in development. This can be bad if it loses its core, but it is often a good thing. The story gets bigger, opens up, and takes on a new life. When it does, you must let the stakes evolve as well. Keep them in sync.

Even if the story does not change, it is still powerful to let the stakes evolve.

EXAMPLE: *RED DEAD REDEMPTION 2*

The stakes at the beginning of the story are simple survival—the player character must act to avoid dying. Survival is certainly a high-level stake, but as the story progresses, the stakes evolve into a high-level confrontation with rival gangs and the US federal government. On a deeper level, the story becomes about the dissolution of the social order—the gang that Arthur was part of dissolves, and an entire way of life begins to die.

Anytime you can escalate the stakes along the way, it gives the story momentum. If you start with the strongest possible outcome as the stakes, that gets your story off to a great start, but it also becomes easy to run out of gas halfway through.

"If we fail, the universe will be destroyed!" is a banger of an opening. But 10 game hours later, it feels a bit tired. "Yep, the universe is still in danger. But I've got to work on my crafting skills for a while…"

The optimum approach is to start with something that feels like the worst possible outcome at the start … and then learn part way through that no, it's so much worse than we thought.

The same is true of the positive stakes. People don't like only fighting to prevent bad things. They want an affirmative reason to strive. They want to make things better, whether it's for themselves, the ones they love, or the whole world.

So it pays to set up positive stakes, and to let them evolve and escalate throughout your story.

TYPES OF STAKES

There are different types of stakes, and you must have all of them working in your story simultaneously. Ideally, they work in harmony or at least complimentary fashion. But that's an advanced technique, and at a bare minimum, just ensure you have all types.

External Stakes

This is what is most commonly meant by stakes. Who will win and who will lose? What does it mean for the world? Will we defeat the evil overlord? Will we prevent the aliens from destroying Earth? Will our new restaurant survive opening night? Will our little village thrive?

Earlier we discussed the film *Rocky* when we talked about Good Endings. The content of that section lends itself to this discussion as well. The external stakes of *Rocky* were: who will win the fight? Rocky, or Apollo Creed?

Internal Stakes

These are the emotional stakes for the character. If the external stakes are "can we save the world," the internal stakes are something like "Am I a person who is capable of saving the world?" or "Do I even care enough to save the world?" They have to do with the identity of the player character. Who are you in the world and are you capable of meeting the moment?

A particular power of RPGs is that players feel they are defining their player character and themselves in the world. That means the internal stakes are tied to the player's view of themselves.

Will you succeed, and will you do so in a way that meets your own expectations? That is to say, one danger is that you fail. Another danger is that you find a way to succeed by cheating—by being untrue to your own values. In terms of internal stakes, this is just as dangerous as failing.

The character can and should grow over the course of the story, so it is fine if they succeed by using a different set of values than they had at the beginning.

EXAMPLE: *GHOST OF TSUSHIMA*

Jin Sakai has been raised to live by a code that allows no deviation. But the first few hours of the game show him again and again that things have changed on a fundamental level, and the entire Bushido Code he was taught to follow is inadequate to the moment. He must adapt, and learn new ways to fight and to think.

But the internal stakes here are quite strong. Making this change will bring shame upon him and his family, in a culture where that is a fate worse than death.

On an even deeper level, it is a change to his fundamental identity, which is a form of death.

But good internal stakes set up a dynamic where the hero's beliefs are tested, and where if they fail, something very important to them will be lost, but something internal (will be gained? Not sure what thought needed to be finished). It might be their own self-respect, or it might be losing the love of someone important to them, or it might be a loss of stature in their tightest circle of friends. As with all stakes, there is a positive side as well. Succeeding means gaining something positive internally. Someone's love, or the respect of a certain group, or just the knowledge that one can achieve things.

In our *Rocky* example, where the external stakes were about winning the fight, the internal stakes were the question: will Rocky go all the way? He's failed at everything he ever tried, gave up too easily, and took the easy way out. In the words of his former trainer Micky, he is a bum!

The negative side of the stakes is that if he doesn't go all the way here, he never will. He will live the rest of his life as a bum. This is his last chance. But the positive side is that if he can prove that he can go all the way, then Adrian, the woman he loves, will know that he can commit, that he will be there for her.

Philosophical Stakes

The story of your game is also about a philosophy. It can be testing the truth of a philosophy, so the positive stakes are that the philosophy is proven true, and the negative stakes are that it is proven false.

EXAMPLE: *PERSONA 5*

This game has several important philosophical stakes, but one of them is about victimhood. The game says "You don't have to be a victim, you can work with others to become empowered."

It expresses this philosophy in many positive ways: each of the main ensemble cast has been wronged or victimized in some way. But when they work together, they can right the wrongs done to them, or at least improve their situation and move past those wrongs.

But of course, philosophical stakes must show both sides, and the game gives us an early antagonist who exemplifies this. Kamoshida is the former Olympian who never got over his failure at the games. Rather than move past it and find a new way to empower himself, he clung to whatever vestiges of authority and power he could find, becoming a predator at a high school, manipulating and abusing children. He is a clear examplar of the negative side of this philosophical stake.

These philosophical stakes are not just some academic idea hanging around as a backdrop. In our example, the heroes should work together, relying on their deep bond as friends, to fight their foes. And the antagonist(s) should rely on the power of hate to forward their agenda, whether sowing hatred among their own troops to drive them into a crazed state, or whipping up hatred in the general populace to oppose the heroes, or some other hate-based strategy.

The philosophical stakes should be omnipresent and are constantly being tested by events in the story.

In *Rocky*, the philosophical stakes are something like "is it possible to change?" If Rocky isn't able to go all the way, if he falls back into his bad habits, then we know that in this world, it is not possible to change or grow. When he does go all the way, we realize that it is indeed possible to change.

How Overt Should the Stakes Be?

The External Stakes should be stated explicitly and reinforced throughout. This is what the player believes the story is about.

The Internal Stakes are the trickiest to express. They should be implicit to the characters and their arcs, and there should be no doubt about these stakes. However, having a character explicitly state what is going on under the surface could be tricky. If Rocky had given a big speech about how he needed to prove he could go the distance, it would have undermined the strength of this powerful story ingredient. It is best to avoid stating them outright and instead make them clear through the character's journey. But they do need to be clear. At the end of the story, players should be able to state clearly what the internal stakes were for the characters. This is what the player comes to realize what the story is really about.

The philosophical stakes should never be stated. They should have a deep impact on the story, but it should be so inherent that players feel it, even if they don't know it. This is what the story is really about, but players don't have to consciously realize it.

SIDEBAR: THE TICKING CLOCK

The ticking clock is a narrative concept that is important enough to be in this chapter, but too simple to warrant its own section.

Every story must have some sort of time pressure. If the protagonist could stop striving against the antagonist, buy a house, raise a family, retire, and then once again take up the cause, the story will have no urgency. Even worse, it won't have stakes. In order to be effective, the story's stakes must be inextricably tied to a ticking clock.

In a game of *Civilization*, if you are too slow to develop the tech tree, a rival will show up with tanks, and quickly wipe out your swordsmen. The same is true of culture, religion, land, or any other feature in the game.

In *Diablo III: Reaper of Souls*, Malthael is working on a plan to use the Black Soulstone to destroy humanity. You must find and kill him before he is able to put this plan into action.

In *Avengers: Infinity War*, Thanos is collecting the Infinity Stones, and when he gets all of them, he will destroy half of all living things in the universe. In this instance, the ticking clock reaches zero—that is to say, the terrible thing that must be prevented happens.

The ticking clock can be tied expressly to gameplay, as in the *Civilization* example. Each turn that the player takes without advancing their tech tree increases the chance that an enemy will irretrievably outpace them.

It can also be a purely narrative device, divorced from gameplay. In the *Diablo III: Reaper of Souls* example, the player can explore the city of Westmarch for thousands of hours, ignoring Malthael's plans, and nothing bad will happen. Malthael will still be working on his plan until the player advances the story.

It's always desirable to have all the elements of a game tied together. But there are sometimes strong reasons to keep the ticking clock apart from game mechanics.

For example, most RPGs encourage players to explore the world and level up different skills and abilities. This requires giving the player space and time to do whatever they want. If the ticking clock was tied to the player's actions or to game mechanics, it would overpower the player while they're off running side quests. Yet you still need some kind of ticking clock to keep narrative pressure and tension on the player.

The ticking clock can be an epic end-of-the-world event, or something as small as a spouse coming home from work, and the player character must get the place cleaned up before they arrive. The scale of your story will give you a sense of how dire it must be.

But every story needs one.

LESS IS MORE

A designer knows he has achieved perfection not when there is nothing left to add, but when there is nothing left to take away.

– Antoine de Saint-Exupery

This quote captures one of the most important aspects of storytelling, and of omit creative endeavors in general. Every time you remove an element from your design, whatever is left becomes stronger, and more pure.

EXAMPLE

"I'm going to kill you! Sucker, you are dead! Your people are going to weep for you, dead guy! You'll be amazed at how dead you are! You'll be all 'holy shit that guy killed me a lot!' You better believe it, dead man! Extreme prejudice, extreme."

vs

Said quietly: "I'm here to kill you."

The first line is certainly funnier and in a comedic game that could be the line to use. There is a type of comedic character, such as Deadpool, whose comedy springs from their nonstop talking. However, if the intent of the line is to be impactful in any way besides comedic, the second line is clearly stronger.

If you met a shadowed figure in a dark alley and they said one of these two lines, which would scare you more? The first line feels like a character who is trying to talk himself into believing that he is going to kill you. The second line is sparse and simple, someone conveying a clear, simple idea.

Less is more, and simpler is stronger.

EXAMPLE

"I've been having terrible nightmares."
vs
"I have terrible nightmares."

In this case the information is the same, but the simpler, clearer construction of the second line makes it more impactful.

Dialogue is handy to use as an example because it can be so mechanical in this way. But the same principles apply to storytelling in general. Keep removing elements until only what is necessary remains. That remainder will be powerful and crisp.

There are many approaches to constructing a story: creating an outline in bullet point format, or an excel sheet; using index cards for scenes, or a whiteboard. Whatever outlining form you use, it's a good idea to step back at some point and consider entire scenes and subplots: Do you need them? Do they add anything? Do they add enough to justify their existence? Can two or more be combined to maximize impact?

Later, in the editing stage, you should look at each scene or moment individually and question whether each beat within them is necessary. Can it be streamlined? Combined?

Finally, when only the necessary scenes exist, and each beat within each scene is necessary, look at the dialogue, and see if it can be cut down or even omitted.

WHAT HAPPENS IF I CUT?

Often we have an internal resistance to cutting material. We've worked hard on it, and we are pretty sure that every little idea is a load-bearing wall. If we cut it, everything will fall apart.

One way to get around this mental block is just to play a game. Take a part of your world, IP, story, or story ingredient, and just ask: What happens if I cut this? Would it require you to restructure the entire middle portion of the game? Or just to change a few lines here and there?

Even if the ingredient in question is entertaining and adds some interesting flavor, it might be unnecessary. If cutting it causes very little patching to gloss over, then it should go. You'll have to shift your mindset from "What amazing and fun element does this ingredient contribute?" to "What is this ingredient leaching from everything else?" If it is not necessary, its presence is taking something away from the whole.

Ask the question "What happens if I cut?" about everything, and be truly open-minded about the answer.

Murder Your Babies

It's ubiquitous advice in storytelling circles that you must be willing to murder your babies. It's also very good advice.

This means that if you have an idea you really like, something you are especially proud of, but it is starting to become problematic or irrelevant, you must be ruthless and cut it. Every creative professional—every single one—has at some point in their career held on too long to an idea that needed to go. They've played defense and run interference to keep the idea alive. But the idea needs to go.

Eventually the idea will be cut. The only questions are: How much damage has been done to the story while you held on to this idea? And, how much damage has been done to your relationship with the rest of the team?

Murdering your babies is a subset of less is more. It speaks specifically to the idea that when you feel protective of an idea, you will hold on too tight. Less is more as a general philosophy is a higher level view of considering every element, regardless of your feelings, and considering whether it is worthy of survival.

DON'T BE BORING

Being boring is the worst sin of storytelling. If your storytelling is cheap and manipulative and your characters are shallow and your dialogue clunky … but players are still excited to see what happens next, you have a chance to correct or improve everything else. If everything else is best-in-class, but your story is just boring, you're going to lose them all, and nothing else matters.

Stories should aspire to be more than just "not boring." But all those other aspirations require the story to first be entertaining. This concept sounds pretty obvious. It is also very easy to violate. Most stories start off exciting. But as development goes on, new elements get added. Someone was confused by this beat— better add a line that clarifies. UX feedback is that people find this character too obnoxious—better tone them down. Someone in leadership really wants a scene added that builds more overall cohesion, so better add that scene.

These forces impact every game story during development. You can fight the most egregious, but you can't fight them all. As we are fond of saying, you can't die on every hill, because there are a lot of hills, and only one of you.

We've discussed elsewhere that these effects can make the story incoherent. But they can also make the story boring. Even without external forces, you may feel some pressure within yourself to smooth out or tone down beats, ideas, lines, or characters.

Before you know it, you've got a boring, mechanically sound story. In fact, if your story is completely clear it will almost certainly be boring. The story needs some chaos, some ambiguity, a compelling reason to keep playing in order to put the pieces together.

Clarity is not the highest aspiration of storytelling. Ambiguity or lack of clarity are often good in their own right, as they provide tension and momentum. But even when that is not the case, clarity can be an important aspect of storytelling without being the primary one.

For example, an analogue watch is made up of tiny, intricate gears that work together in harmony, and while it can be a stunning achievement of engineering, nobody enjoys observing the inner workings of a watch for more than a few seconds.

Better to Confuse Than to Bore

Boring stories are often the result of a desire to achieve clarity. These include more information so that no one can possibly misunderstand!

The perfect balance in storytelling is as follows:

- The stakes are clear.
  - But the potential of the stakes to change is ambiguous.
- The character relationships are strong and well defined, even if they are constantly evolving.
  - But there is some uncertainty around the edges. What did he mean by that one comment? What does she really think?
- The goals are clear, although they also should evolve.
  - But there may be conflicting goals between different characters or factions.
- There is some degree of unclear or ambiguous energy in the story.
  - This can be plot, character, or world related—or all three.
  - This provides tension and intrigue, hooking players and driving the story forward.

It becomes quite tricky to find that perfect balance of solid clarity and murky ambiguity. As with any tricky balance, you should strive for the perfect target, but also know which side to err on. If you have to go too far in one direction or the other, which one do you favor?

In the case of boring vs confusion, the answer is clearly that it is better to confuse players than to bore them.

If you confuse players too much, they may get angry and stop playing. That is a real danger. But that is a threshold: mildly confused players will be intrigued and want to know more. Thoroughly confused players will be annoyed, but will still try to piece together what is happening. Finally, only at the highest level will you lose them.

Bored is a binary state. If you bore players, most of them will stop playing. Or they will keep playing to experience great gameplay, but they will completely check out of the story. Either way, you've lost them.

Many of us have an instinctual dread of hearing that we've confused a player or tester, but in the end, it is a far better problem to have than boring a player or tester.

Consider it in terms of your skill and reputation as a storyteller. If you confuse players, some of them will think it's their fault. They may think they're not smart or quick enough to follow what is happening. If you bore them, 100% of players will know with certainty that it's your fault, you're a bad storyteller.

BE BOLD

Another trap that narrative folk fall into and get boring is to write defensively. When your writing goes into the build and you start getting comments from the rest of the team, almost always critical, snarky, badly worded comments, it can be easy to start writing defensively.

This is a mindset where you examine every idea or creative impulse through the filter of "What will the team say? What rocks will they throw at it? How can I write this to avoid criticism X or Y, or to avoid teammate X or Y taking a massive dump on this?"

You may insulate yourself from day-to-day criticism, but you will also ensure that your writing is boring. The sooner you can get to a place with the team where you are saying "These are my creative instincts, backed up by experience and creative reasoning. I am happy to hear all your feedback and consider it, but I will have to go in the direction I think best," the better. It's about establishing some boundaries.

Disclaimer: Don't do or say anything that will alienate your teammates or risk your job, and the above relationship advice applies to the wider team, not to your direct manager. Taking feedback and direction from your manager, or their manager, is a whole different ball of yarn.

ACTIVE VS PASSIVE MINDSET OF PLAYERS

Humans absorb narrative in either a passive mindset, or an active one.

A person in a passive mindset is like a sponge: they absorb everything. There may be a corner of their mind that is active, thinking "Ah ha! I bet this is going to happen!" or "I wonder if that story beat means that someone else in this scene knows the truth?" But they are still simply waiting for the characters and story-teller to reveal what happens next.

In this mode, their absorption and retention of information is high. Information in this case might be plot points, scenes, beats, or twists. It can mean character backstory, choices, emotions, or arcs. It can mean subtext or foreshadowing. It can mean music, sound effects, setting, or time-of-day. Storytelling has thousands of channels with which to communicate, and passive audiences absorb them all. In a scene where everyone is happy and upbeat, but the music is ominous, audiences will absorb that, note it, and file it away.

A person in an active mindset is quite different. They also absorb information, but they rank it in terms of importance and discard any that is not relevant. You might think of this as a survival skill. If you were in the wilds and noticed a lion standing on the nearby ridgeline looking at you, your mind would strain to absorb some information, but would ignore other information.

You'd try to note how far the lion is from you. How fast could it reach you? Where is the rest of the lion's pride? Are they sneaking up from behind? Is the lion acting threatening? Does it look hungry? Are there sticks or other possible weapons nearby? Are there other humans you can call out to for help?

In that same moment, there might be a beautiful sunset taking place. There might be a gentle, cooling breeze, and some delightful birdsong occurring from a nearby stand of trees.

A viewer, watching the scene with a passive mindset, will absorb all of these things as well. Sunsets are visually compelling, and the onset of night might be important information for later.

You, in the moment, with an active mindset, will dismiss all of this other information as not helpful. Beautiful birdsong will not matter if a lion is ripping your intestines out in 30 seconds.

One of the hardest things about game narrative—aside from everything else about game narrative—is that it is perhaps the only storytelling format where the audience is in an active mindset.

Someone reading a novel is completely passive. They can even put the book down and consider what they've just read. Someone watching a movie is still passive. They do not believe that their participation will change the outcome of the movie. In a theater, the movie will keep going regardless of the viewer's feelings, so they are compelled to keep up, but they "keep up" in a passive fashion.

Players, on the other hand, are in an active mindset. Playing a game is problem-solving. The core loop of every game involves solving problems. This is true of a first-person military shooter or a dating sim. It's true of a cooking game and a fighting game.

The player's mindset is that they can alter the outcome of events through action. This is true when the story is interactive, and true when it is not. It's not about logic, it's about mindset.

EXAMPLE

A player can binge an entire season of a television show over the course of a weekend. Let's say each episode is 45 minutes, and there are ten episodes. That is 450 minutes during which the player sat, rapt, taking in the story.

When that same player is asked to watch a 2-minute cutscene, they look for the skip button as fast as possible, or go to refill their drink, or grab their phone to go to reddit and complain about these interminable cutscenes.

The problem is not that players have a low attention span, even if that is a civilizational problem at the moment. The problem is that players are in an active mindset. Putting the controller or mouse down, sitting back, and watching a cutscene requires a shift in mindset and mode.

WHAT IS THE PRACTICAL EFFECT?

Trying to tell stories to players in an active mindset means being aware of how their mind is working. Subtlety and implication will be lost, because practical, actionable data are what the mind requires.

As a storyteller, you must find a way to wrap any information you want to convey into the game seamlessly.

Gameplay

The best way, as always in game narrative, is to try and convert your narrative beat into gameplay. If the player's active mindset categorizes a story beat as something that will affect their gameplay decision making, you will have their full attention.

Case Study: *Baldur's Gate 2*

In this game, there are two party members who dislike each other intensely: Minsc and Edwin.

If you have both in your party while playing, they will periodically squabble, and each interaction will get stronger and stronger. This is a character-based part of the game—they have lore reasons to not like each other.

However, an experienced RPG player will know that this ingredient is here for a reason. Trouble is brewing, and it is going to affect the player's party.

Eventually, Edwin's taunting will break Minsc, and the good-natured Ranger will go mad and kill Edwin. If the player has invested time and gold in leveling up and equipping Edwin, this can be devastating.

Someone reading a book or watching a movie will be fascinated by this result. But a player with an active mindset will be paying careful attention to all the clues, implying that this is going to happen, and be looking for solutions the entire time.

The storytelling is wrapped tightly into gameplay.

Not all story ideas can be layered into gameplay, but it's always worth the time and effort to try and find a way.

Environmental

Environmental storytelling is another way to get through to an active mindset. In *Portal*, the player was:

- Trying to solve puzzles,
- Trying to understand what was happening at the facility in which they were trapped, and
- Trying to understand why they were at the beck-and-call of a clearly insane AI.

Questions 2 and 3 on that list are narrative-related, but because the answers could have an impact on the type and difficulty of the puzzles the player would face, and particularly on the danger the player would face if they failed, the player's mind pays some attention to questions 2 and 3.

In that game, the player discovers a back room where someone has written "The Cake is a Lie" over and over on the wall. This bit of environmental storytelling reinforces that something has gone terribly wrong at this facility, and that the AI, GLaDOS, is indeed insane. It has zero impact on gameplay. But because it is found in the environment where the player is looking for clues, it is tangentially related to questions 1 and 2 on the list above.

In that way, it makes the cut for an active mindset.

Don't Ask the Player to Shift Mindset

Earlier we mentioned how a cutscene requires the player to shift from active mindset to passive, and there are times it is desirable to do that, as well as best practices for doing so.

However, it is always preferable to convey a story without trying to shift the player's mindset. Even when you cannot wrap story into gameplay or the environment, you can still try to find a way to convey it without asking the player to stop playing.

EXAMPLE

Audio Logs. It may be hard for modern audiences to believe, but when games introduced the idea of an audio log you could pick up and let play while moving, it was quite an innovation.

Now players did not need to stop playing the game and listen to character voice over. They could simply pick up the log, and keep playing while the log ran. If they got into intense gameplay, they would probably lose track of the log, but if it interested them enough, they could choose to go into a menu and replay it. This second course of action does involve a mindset shift, but it's one that the player has initiated.

Approach a Mindset Shift with Care

When you do need to play a cutscene or cinematic, consider how to get into it from gameplay. In the Cinematics chapter, we will go into more detail about how to start a cinematic from gameplay. But for this discussion of mindset, it is worth just noting that you should think about the change in tempo.

If the player has just finished a high-adrenaline fight and has an elevated heart rate, don't start the cutscene with a close-up of leaves floating down a stream, which transitions into a long pan. You should try to match the tempo, energy, and pace that the player is feeling, and then turn all those dials down carefully in the first third of the scene.

CHARACTER NOT PLOT

Ideally, plot and character work together harmoniously in your story. Each supports and advances the other. Often however, these two are omit at odds. Taking time to develop a character, to give us a view into their inner world, requires slowing or even stopping the plot. To keep the plot moving, you won't have time to develop the characters.

An easy way to understand this tension is to think of a favorite TV show. Most episodes are heavily plot-based: they must introduce a conflict, develop it, and pay it off before the end of the episode. Even shows that have a continuing overall story usually try to resolve some smaller conflict before the end of the episode. That just makes it more satisfying.

Along the way, there is not much room for characters to develop. Over the course of a single season, the main protagonists of a TV show will have much more screen time than the protagonist of a movie—several orders of magnitude more. Yet they will not have changed very much.

Over the entire run of a show, a character could change quite a bit, but it is a slower change, due to the needs of plot in each episode.

Plot Is a Trap

Depending on what game genre you work in, you likely won't have much control over the ratio of plot to character development in your game. But it is still useful to remember that character development is freeing, while plot is a trap.

Case Study: *Blue Eye Samurai*

Mizu, the protagonist of the Netflix show *Blue Eye Samurai*, swears as a child to get revenge on each of the four men who may be her father. To do this, she must become the best swordsman in the world. There are flashbacks where we see her growing up, but most of these are focused on her learning sword smithing, or life lessons.

If we tried to rely on plot to convey her journey to sword mastery, we would have to devote many episodes to her discovering new and different sword disciplines, learning from different masters. In doing so, we would map out a timeline of her youth that could possibly cause problems for us later. If we wanted to add a story into her background at some later date, we'd need to figure out when and where in her backstory it falls, what her skill level is, and where she was.

Instead, her motivation makes everything else viable, with very little information or detail required. After giving her a motivation, and then telling us that she will focus her life on learning sword skill, the show does not need to belabor the point. We believe that she has made herself into a sword wielder who can defeat mercenaries, assassins, and samurai. We believe this simply because her motivation is strong enough.

In games, that character approach requires less time, fewer assets, and less budget to get the player in the right mindset.

Character development is also less prone to criticism. Will-to-power is one of the most powerful forces in fiction. If a character swears they will accomplish something with enough fervor, and later we see that they've accomplished it, we believe that their determination made this happen.

Meanwhile, if we construct a plot to bring about a certain outcome, it is quite likely that along the way, a playtester will say "wait a minute..." and then deliver a well-reasoned criticism of the plot construction. Now you've got to add a new idea or beat to patch up your plot. But it will happen again and again.

Setting up strong character motivations and letting those motivations manifest things in the world speaks to a different part of the player's brain.

Your story will always have plot—sometimes quite a lot of it, unavoidably. But as much as you can, think in terms of characters.

UNDERSTANDING THE SCALE OF A PROBLEM

Be cognizant of the fact that you cannot solve every problem. Some narrative problems crop up for 10% of players, but to solve it for that 10%, you will have to add an ingredient that will be seen by 100% of players. The solution, seen by 100% players, may cause confusion for the 90% that didn't have the problem to start with.

Let's say we have a scene where the player character who used to be a detective but is now retired, tracks down someone who is in hiding.

After a team playtest, a colleague comes to you:

Colleague: I don't get it, how did she find that guy who was in hiding?
You: Well, she was a detective for many years.
Colleague: Oh that's right. But that's just backstory stuff, not who she is in the game, so I didn't really think about that. Can we maybe add something to remind players of that?

They make a good point; the backstory is probably not on most player's minds. Yet, of your ten teammates, only one had this concern. Among the other nine, some just didn't care and didn't think about it, while others remembered that she was a detective.

To address the colleague's request, you'd have to add an interaction like this:

Character-in-Hiding: How did you find me?
*Player Character: Twenty years in the Atlanta PD, homicide detective, how do
        you think?*

Now the 10% of players who were wondering this will have their answer. And
90% of players will have watched you violate two of the narrative concepts we've
discussed:

- Less Is More
- Don't Be Boring

In addition, 90% of players may think that you included this exchange because
her status as an Atlanta PD homicide detective is going to be important to this
scene. But it isn't, and when the scene ends without that ever coming up again,
they will be left confused. Now you've got a problem for 90% of players!

Consider carefully if the problem is worth the solution. Sometimes you'll have
to accept that 10% of players will have a question mark over their head for a few
moments, then shrug and keep playing.

GO TOO FAR, THEN PULL BACK

In Animation, there is a creative concept of "going too far, then pulling back."
This means, rather than trying to inch up the right idea, just come up with something that is over-the-top, then keep pulling back until it feels right.

Let's say in your story, there is a scene where a character embarrasses himself
in public. A real low moment.

The cautious approach would be to ask: okay, what's exactly the right level
of embarrassment? Could he perhaps forget to zip his pants up after using
the restroom? Maybe he trips and falls flat on his face in the middle of the
restaurant?

The Too-Far-Then Back approach is to ask: How bad can we make it? Could
he accidentally set fire to the restaurant while in the restroom, leading to an
evacuation into the cold snowy night, and his pants are stuck down around his
ankles?

Unless the game is a zany comedy, the above scenario is probably way too
much. But now that you've mapped that out, you don't need to carefully slide
up to the line—you're already way over it. Now start pulling back until it
feels right.

In all honesty, we are not sure why this process works better than the
other way. But for us, and for many other creative professionals, it has indeed
worked better.

However, every creative is different, and your mileage may vary.

PHASES OF CREATIVITY

The creative process is different for everyone. However, most creatives find that the ideal process involves several phases, where the creator shifts back and forth between a loose, organic, intuitive experience, and a more cerebral, analytical experience.

Here are the stages as we see them:

- Free Association. You have a nearly blank page. There may be a few requirements for the story ingredient, but most of what you need to figure out is undefined. So completely open-ended dreaming or brainstorming is called for. In this context, dreaming means brainstorming by yourself. You shouldn't focus on what the ingredient "needs to be"; just find something that gets you excited.

- Editing. You have found an idea for the ingredient that you want to pursue. Now you pull back from it, disengage the creative, loosen part of your mind, and engage the critical, editorial part. You will immediately see many flaws. It's not as fun as you thought, and it breaks other things in the story, or it's just like that thing that happened in that other game. It can be tempting at this point to throw the idea out and start over—but that usually leads to a doom cycle. Instead, think of it as problem-solving: How can you shape or alter the idea to address those flaws while keeping what you loved about it?

- Directed Brainstorming. As you develop the story ingredient, it will change subtly and the way it relates to the rest of the game story will change. However, if you continue to work on it analytically, it will stiffen up. Instead, drop the concerns, the rules and all of that, and just dream or brainstorm. This is different from step 1 in the sense that you are somewhat directed. You know what the idea for this ingredient is, but you are just opening yourself to new takes on it, new directions for it, new stuff all around.

- Problem-Solving. After step 3, you've got a more solid idea, with a strong foundation. So it's time to go back into analytical editorial mode. But now you are identifying and solving specific problems.

- Step Back. Late in the process, it is good to return to an idea you haven't looked at or thought about in a while, and examine it from a distance. You may see it in a different light. It may suggest new ideas. This is a dangerous step, because you may want to throw the idea out because you've become bored with it, which is obviously the wrong step. But if the idea has truly become anemic, or is in some way just not suitable for the game anymore, then you either need to throw it away or adjust it.

- Walk Away. It is also vital to know when to leave an idea alone and stop tinkering with it. Creatives often can't stop, and they ruin a perfectly good idea by overworking it. Stop!

SIDEBAR: OH, JUST LIKE IN THAT OTHER GAME!

Many game teams have a vampire, and you must be wary. This person, sometimes with good intentions and sometimes with bad, will hear your fledgling idea and immediately say "Oh! Just like in recently popular game X!" When they do this, all the wind goes out of your sails, you feel like your idea must be derivative. You didn't even play game X, but maybe you saw a clip on YouTube somewhere. That idea that you loved a moment ago is now toxic—no way you can use it. Everyone will point at you and declare you're a plagiarizer.

Sometimes, this vampire is you! You, as the idea's creator, have a propensity for seeing similarities even when others don't. Red Car Syndrome is the cognitive tendency to be unaware of how many red cars there are on the road until you've bought one—then you see them everywhere. The same happens with ideas.

Take a deep breath. In its fledgling state, any idea can be accurately compared to a hundred ideas. The similarities will loom large. But they are not real.

If you can look at a story and say "It's just 'boy meets girl, boy loses girl, boy gets girl', so it's a copy of every other love story ever," you're also saying that *Romeo & Juliet*, *Natural Born Killers*, *While You Were Sleeping*, and *Princess Bride* are all the same story. It's patently absurd.

Your "derivative" idea is just in its infancy. As you add to it, it will take on a life of its own. A critical idea that "Game X" does not have is you. Your creative tastes and instincts will guide the idea into something unique.

Unless you were the main creative on Game X. Then if someone tells you "That's just like in Game X," you have a real problem.

CHAPTER SUMMARY

In this chapter 2, we discussed the following topics:

- Storytelling is about trust between storyteller and audience.
- The storyteller must trust their audience.
- The storyteller must also earn and keep the trust of the audience, in order to tell the story in a dynamic fashion.
- The Stakes of a story: What is lost? What is gained?
- Less is more. Let your audience participate in the story.
- Don't be boring. This is the first duty of a storyteller. If the story is engaging, your audience will go along for the ride, even if it doesn't make sense. If it's boring, they'll drop out.
- Active vs passive mindset of players. Someone playing a game is in an active mindset, meaning they will latch onto information that is useful for solving problems, but have less focus on information that is not relevant to solving their problems.

- Character over plot. Characters and their motivations are a sharper and more powerful way to move the story forward than plot.
- Understand the scale of the problem. Not all problems are worth solving. If 10% of players have an issue with something, but putting a solution in will degrade the experience for 90% of players, it may not be worth it.
- Go too far and then come back. Rather than inch up to the line to find the right intensity for an idea, start by going too big, then tone it down to the right point.
- Phases of creativity. Understand that a creative process means moving back and forth between freewheeling creativity and analysis.

3 Ideas

- What makes a strong concept for an idea
- How changing the original idea for a game can be dangerous
- How ideas should always support the game overall

Ideas, where do they come from, and how can you tell the good from the bad? In this section, we often refer to "idea" and "concept." These terms could mean the basic concept of your world or your story. But it can also mean any idea that drives a scene, a beat, a character, or any aspect of your world and narrative.

An inherently great or terrible idea is rare. Most ideas in their base state are serviceable. It's how they are developed, how well or badly they serve the project, and how much they excite the rest of the team that determine their true worth.

Great ideas are made or lost in how they are developed. Are they put into a structure that supports them, highlighting what is great about them? Is a counterpoint incorporated into the world, to stand in contrast? Are the compelling aspects of the idea centered in the presentation? Are the boring or unexciting parts cut away surgically?

Here are some nuts and bolts:

A STRONG LEAN CONCEPT

A strong concept is deceptively simple at first glance. You feel like you can get it in 15 seconds. What makes it powerful and useful is that it is deep. As players reencounter the concept over the course of the game, they begin to see new sides to it, new shades of meaning. Affirmations, but also contradictions, are contained within it.

Case Study: *Bioshock*

The premise of this game is that a group of rich objectivists retreat from society to form their own utopian underwater civilization. While grand, it also sounds pretty straightforward. But as the player explores the city of Rapture, they begin to see more sides to the concept, and more deeply beneath the surface, no pun intended.

DOI: 10.1201/9781003624882-5

How did this society break down? What was its original sin, and how was its doom written into its DNA at the outset? What different forms did its weaknesses manifest?

This is why a strong concept is hard to realize, and so rare: most dev teams want to keep piling on more ideas, more twists and turns. They are not able to see the concept in its nascent stage and understand what it will become. Instead, they simply see something "too simple". So in a well-meaning attempt to fix it, they want to pour more and more onto it.

When the game is close to being finished and all the experiential elements of gameplay, art, sound, and UI begin to mix with world and narrative, it becomes too much. At that point, it is either too late to pull out all the excess, or the team is so close to it that they cannot see it for what it is. And this is how you get a huge, unholy mess.

Case Study: *World of Warcraft*

This game is a massive IP. And *World of Warcraft* is a massive game. There are thousands of things a player can do in that game. It is possible to play for dozens of hours without ever repeating an activity. Yet the IP and game have a strong, clear conceptual impact.

Why? You could ask anyone who has played WoW what the core concept of that game is, and they will tell you "Horde vs Alliance." Or more likely, they will shout "For the Horde!" or "For the Alliance!", depending on their own proclivities. That is a seemingly simple concept that has sunk into every corner of the game and informed every action a player takes.

Horde vs Alliance sounds simple, yet it has defined and powered one of the most successful IPs in game history.

SIDEBAR: WHERE DO IDEAS COME FROM?

You may have noticed that this chapter has centered around evaluating ideas rather than discussing their origins. Yet "Where do ideas come from" is one of the questions most commonly asked of writers and storytellers.

The truth is that they come from many places, and that it's different for everyone. A book can't answer this question for you.

As mentioned below, ideas should hold some meaning for you, and this means that for you, ideas will come from something you think about quite often. Do you always wonder what your cat or dog is thinking? Do you brood about the ways in which people are harder on those they love than those they don't care about? Do you read classical history obsessively?

These and any topic that interests you can be the springboard for an idea that holds meaning for you, and thus an idea you can do something with.

Another important factor is simply observation. Keep your eyes and ears open, and you will see things in your life all the time that can make the basis for a great idea.

MEANING

An idea will generally resonate with others if it has some kind of meaning for you, the creator. "Meaning" should not be confused with "message." The concept or central idea of your game does not, and should not, intend to convince others of something. Rather, it is just something that is important to you.

Ken Levine, the creator of *Bioshock* has said that his intent with the first game was to look at what happens when people's ideals come face-to-face with reality. He went on that the problem with any philosophy is that it must be carried by humans, who are imperfect by nature.

That captures this point perfectly: the core concept of *Bioshock* clearly holds meaning for its creator, and it grapples with the depths of this idea. But it is not out to convince you, the player, of a particular viewpoint.

If the idea has meaning to you, your mind will find all the ways the idea is interesting, or can be tested.

On *StarCraft II: Heart of the Swarm*, Brian was trying to understand what free will looked like in a hivemind structure like the Zerg Swarm. All of the characters in that game, Abathur, Izsha, Nafash, Z'gara, Dehaka, and Stukov, swirled around the protagonist, Kerrigan, with greater and lesser degrees of free will, and greater or lesser degrees of interest in it. Likewise, Kerrigan and James Raynor both struggled with being the victim of events and then in turn taking control of events. By doing so, they sometimes turned others into the victim of events.

DAMAGING IDEAS

In story development, all new ideas and concepts should be considered. By themselves, nothing is dangerous. A new concept is either useful to the greater whole, or it is not. However, teams who must work collaboratively on ideas can fall victim to an exciting new idea that feels better than the existing idea but is actually worse.

THE THRILL OF A NEW IDEA

One danger is that when a team gets together in a room to solve a problem, someone will often propose a new idea, and everyone will get excited. It seems to solve everything! With no baggage!

This is almost never true. But there is a surge of adrenaline in the moment when the new idea emerges. The surest sign that this is a false positive is the fact that hours or days later, the idea not only does not seem as exciting, it actually turns out to break certain things in the story that the previous idea supported.

In that scenario, it is usually the narrative person sitting at a screen days later saying to themselves "wait, this doesn't actually work..." But now they've got a real problem because all the other stakeholders on the game remember that dopamine hit and in their minds, it's all sorted! If the narrative developer comes back to them to criticize the solution that "everybody loved in the room," there's going to be trouble.

Often, the stakeholders go back into a room and grudgingly bat around new ideas until someone finally comes up with a new idea … and everyone gets excited! Then the whole process repeats.

As a result, many teams stumble from new idea to new idea for years, never seeming to see the pattern. Such is the rush of dopamine.

As a veteran narrative person, you should learn to give new ideas a cooling off period. This will not win you many friends on the dev team, but over time, others will see the pattern. Try to share with the team the discipline of waiting a few days to fall in love. As with many topics, it's possible to speak to the other disciplines in ways they understand.

Every artist has gone to bed loving the work they just did, only to wake up, look at it and sigh in frustration. Every designer has built a level or system that they were convinced was great, only to playtest it the following week and see just how broken it is.

If you can convince a team to give ideas a cooling off period and have a follow-up meeting to review the merits and drawbacks of the idea in a clear-eyed way, you will have done yourself, the team, and the project a huge favor.

PUTTING A HAT ON A HAT

Writers love to add an extra layer on to a concept, fearing that simple equals boring. In film, this is referred to as "putting a hat on a hat," which means adding a second, completely separate concept on top of an original. This second concept performs the same function as the underlying concept. Then these two concepts compete with each other and muddy up the entire experience.

It is particularly noticeable in comedy, where people often try to just throw extreme and absurd ideas together, hoping they all stick. However, it is a similarly bad idea in other genres of storytelling.

Occasionally, two unrelated ideas can be combined in an interesting way, when it is core to the premise. When done well, this can grab attention. For example, the film *Snakes on a Plane*, was reportedly sold based on just those four words. However, much more often, it just ends up being a giant mess of half-realized, competing ideas.

EXAMPLE

Comedian/director Bill Hader was interviewing with talk show host Seth Meyers, and recalled a skit he proposed for *Saturday Night Live*, which Meyers, then the lead writer, told him was "a hat on a hat."

The skit was Peter Falk showing Natalie Portman how to do Star Wars impressions. Presumably, Hader would be imitating Peter Falk, and Natalie Portman would either be the real actress or another SNL cast member impersonating her. Then both would do impressions of people or creatures from *Star Wars*. Hader thought the idea would be incredibly funny and ignored Meyer's warning. Then the skit died in rehearsal and nobody laughed. It was a funny thing—celebrity impressions—on top of another funny, unrelated thing, Star Wars impressions.

OUT WITH THE OLD, IN WITH THE NEW

It takes some time to make a game. Near the start, the team will put ideas in the game that are new, fresh, and exciting. Everyone likes them. A year or two into the process, the team will declare those same ideas old and boring. Very predictable. Players will hate it!

What happened? The team plays builds of the game every week, sometimes multiple times a week. They have seen this idea over and over. They've gotten bored of it, and they want a new idea that excites them.

What they have forgotten is that players have never encountered this idea. It will be fresh and new to them. Players will experience this idea the same way the team did years ago when the idea was first put into the game.

Over time, structures and flows have grown up around the original idea. Replacing it will have unintended consequences. As a narrative professional, you must try to evaluate the ideas in a cold light. It does actually happen that a new and better idea comes along, and you must evaluate the idea fairly, but you should at least be aware that the team's antipathy to the old idea is not rooted in a careful analysis. It's rooted in boredom.

Note that this problem is similar to "The Thrill of a New Idea" concept above, but slightly different, in that it occurs over years rather than weeks, and comes from a negative impulse. That is to say, rather than being excited about a new and possibly suspect idea, the team is bored of an old but possibly solid idea.

THE RULE OF COOL

One of the most pernicious and damaging concepts out there has a breezy, rhyming name. The Rule of Cool states that if something is cool, put it in and bend everything else to justify it. This will make the project better. It's a vague enough statement that it's hard to argue with; of course you want every ingredient to be cool, and a cool idea is better than a not-cool idea. Many game developers use this mindset to complain that the narrative team is not open to their "cool" ideas, or worse, that the narrative team is defensive and protective of their own, not-cool ideas.

An environmental art lead on the Reaper of Souls team used to plaintively announce once a week at the leads meeting "I can't believe we can't do cool stuff on this game because the story says we can't."

As is so often the case, the details matter. Anyone can decide that their idea, or their friend's idea is "cool," but that doesn't actually make it cool. At the professional level, "cool" is a very high bar.

To be cool, an idea must be exciting and surprising. And that means it must withstand the cooling off period. And it must be better than the idea it is replacing. If the previous idea worked well when we put it in 6 months ago, but now we've grown bored of it, a team can easily assume the idea that is new to them is better and more exciting. But that emotional reaction is not an accurate assessment: the old idea will still be new and exciting to players when they first encounter it.

The more accurate way to assess an idea is: does it support the plot, themes, ideas and character arcs of the greater story? Often the new idea, buoyed by excitement, does more damage than good.

Finally, to be cool, an idea must fit in the tone, mood, genre, and world of the story. This seems obvious, yet those who cite the Rule of Cool are almost always violating this tenet.

If we'd suggested to that environment lead on *Diablo* that it would be "cool" to create a map tileset on the moon, he would have told us we were being stupid. Yet he seemed sure that his ideas, the ones that didn't fit into the world or IP of the game he was making, were cool. Of course, they were not cool.

Emotional feeling about an idea is not a substitute for thoughtful, careful analysis of what an idea is and how it serves or damages the story. Yet the notion of "cool," an entirely subjective standard, is 100% based on this emotional reaction.

In summary, cool is a fine goal, but a dangerous and potentially misleading one. A cool idea meets all criteria of being exciting, new, fresh, and surprising … but it must do so while also meeting the baseline standards of living within and supporting the IP of which it is a part.

SUPPORTING AN IDEA

Several times in this chapter, we mentioned that ideas work better or worse depending on how they are supported in the game. So, what does that mean?

An idea is part of a structure and a flow. It fits within a narrative, which in turn fits within a game. You might think of it as a single ingredient in a very large and complex stew. If you add the wrong amount or add it at the wrong time, it will simply disappear. Or perhaps it will overpower and ruin the entire dish.

There are specific steps one can take to make an idea successful. The first is to follow the advice at the top of this chapter: make the idea lean and simple. This is good in its own right, but it also makes the subsequent steps easier.

THE ONE-TWO PUNCH

One way to make an idea shine is to introduce another idea or concept that seems good, and then introduce the main idea, showing that it is even stronger.

This progression makes the main idea more impactful through contrast.

Case Study: *The Seven Samurai*

Two samurai, Kambei and Katsushirō, are trying to recruit more samurai to their cause. The experienced Kambei tells the young Katsushirō that they will test prospective samurai. Kambei will call to passing Samurai, bidding them enter his hut. Then Katsushirō, hiding behind the door, will hit them with a club from behind.

Katsushirō is understandably nervous about this plan, but follows orders. When the first samurai passes by, Kambei calls to him. The samurai enters, and Katsushirō swings the club. Without missing a beat the samurai spins, grabs the young man, and throws him across the room.

Kambei apologizes and explains that they need his help. When this Samurai finds out that they will only be able to pay with a little rice, he rebuffs them and leaves. Katsushirō is devastated: that samurai's reflexes were amazing. Surely he's the best around!

But when the next samurai passes by the hut, Kambei again calls out. This samurai stops in the street, looking into the hut. Rather than enter at all, he says, "Let's not play games." Kambei tells Katsushirō to stand down, and Kambei shares a laugh with this new samurai. He enters, and they recruit him to their cause.

The second samurai was so sharp that he detected the trap and refused to walk into it. This idea is impressive by itself, but the beat really shines in comparison to the first. We were like Katsushirō: impressed by the first samurai's quick reflexes and sad that he wouldn't join. But when we see the second samurai operating at an even higher level than the man we were impressed with, an exciting beat becomes truly epic.

This is the power of the one-two punch.

THE OPPOSITE

Another important way to support an idea is to show the opposite or contrary concept. The idea stands in stark contrast to its opposite.

Make the idea the exception, or in some way against expectations, and it will stand out.

Case Study: *Pirates of the Caribbean: Curse of the Black Pearl*

This story continually tells us that Captain Jack Sparrow is a drunken sod, and a buffoon. And it gives us plenty of scenes that reinforce this idea.

But it also gives us a number of scenes which imply that under the surface is a dangerous, crafty, competent operator. If this latter category of scene had come too late in the story, it would have felt like a convenience for the story tellers, and fallen flat. Instead, the filmmakers pepper early scenes with these kinds of moments, and many of them work by contrasting Jack's appearance and manner with what he actually does.

When Sparrow is captured by Lieutenant Norrington, Norrington takes inventory of his possessions and comments, "You are without doubt the worst pirate I've ever heard of." Sparrow famously replies, "But you have heard of me!" The moment is amusing and works by itself. It does not seem like a setup for anything else.

Yet not long after, as Sparrow sails out of the harbor with one of Norrington's prized ships, an aide to Norrington comments: "That's got to be the best pirate I've ever seen." Norrington must grudgingly agree.

This contrast, going from "you are without doubt the worst pirate I've ever heard of," to "that's got to be the best pirate I've ever seen," in a few beats, drives home that Sparrow is a dangerous and capable pirate.

A side benefit of the Opposite approach is that it can actually highlight two things at once. The scene above highlights Sparrow's competence, but also develops Norrington a bit. He's not happy to admit he was wrong, but admit it he does, which is telling.

THE RIGHT PLACE AND TIME

A critical part of featuring an idea is knowing when and where it should appear in a story. There is always a temptation to introduce a cool or exciting idea early, for fear of "losing" players if you wait too long. Likewise, there can be a temptation to hold off on a cool idea for a long time, building up to it.

It is important to understand the right moment to introduce or develop an idea. It's difficult to give more guidance on this point because everything about finding the right timing depends on the rest of the project. Structure, pace, tempo, character arcs: all of these affect what makes the timing good or bad. It is too project-specific to give meaningful insight.

EXAMPLE: *THE THING*

In the 1982 film version of this story, there is a slow burn as characters realize that a shape-shifting alien has infiltrated their group. Now they are unsure if those around them are what they seem. Tension rises, trust erodes.

The audience has seen a few explicit examples of the alien's biological horror processes, but it was always quick and somewhat obscured. As the film goes on, anticipation builds about when the alien will fully reveal itself.

Eventually, everything explodes in several intense scenes. We would recommend watching the movie twice. Once just to experience it. On the second viewing, you will be able to put on a more analytical hat and see just how expertly John Carpenter and Bill Lancaster construct the entire story around the tension and expectation.

Finding the right moment for an idea is one of the most important aspects of supporting that idea. A powerful idea, well set up in every other way, will fizzle if it plays at the wrong moment.

"Moment" can be influenced by structure—what does the player know, and what don't they know? It can be affected by tempo—does the idea's placement take advantage of the current momentum? Or is it undercut by that momentum? It can be affected by tone, feel, mood, and many other factors.

As everything else in your story comes into focus, take a look at where the key ideas live, and see if that is the right place for them.

AN IMPACT

The final way to properly support an idea in the narrative is to make sure it has a big impact on events and upon the characters. This may sound obvious, but it is quite easy to reveal a concept in your story and then have all the characters react to it for a beat ... and then carry on with the overall conflict.

The introduction of a major and important idea must change the direction of the story and/or change the way characters feel about the conflict, themselves, each other, and the story in general.

If you find that a major idea is not accomplishing this, it may mean the idea is not as good as you'd hoped. But it may also mean that you are not properly supporting the idea.

Are you introducing it in the correct spot? In the correct way? What changes would you need to make in order to give it this kind of impact? Are there unexpected side effects? What ripples did the idea create in the story?

CHAPTER SUMMARY

In this chapter, we discussed the following topics:

- A strong, lean concept. Simple, impactful ideas are always better and more durable.
- An idea should hold some meaning for you. If it does, it will likely hold meaning for many of your players.

- Damaging ideas. New ideas crop up during development, and you should be open to them, but be careful that the excitement of a new idea doesn't override your analysis. The new idea may do more harm than good. Keep a clear mind.
- Supporting an idea. Most ideas are not amazing or terrible on their own merits. Usually, an idea needs support to really shine, and there are some straightforward ways to achieve this.

4 Basic Structure

IN THIS CHAPTER

- Learn the basics of story structure
- What are the different events that signify the start and end of an Act
- How differing philosophies drive storytelling

BASIC STRUCTURE

As with the other story basics we touch on here, a great deal has been written about structure, and we encourage you to seek out some of that writing. You may agree with some, all, or none of it, but it is good to know. What we've written here is just the briefest essay on structure as it applies to all storytelling. Structure for game narrative has some key differences, and we will go into more detail on that later.

A key concept to understand about structure from the get-go is when it's important to think structurally and when it is not. Structure, or plot, is just the things that happen in the story, what order they happen in, and with what momentum.

More than anything, structure is a diagnostic tool. That is to say, if you have developed powerful characters with real problems which they are trying to solve in a way that is true to them, and thus learn lessons that cause them to grow until they can—or definitely cannot—solve that problem, then the structure will just happen. It's not useful to think about structure at that stage. If you do, you're trying to impose rules from the outside because you think you're supposed to.

But structure is invaluable in second and later drafts, when you are trying to solve problems in your story. Many of the character-driven decisions of the first draft will have the right spirit or intent, but they'll be a bit off, or too slow, or too fast. There are a number of ways that you will need to fine-tune a second or later draft of a story, and understanding structure is a key tool for doing that.

Note that for game narrative, structure is important as an independent concept or tool, because your story must fit perfectly within the bigger structure of the game. You have less freedom—but we'll get to that later.

We've discussed protagonists with a problem that brings them into conflict with an antagonist, leading to escalation and eventually resolution. This already suggests a structure, the classic "Beginning, middle, end" story.

That trio of states—beginning, middle, end—suggests a three-act structure. However, the classic three-act structure has a good deal more to it than that. We will cover it because it is the most commonly used act structure in general. Film uses the three-act structure almost exclusively.

 DOI: 10.1201/9781003624882-6

What follows is a summary of the film industry's concept of a three-act structure. It's not the only way to realize a three-act structure, and if applied mindlessly, it just becomes formulaic. But consider this a guideline to spark some thought on your part. It's also useful because you may have teammates who are familiar with this paradigm and will want to discuss it, or even enforce it, on your project.

It behooves you to know it better than they do!

It goes like this:

ACT I

We meet a character in their normal world. Everything is the way it has always been. This may be good, or it may be terrible. The character may be hopeful and happy, or they may be hopeless and sad. But they regard their current circumstance as their normal state of being.

Then, a change occurs that throws the normal state of things out of balance. This change is almost always for the worse. This is called the Inciting Incident, and it is where the plot begins.

Note: The story begins before the plot, because we have met our hero in their normal world before the inciting incident. In very rare circumstances, having lots of time between the start of the story and the inciting incident may be desirable, but most of the time, you want this interval to be as short as possible. Get things moving!

This world-changing event can be anything from an orphaned kitten wandering into the house, to losing a job, to aliens showing up and destroying entire continents. There is no requirement for scale, so long as it is impactful to the character.

The character decides to do something in order to bring their world back into alignment. They take action to fix the problem—perhaps they want to restore the norm, or to change things for the better, but either way, the change must be dealt with.

In some models, the character actually resists taking action, hoping to just muddle through. These concepts have been described as "the Call to Adventure" and "the Refusal of the Call," although they have been overused and misused to such an extent that they are almost devoid of meaning. So let's just refer to them descriptively.

Then, disaster strikes: the worst thing that can happen … happens. In the poetic language of film structure, this is sometimes referred to as "Plot Point One," or "the act one break."

As a result of this terrible event, the protagonist realizes or finally accepts that they must set out on a real journey to restore the balance of their world. This journey can be metaphorical, emotional, geographical, or anything else. In most adventure stories, it's a literal journey, but it can easily be one of self-discovery, or a journey to reimagine a failing business. The term journey is meant to signify that the protagonist must move away from everything they know to solve this terrible problem. They will not have their usual support system as they begin to take action.

Case Study: *Horizon Zero Dawn*

Normal Life and Normal world: Aloy is an outcast from her tribe, the Nora. She is being raised by another outcast, Rost.

Inciting incident: In a playable flashback, young Aloy finds an augmented reality device called a focus, which gives her special perceptive abilities. In the present day, this leads Aloy to question her own origins, and Rost tells her that if she wins the coming-of-age contest, the Proving, the Nora will have to accept her, and perhaps the matriarchs will tell her about her origins.

Note: The inciting incident is a playable flashback. So it is in Aloy's past, but the player's experience of the story beat falls in the correct spot for an inciting incident.

Initial steps: Aloy participates in the Proving.

Disaster strikes: Masked cultists attack, derailing the Proving and killing Rost, the only person who has ever cared for her.

Setting out on the journey: The matriarchs appoint Aloy a "Seeker," allowing her to leave the Nora lands to pursue the cultists. With Rost dead, Aloy's only tie to the location and people has been severed.

She sets out on the journey.

The End of Act I

This moment, when the character takes action to deal with the change, is the end of Act I, or the end of the beginning.

There is no going back.

SIDEBAR: FOUR- AND FIVE-ACT STRUCTURES

Is three-act structure the only way to go? Not at all. There are models for four- and five-act structures. They are not as common, but you may run into them.

The rarest of all, the four-act structure, is essentially the three-act structure, with a surprise act thrown on at the end. The protagonists achieve their goal, and it seems as if the story should be heading for resolution, but there is a surprise development that extends the story.

The 1998 film *Saving Private Ryan* uses the four-act structure. The protagonists spend the entire film searching for private Ryan. When they finally find him, it's time to bring him back to base and, in keeping with the title, save private Ryan. The story should be over. But there's one problem: Ryan refuses to leave his unit, as they are defending a town and are about to be attacked. Now the protagonists must stay and help defend the town, while continuing to save private Ryan. This surprise act at the end of the story can serve as an interesting development in the story, or feel like a tacked-on, superfluous idea. It all depends on the skill of the storyteller.

More common is the five-act structure. All of Shakespeare's plays used this structure, and many 45–60-minute dramas on television also use it.

A brief summary is as follows:

Act 1: Introduction
Act 2: Rising Action
Act 3: Climax
Act 4: Falling Action
Act 5: Resolution.

From that breakdown, you can see that the five-act structure uses the same beats, in the same order, as the three-act structure. In the three-act structure, several beats are contained within one act, while in the five, they are broken out.

Some games would benefit from a five-act structure, and it is certainly worth investigating. However, it is a bit too specific for us to delve deeper into it here, since the three- and five-act structures are really variations on each other.

Act II

Act II, or the middle, is structurally very difficult. This is a series of escalating events where the protagonist takes action, is foiled, suffers defeats and setbacks, learns, tries new things, grows, meets new characters, and perhaps even sets new goals or acquires new problems, which grow out of the old.

Act II is characterized by exciting action. As with other elements, action here does not necessarily mean car chases. Action could be an intense argument, or discovering a dead spouse's secret diary.

It is also the place in the story where we meet other important characters, and learn more about them, as well as more about our protagonist and our antagonist.

It is also where we see our antagonist take more actions. As covered earlier, the protagonist and antagonist react or try to proactively outdo each other.

Finally, it is also where subplots are introduced. Subplots are character-driven plots that will be introduced and resolved in the course of the bigger story, and often reveal variations on the main themes of the story.

Beware Episodic Construction

The danger in constructing Act II is that it can become episodic—a series of smaller problems/situations that technically contribute to the overall storyline, but actually feel like modular bits that don't have much meaning in the overall picture.

Essentially, episodic construction in Act II can feel more like a short story collection than a novel.

The Midpoint

In most three-act stories, there is a major tent pole right in the middle of Act II—which is also the middle of the story.

This midpoint is a major reversal or setback. The protagonist learns something about themselves, and must regroup, finding renewed determination, or new purpose.

Some variations of the midpoint bring the underlying theme into greater focus. If your story is about how love and hate are two sides of the same coin, then the midpoint hinges on a moment where two people who once loved each other now wish to destroy each other. Or how an old enemy may sacrifice themselves to save their old rival.

EXAMPLE: *BIOSHOCK*

In this game, the midpoint is the revelation that the character you thought was helping you all along is in fact the antagonist, and he has gained mind control over you, and now forces you to take actions you don't wish to take.

The End of Act II

In the classic three-act structure, the end of Act II is defined by a major, disastrous set back. The worst thing that can happen does happen.

If you notice the similarity to the end of Act I, that is absolutely on purpose. The "worst thing" from the end of Act I, which seemed so awful at the time, is now dwarfed by the worst thing at the end of Act II, showing how much the stakes have increased, and how much the character(s) have grown and gone through.

In film this is elegantly referred to as "Plot Point Two," or "the act 2 break."

In the 1998 comedy *The Wedding Singer*, the worst thing that could happen at the end of Act I was that the protagonist's girlfriend leaves him. At the end of Act II, he has learned to move on and fallen in love in a more profound way, and then the worst thing happens: his girlfriend returns, willing to take him back, which destroys the new relationship he's forged.

In the 1988 comedy *Working Girl*, Tess McGill has been leading a double life, pretending to be an executive when she is actually an assistant. At the end of Act II, the antagonist publicly reveals Tess's deception, causing everything Tess has built to come tumbling down.

Act III

This "worst thing" event sends us into Act III with a great deal of momentum. For all that our protagonist has achieved, for all that they have accomplished and grown and learned, the situation is now more desperate than ever, the stakes higher.

And so they enter Act III needing to rally around their cause, and form a plan to fight back, using all the things they have learned in the story—whether practical skills like "how to fight" or philosophical skills like how to be strong in the face of overwhelming adversity.

The Act III Rally

The antagonists seem to have won. But the protagonist(s) rally and take the fight to the antagonists.

A Bad Turn

There is at least one more major setback or turn, which throws the protagonist's plans from the beginning of Act III into chaos. This requires the protagonist to adapt, using skills, wisdom, and knowledge learned in Act II to give their cause one more try.

The Good Turn

The antagonist's reaction, or that of their group or allies, overcomes the bad turn, or fails to overcome it.

The Climax

All of these ingredients come to a head in one key moment, where the protagonist succeeds, or the antagonist does.

The Resolution

Endings and Resolutions were covered elsewhere at length, but this is where they fall in a three-act structure.

Case Study: *Star Wars: A New Hope*

In *Star Wars: A New Hope*, during Act III, the rebels plan to send small fighters out to meet the massive death star, hoping to shoot a torpedo into a very small opening, which will set off a chain reaction and destroy the death star. This desperate, doomed-to-fail plan is the Act III Rally.

Their plan has setbacks, but the real problem arrives when Darth Vader takes his personal ship and two additional pilots out into the battlefield, destroying the rebel ships before they can get a shot off. All seems lost. This is the Bad Turn.

Then the mercenary Han Solo, who had earlier abandoned the cause, returns to help, damaging Darth Vader's ship so that he is out of the fight.

This is the Good Turn, and it is important to note that it is motivated by the camaraderie and friendship that our protagonists Luke and Princess Leia inspired in Han Solo. He has come to believe in their cause, or at least in them. So their actions in Act II have paid off here.

But removing Darth Vader from the fight is not enough. There is still that nearly impossible shot—Luke must shoot a torpedo into a tiny exhaust port. As he approaches on the same vector as a previous pilot who failed to hit the mark, Luke hears the voice of his dead mentor, telling him to turn off his computer and trust in the force. He does so and is able to make the shot.

This is the climax, and a vital beat, because so much of the story centered around Luke learning to trust and believe in the force. He is not the protagonist because he is a better shot than the other pilots. He is the protagonist because he believes in the force and has sought to better himself through its pursuit.

Having destroyed the Death Star, Luke and his allies return to the rebel base, where he is awarded a medal. This is the resolution, and it lets us know the story is over.

SIDEBAR: A SIMPLE STRUCTURE TOOL

One way to think about how different plot points, scenes, and beats are connected is to remember the "and therefore" or "but'" rule. This concept has been articulated in a number of places, but we first heard it mentioned by the creators of *South Park*.

Simply put, two story beats should be easy to connect with the words "and therefore," or "but."

Examples

Early in the story of *Ghost of Tsushima*, the protagonist Jin Sakai goes straight to the stronghold of his enemy, Khotun Khan, to confront him. Khotun quickly defeats Jin, and therefore, Jin realizes that the traditional way of the Samurai will not work against this new enemy, so he begins to plan a new way to fight back. The rest of the story flows logically from the events of the scene where Jin and Khotun fight.

Or

In *World of Warcraft: The War Within*, the heroes gather in Dalaran and teleport the city to Khaz Algar to set up a war base like they had in the Northrend and Legion campaign, but are attacked by the Nerubians and Xal'atath, and the floating city is destroyed forcing them to regroup in the new land and make new allies.

In other words, beats should connect with the logical follow through. X, and therefore Y. Or, the logical follow-through should be interrupted by an unexpected event. X, but Y.

This tool prevents randomness from creeping into a story structure.

Multiple plotlines are more common in film, TV, and novels than in games, but they do still exist, so we should address that here. In the case of multiple plot lines, you may have a structure like:

Plot A, beat 1
Plot B, beat 1
Plot A, beat 2
Plot B, beat 2.

If that is the case, you can still use the rule by connecting the Plot A beats with "and therefore" or "but," and connecting the Plot B beats the same way. Players will still inherently understand the connections, even if they occur farther apart.

This is the classic Act III construction. If you watch and analyze the final act of many Hollywood movies, particularly from the 1980s and 1990s, you'll see how many variations can exist while still containing the basic steps outlined here.

A WAR OF PHILOSOPHIES

Another element common to almost all narratives is that under the surface is a war of philosophies. Your protagonist and antagonist are not merely opposed because of their goals. They are each the avatar of a competing philosophy. These two philosophies cannot coexist, and so there will be conflict between them.

Selfishness vs selflessness. Rage vs balance. Change vs conformity. Freedom vs oppression. In some cases, the two may not be diametric opposites, but still philosophies that clash. You could have a story where Lust is opposed by Meaningfulness. While the opposite of lust is something more like restraint, or lack of lust, the deeper idea is that lust is a powerful drive that ultimately lacks meaning. And so the philosophical counter to unrestrained lust is meaningfulness.

Based on your own inclinations, you may think some of the X vs Y scenarios above have a good-and-evil-by-default cast to them. But if you analyze enough media, that is simply not true.

Take change vs conformity. Gattaca tells the story of a young man living in a deeply conformist society, who creates change in his own circumstance through sheer force of will. In this scenario, conformity is the "evil" force, while individualism and change are the "good."

But in *Lord of the Rings*, Frodo seeks to reestablish the harmonic order to "the way things should be." In that scenario, Frodo is seeking to create conformity to an ideal world order, while Sauron is seeking change.

This concept also applies to IP building, on a much grander scale, which we will go into more detail on later.

CHAPTER SUMMARY

In this chapter, we discussed the following topics:

- Three-Act Structure:
  - Act I: Introduce the protagonist in their normal world, until something upsets the established order.
  - Act II: The protagonist sets out to correct the problem, meets new friends and enemies, undergoes a series of trials or conflict, and the stakes keep rising.
  - Act III: The situation is as dire as it can get, and the protagonist must rally themselves and their allies, harnessing everything they've learned and all the growth they've experienced through the whole story.
- A war of philosophies. The protagonist and the antagonist should each be an exemplar of a philosophy, and these philosophies should be opposed. This underlying current will frame everything in the story.

Section 2

Game Storytelling

Building off our discussion of the foundations of storytelling, we move into storytelling in games specifically.

DOI: 10.1201/9781003624882-7

5 Storytelling That Is Unique to Games

IN THIS CHAPTER

- What is interactive, environmental, and emergent storytelling
- What is prioritized storytelling
- What is nonlinear storytelling

Games are a new and unique medium. They share characteristics with other media, particularly in the storytelling arena. We covered the more universal storytelling principles in the previous section. But the most important aspect of game storytelling for you to understand, and the hardest to truly grasp, are the types of storytelling that are unique to games.

Like any new medium, games began by copying what came before. Early films copied theater. It was some time before filmmakers realized, "Oh, I can move the camera around! It doesn't have to be locked down the way a theater audience is stuck in their seats!"

When games started, storytelling was mostly done through cutscenes, in other words, like a film. There was also some story in mission briefings and load screen text. But that was marginal. Game manuals also contained a story, but it was IP and world story, not the story of the game.

Over time, we have learned a few storytelling techniques that are unique to games, which makes them extremely powerful. But games are a young medium, and in the coming years, hopefully, we will discover more new techniques.

For now, these are the ones we know about.

INTERACTIVE

The first type is the most obvious: players can interact with the story. Novel readers, theater, ballet, and film audiences can consume the story, but they cannot affect it.

Players participate in the story. In the most structured and linear games, the story is set, but the player's participation is still required. In many games, such as RPGs, the player actually alters the course of the story. It can be as momentous as deciding if the world will be a utopia or a hellscape moving forward, or as human as nudging a companion into being a better or worse person.

Whatever level of interactivity your game story has, you must find a way to highlight it at every stage.

DOI: 10.1201/9781003624882-8

In *StarCraft II: Heart of the Swarm*, we had an upgrade tree for zerg units. It's a design-forward feature, where the player is offered two short missions with alternate versions of an upgraded unit. Afterward, the player must choose one of the upgrades. The other is discarded.

Each of these short missions had a brief level of story involved. Where did the upgrade come from? Who are we fighting? The purpose of the mission is to test out the upgrade, but this is no lab simulation: we are on a real planet, fighting real opponents. Our advisor, Abathur, has opinions about the benefits and drawbacks of this particular upgrade.

There was also a story element to the way the overall choice was presented. This was the future direction of the Swarm. Now, players didn't just feel as if they were making a design choice to tailor their own play experience. They felt that they were charting the evolutionary future of the most adaptable race in the galaxy.

Adding narrative to a simple interactive design choice immersed the player deeper into the StarCraft universe and made for a more powerful experience overall.

In cases where there is deeper and more interactivity, it is still important to keep it front and center. The player should feel that everything they do is having an influence. In some squad games, the player makes choices about what to say or how to react to squad members around them. In some setups, every choice really matters. In others, only a few consequential choices matter, and the rest are just flavor. Regardless, the constant choice gives players a powerful feeling of control and influence on the world around them.

ENVIRONMENTAL

Environmental storytelling happens when the player assembles the story, or part of the story, from clues found in the environment. It is present in other media, but it is included on this list because the player experiences it so differently in games.

Environmental storytelling in games is truly unique. To start, we can consider an example of great environmental storytelling from film, and then contrast it with games.

Case Study: *Back to the Future*

The first scene in the film is a long pan across a set. In one continuous shot, we see the following:

- Many clocks, setting up the importance of time.
- A radio alarm goes off, but the bed it is next to is empty.
- An automated coffee maker starts brewing, but there is no pot on the heat pad.

- A television turns on and tells us that officials deny the rumor that plutonium was stolen from their facility.
- A toaster, which pops up some badly burned bread—it has clearly been toasted many times.
- A homemade gadget that opens a can of dog food and empties the can into a dog food bowl, which is already heaped with older dog food.
- A doorway, where the protagonist, Marty, enters, calling out to "Doc," and a dog named "Einstein."
- He kicks his skateboard across the floor, where it bumps into a case under the bed marked "Plutonium, Handle with Care."

In the course of just a moment or two of screentime, we see that

- This is the home of an inventor.
- He has automated much of his life.
- He is obsessed with time.
- He loves his dog.
- He has stolen Plutonium.
- He has been gone for some time, at least a day or two.

This is powerful environmental storytelling for film. It's compact and economical, it is "show don't tell," and it invites us to add up different ingredients, so we feel smart.

All of this would be fundamentally different and more powerful in games because of one concept: interactivity.

Players move through the environment under their own control. Each element the player examines is by choice. In the film example, the director chose what we see and when we see it. But with the player in control, every part of the experience is different and more powerful.

Players can linger on some parts of the environment, absorb others in passing, and completely ignore others. Thus, the player picks up the clues that matter most to them. And because they can encounter them in a nonlinear order, they also piece the story together in their own way, with their own flavor.

In an interactive world, environmental storytelling is one of the strongest tools you have, and you would be wise to make the most of it.

Games that use environmental storytelling almost exclusively are titles like *Gone Home* and *What Remains of Edith Finch*. But even big AAA games with hundreds of different story channels still rely heavily upon environmental storytelling. Some of the true power of the historical feeling in an *Assassin's Creed* game is simply walking through a place that feels like it is in the past. There is a reason that Ubisoft's environment artists are so diligent about accurately capturing the historical locations they set their games in.

EMERGENT

One of the most mysterious and interesting storytelling types is emergent story. When multiple game systems, along with the player, all crash together in new and unexpected ways, a story emerges.

It was not planned. No one wrote it down. It emerges from the world.

What follows is a hypothetical story that could have emerged from the systems in *The Elder Scrolls IV: Oblivion*.

Case Study: *The Elder Scrolls IV: Oblivion*

You, the player, enter the prosperous town of Bruma. You decide you want to steal a valuable jewel from the Mages Guild Hall. Using stealth, you sneak into the hall, lift the jewel, and are making your way back out with your ill-gotten gains.

But one of the mages has an amulet of perception, and she sees you. She chases you out into the street, and as you flee, she hurls a fireball at you. This was ill-advised, because you were running into a crowd of villagers to hide. You survive due to your fire-resist gear, but 20 villagers are instantly turned to a crisp. The survivors all scream and run away!

But a Bruma town guard just witnessed a mage incinerate a group of villagers. He calls upon the other guards, and they all charge at the mage. More mages come spilling out of the guild hall. They don't know what is going on, but they see one of their own being attacked by the Bruma guards.

You flee into the hills. You stop on a nearby hilltop and see a huge battle between 6 mages and 40 guards. The town is on fire and people run screaming everywhere.

It's a pretty straightforward story about the day that the city of Bruma suffered a cataclysmic event. But no one wrote this story. No one planned it.

Instead the following game systems all crashed together:

Stealth: This is how you snuck in.

Thieving: This establishes the concept of property, and so the mage could see you had something that belonged to her guild.

Area-of-Effect Damage: This is how the fireball killed innocent villagers.

Special Gear: This is how the mage detected you, and how you survived the fireball.

Factions 1: The mages, the cityfolk, and the guards were all different factions, which is what set up the carnage and the fight.

Factions 2: While the cityfolk faction AI said to flee from the violence, the guard's faction AI said to protect the cityfolk, which is what caused them to attack the mage.

Factions 3: The mage faction AI told her to call for help, and told the other mages to come to her defense.

All of these systems clashed together in a new and unexpected way, and now you, the player, just caused a massacre in the city of Bruma. Congratulations.

Emergent stories can end up being lame and simplistic or deep and incredible. But they are always impactful because the player can tell that they are discovering it as it happens, and usually that they are the catalyst.

WHY TALK ABOUT EMERGENT STORY IN A NARRATIVE BOOK?

We said that no one wrote these stories, and it sounds like something that happens without a narrative developer involved. So why talk about it? Is it just a way to taunt everyone with their future obsolescence?

No. Emergent stories will happen if enough systems come together, but the stories produced purely by chance will often be lame. The example above was the product of many systems that all worked quite well by themselves, but were also designed to work together in order to create great stories. It's not a pure coincidence that great stories emerge from these systems.

If a gameplay designer works on this without your help, their focus will likely be on producing really fun and interesting gameplay outcomes—as it should be. But you are the one who can consider how and why different systems might combine.

Setting the stage for a great story without being the one to tell it is a big part of game narrative anyway. You will always want the player to feel like they are the one telling the story. This is just a more extreme version of that.

As a next step, you can even try to predict certain outcomes and acknowledge when they happen. Imagine if the player who caused the massacre in Bruma was walking through the central square in Imperial City, and heard a crier: "There's been some trouble in Bruma, with casualties!" You don't even need to specify what happened, because there might have been many different bad things that could have happened in Bruma. Or any of the other cities, which is why you would write lines for all of them.

Or perhaps you could generate text for a notice that would do the same thing. Players will fill in the details of what happened, because they were there! And now they'll be amazed: the game is reacting to them!

AMBIGUOUS

We should note the distinction between vague and ambiguous storytelling. Vague is just muddy, confusing, and ultimately unsatisfying in any medium. It is usually the product of a clumsy storyteller who is not even aware that they are being confusing. Ambiguous, on the other hand, is a story beat where either one thing happened, or another happened, and it is not clear which. But it's definitely one of those two. There may be a wider field of possibility than just two options, but it is more heavily structured than a vague story.

Many media experiment with storytelling that is ambiguous. Yet we've listed ambiguous storytelling under "specific to games," and this is because the way players engage with ambiguous storytelling is completely different than consumers of other media.

In film, theater, and books, there is some interest in an ambiguous story. One of the most iconic examples of this is the briefcase in *Pulp Fiction*. What is in the briefcase? Quentin Tarantino never tells us.

This example is iconic partially because it is so rare. For the most part, someone who has watched an entire movie, television show, or play, or who has read an entire novel, wants some concrete understanding of what happened. Experimental forms of these media play around with ambiguous storytelling, but the mainstream of each has a hard time satisfying their audiences with an ambiguous story. Thus, ambiguous storytelling is limited to experimental genres for those media.

In games, ambiguous storytelling is in the mainstream. Giving us the ingredients of a story without telling us exactly how it played out is quite common. Most open world games are huge, mainstream hits. They are big games with a wide-ranging audience, and they have ambiguous storytelling everywhere.

EXAMPLE: *THE ELDER SCROLLS V: SKYRIM*

In this game, the player can come upon a burned-out hut near Riverwood. There is a charred corpse and a scroll of Summon Flame Atronach.

The broad strokes of what happened here seem clear: someone tried to summon a Flame Atronach and immolated themselves instead.

But the story that led to this outcome is ambiguous. There are specific events that happened, but we don't know what they are. Did a farmer find the scrolls and attempt to summon the Atronach, thinking it could help clear his fields? Did an apprentice steal her master's scrolls to prove her worth? Maybe an aged, doddering summoner was seeking to prove that he still "had it," except that he didn't?

The game has not told you a story. Instead, it gives you all the ingredients for a story, and you can assemble them in a way that makes sense to you.

You may ask, Isn't this environmental storytelling? It is, but many of these concepts have overlap. Ambiguous storytelling can be created using many other types of storytelling, and vice versa.

Why do players who would be frustrated by ambiguous storytelling in a film accept it and even relish it in a game?

The simplest explanation is that the player is invited to participate in the story: you examine all the elements, and put the pieces together. You figure out what happened.

Of course, the same thing is true of an ambiguous movie. So there must be something deeper. The real difference is the player's mindset that we discussed in Chapter 2: "Narrative Concepts."

Someone watching a film or reading a book is in a passive mindset. They are waiting for the storyteller to present them with all the information needed to consume the story. Suddenly, the storyteller is asking them to shift modes, to become active participants. We discussed in Chapter 2 that asking your audience to shift modes is difficult.

Games, on the other hand, are telling stories to players who are in an active mindset. Players are expecting to solve problems, so presenting them with a story beat that isn't fully defined doesn't require a mindset shift. It fits in perfectly with their current mindset: "Oh, there's a problem of incomplete information? I bet I can deduce what happened!"

This openness to a type of storytelling that invites the player into the creative process makes ambiguous storytelling powerful and widely used in games, in a way that it simply cannot be in other media.

Having players with an active mindset causes other problems, such as their impatience with cutscenes, so you may as well take advantage of the mindset they do have and invite them to piece together a story in their head.

PRIORITIZED STORYTELLING

Games can tell stories on multiple channels during the player's experience.

In a Real-Time Strategy game like *StarCraft II*, you can communicate story to the player in many different ways:

- In-mission cutscene
- In-mission Ambient
- Briefing heading in to the mission
- Debrief after mission
- Log Menus
- Story mode Conversation
- In-Engine Cutscene
- Pre-rendered Cutscene.

Over time, players begin to attach significance to the channel used to convey something. The above list is prioritized in order of gameplay importance.

If you trigger an in-mission cutscene, where you take control of the camera away from the player to convey something, it is vital for gameplay. You should only rarely do this, because in RTS it's pretty enraging to have control taken away.

There is a lot of ambient VO on a map, and some players tune it out. But if you add too much ambient VO to try and tell character stories, players will tune it out even more. So you should reserve this channel mostly for gameplay-critical communication. One exception to this rule is during a hero mission, where you are directly controlling a character like Jim Raynor or Sarah Kerrigan, because the core fantasy of the mission is to experience more with that character.

If players only care about useful gameplay information, they can pay attention to the first three channels on that list, and they will have everything they need to know. They can tune out or skip all the other incoming messages, confident that they're not missing anything.

If they have forgotten something and want to relearn it, they can go to the log menus, which are a part of the game where the developers have listed things like enemy types, with their vulnerabilities noted, etc.

If players are interested in the story, the priority of the list is different. It would go like this:

- Pre-rendered Cutscene
- In-Engine Cutscene
- Story mode Conversation
- Debrief after mission
- Briefing heading into the mission
- In-mission Ambient
- In-mission cutscene
- Log Menus.

The effect of having all these different channels is that players, who have a split-focus most of the time, can intuitively understand how important or unimportant a particular communication from the game is.

Not all games have as many channels as an RTS, but as you play different genres of game, you will start to notice that there are multiple channels by which the game can communicate with you, and that you develop your own priority list of how much to pay attention to different channels.

Other media, such as film or books, cannot do this. They have only one focus. It's true that films can have ambient or background voices, but those are used to convey a sense of the location—a busy train station or loud lunch crowd at a restaurant. Nothing those characters are saying is meant to convey story to you, the viewer. If they were, they could not be background, because you might miss them.

You might say that films communicate with visuals of the characters and environment, and audio of the musical score and sound effects. And that's true, but all of those channels are still intended to form into a cohesive whole for the viewer. Even when they are discordant, like ominous music over a happy scene, they are intended to convey one feeling. *It seemed like a normal day in the park— but it was not!*

Meanwhile, the channels in games inherently come with a priority list for a split-focused player. We discussed active and passive mindset for players, and this prioritized storytelling is a tool to help the active mindset player find the correct focus.

NONLINEAR

Everyone in games is fascinated by nonlinear storytelling, even though the name is a bit of a misnomer. In one sense, all story is linear. Information is presented to a player in some fashion, and their mind constructs a linear understanding of what happened. So that story, in their mind, is linear.

Let's present players with five story beats in this order:

- The player character gets in a fight behind the local ShopMart.
- The player character wakes up to his morning alarm clock.
- The player character gets arrested at a local bar.
- The player character buys some snacks at the ShopMart.
- The player character eats breakfast and decides to go to the ShopMart.

Clearly, some of the beats are out of order, and the player can impose an order: The first beat is the character waking up to his morning alarm. The second beat is probably eating breakfast and making plans. The final beat is very likely the character getting arrested.

The beats about buying snacks and getting into a fight are in the middle, but it is impossible to know which comes first. Did the character get in an altercation, then go inside and buy a snack, and then head to the local bar before the police caught up? Or was it: buy snacks, get in a fight, then head to the bar? Or is the beat of getting arrested completely independent of the fight? Maybe something else happened later in the day?

However, players will assemble this story into a linear series of events in their mind, with cause and effect. This is simply how the human mind works. So, "nonlinear" refers to how the story is presented, but the final shape it takes in the player's mind is still linear.

In fact, some players will assemble it into a linear story so instinctively that it will never occur to them that there was another interpretation.

If that is the case, what is the value in presenting the story in a nonlinear way? There are a number of benefits, with the key one being that it invites players to participate in assembling the pieces, and anytime you can invite the player to participate, you draw them in deeper. Another benefit is that each player can assemble the pieces the way they want, creating their own interpretation, which might be different from other players. This gives each player a feeling of a customized experience.

The crucial aspect of presenting a nonlinear story still involves the order in which you present the pieces. It matters!

First, because of anchoring bias. Anchoring bias is the tendency to give greater weight to the first piece of information presented and to gauge all subsequent information from it. If a player hears multiple pieces of information, they will weigh its importance based on the order they heard it in. Particularly, when there are contradictory pieces of information, anchoring bias causes people to believe the first piece of information they heard, regardless of its veracity.

In our scenario above, players would most likely assume that the character got into the fight before buying the snacks, simply because the information was presented in that order.

Second, players construct the story as they gather information, rather than waiting until the end and putting all the pieces together. This means that the connections between pieces of information feel different, based on what else the player knows.

In the scenario, players would guess that the character was arrested because of the fight, since the fight was presented first. The arrest seems like a consequence. However, if we showed the character getting arrested first, players would be more open to the idea that the two beats are not strictly related. Or that perhaps the character got arrested, was released later, and then ran into the person who got him arrested, and picked a fight.

SPECIFIC TO GAMES

In other media, the story must be presented in a linear fashion. Even a film that is edited out of chronological order, such as *Memento*, is presented in a linear fashion to the audience, and they must construct the story in their minds.

But games can let the player determine the linear presentation of the story.

To reach once again for our scenario above, imagine our game has a chapter called "The Events of August 10." The player is presented with a menu of five gameplay sections. Each section must be played to advance the game. But the player can choose which order to play or experience those events.

All of the permutations we discussed above, all the different scenarios that will affect how the player experiences the story, are now under the player's control. Each player will chart their own course and experience the story in their own way.

No other media can do this.

CHAPTER SUMMARY

In this chapter, we discussed the following topics:

- Interactivity. All game narrative is interactive to a greater or lesser degree. Finding any way possible to let the player interact with the story will make it more powerful, including adding narrative to interactive design choices.
- Environmental. Players move through an environment with an active mindset, meaning they are excited to gather clues from their surroundings, in any order they find them, and piece them together to create the narrative in their head.
- Emergent. When complex game systems crash together due to the actions of the player, a story that was never written by anyone emerges, often with unsettling or hilarious consequences. While the storyteller did not construct the story, a narrative designer can work on the systems with an eye toward how they can collide.
- Ambiguous. Stories that are ambiguous are generally considered unsatisfying in other media, but are perfect for games. The player's active mindset makes them excited to construct theories about what happened.
- Prioritized storytelling. Games can communicate narrative to players on multiple channels. Players will naturally develop a hierarchy about which channel means what. Prerender cinematics may indicate important story beats, but no gameplay information. Mission briefings may have minimal story, but critical gameplay topics. Ambient dialogue may just be pure flavor in every way.
- Nonlinear. Through interactivity, games can achieve nonlinear storytelling in a way no other media can. Players can experience parts of the story in the order of their choosing, allowing them to construct their own version of what happened.

6 Interactive Structure

Interactivity is a defining feature of games. And so, all story in games is also interactive. Even the most tightly controlled story requires the player's participation to advance. If the player doesn't play, the story doesn't advance. Maybe a simulation will evolve and develop without player input, but even those games are deeply interactive. The point of the game is for the player to change the simulation.

THE BASICS

There are a few key concepts about interactive structure that we need to understand at the outset.

CEDING AUTHORIAL CONTROL

As someone interested in storytelling, you probably have a strong sense of how you want the story to go. Maybe you can think of several scenarios, but even then you probably have a favorite.

One of the hardest things you'll have to do in game narrative is to cede authorial control. Your role is not the same as an author, or even a screenwriter. You are more akin to a Dungeon Master in a tabletop game. Your players are driving the story, not you.

You are setting the stage for the story, giving players all the tools, props, and stage dressing to put together a story. You are also defining the edge of the stage. But the player is the improv artist who walks on to that stage and makes up a story using all the material you've put in place. The material you provide can strongly suggest a story, but in the end, they're in control.

That can be kind of a tough idea to accept. As a storyteller you naturally want control; that's how you'll grab players, move them, and share amazing moments with them. To be blunt, if ceding authorial control is a deal breaker for you, then take that knowledge and focus on a different creative outlet. If you stay in game narrative, you will be perpetually frustrated. You will struggle against the basic premise of the medium you're in.

If, on the other hand, you get a thrill out of arranging the pieces in such a way that players can come into the mix and surprise you, then game narrative is the medium for you!

Fortunately, it is not an absolute, binary state. You can experiment with your own comfort zone, and get a sense of where you, as a storyteller, land on that spectrum. It is certainly a good idea to push yourself outside of your immediate comfort zone, and see if you might develop an affinity for a type of storytelling that you would have expected to hate.

DOI: 10.1201/9781003624882-9

Now that we've gotten that bit of tough-love out of the way, there is good news. There are different degrees of player agency in different types of games. While some give players a high degree of agency, which in turn steals agency from you, there are other game genres that do give a higher degree of authorial control, even if it will never be as much as a novel.

PLAYER TYPES

To serve the needs of all players, it's useful to understand different player types. We have identified three player types, although there may be more.

Bud

Bud is here for the gameplay. He doesn't care about the story, skips past every story element he can, and scrolls reddit during the ones he can't. He doesn't care about the world, story, or characters. If you force him to engage with the story, you're doing him a disservice, because he just wants to play a game.

Bud is usually quite loud and emphatic about his disdain for story. If forced to consume any amount of story, especially if he deems that amount to be "bad" or "predictable," he will be angry.

Case Study: What Happens When Bud Gets What He Wants?

We worked on a game that had a lively, engaging amount of story in each zone. One of our teammates was a Bud, who always complained about the extra time and effort of incorporating narrative into the levels he worked on. Yet when we held a playtest for a zone that had no story or even voice over in it, but was otherwise complete, his feedback was that something was missing from the level. When he later played the same level with narrative and voice over added, he said the level had "come a long way."

The moral of that story is that even Bud values narrative. This only makes sense, since story is an inherent part of the human experience. It turns out that what Bud truly hates is a story that he feels is forced on him.

We'd characterize Bud as hostile to story, and impatient with being forced to engage with it, but unconsciously needing at least a little narrative to provide context.

Courtney

Courtney is not that interested in the story or world, but she wants enough for context, and she wants it to make sense. She enjoys a good story moment, but she's not going to read journal or codex entries, and certainly not novelizations or wiki pages. She'll watch a cutscene, but if it goes on too long, her attention will wander, and if it's egregiously long, she'll skip. She wants to play the game.

The key difference between Courtney and Bud is that she does want some context for her actions, and she does want the world to make sense. But she wants a concise, economical story that does not require too much work to engage with.

In other words, it's not enough to slay the epic boss, she wants to know why she's fighting the boss, why it matters, how it will affect the world moving forward, and she wants all of that to make sense. If it's lame or nonsensical, she will not be happy.

But she doesn't need to know the backstory of the boss, nor how he came to be evil. If she can get the boss's whole vibe from context and a very short cutscene, that's perfect. The story must be contained within the game and within the mainline of the experience. She is not going to search out rare audio logs in obscure corners. The story must come straight down the middle at her.

Korbin

Korbin wants to know it all. If you're interested in game narrative, you are likely a Korbin. They will read every tooltip, loading screen, codex or journal entry, and optional dialogue. They may very well know the lore better than most of the game devs, and will not hesitate to say so.

Korbin may lurk on the game's subreddit, or they may get in flame wars with those who disagree with them, but they are certainly involved with a community one way or another. They will catch implied character and story elements, and be able to put together hints and clues to see the bigger picture. Sometimes they do this accurately, other times they form opinions based on plausible but incorrect associations between ideas.

After Korbin falls in love with an IP, they become a proselytizer for it. They tell their friends, family, and online community about it. They find other Korbins online and create/moderate/post to subreddits. In extreme cases, a few Korbins will get together and create a fan wiki for an IP. Having such a wiki is invaluable, as it gives new users a place to land and look around after they've become initially intrigued by the IP.

Because Korbin knows all the obscure lore bits, they can, and are eager to, jump in and help people understand. When a Courtney shows up in some online community and says, "This part of the game doesn't make sense," a Korbin will jump in to share the little-known fact or long-ago-revealed lore that explains it. This can be incredibly useful, as communities often have long-running misunderstandings of the lore, and the devs should not weigh in to correct it. As a narrative dev, you'll really wish there was a Korbin out there to explain the full picture. Depending on individual personality, Korbin may explain the lore to Courtney in a helpful way, or correct her with a "Well, actually…" You cannot control which Korbin shows up, but hope for the former.

Korbin truly loves the game and IP. That love can remain pure, or it can turn toxic.

Proportions

Different game genres naturally attract a different percentage of each player type. *Baldur's Gate 3* will attract more Korbins and fewer Buds, while a FIFA 24 will attract more Buds and fewer Korbins.

Courtney is the most common player type, usually by far. Courtney is also the least vocal player type. She may share her opinions with her friends, but for the most part she's either enjoying the game or has already switched to another game.

Note: It is very important to remember that you don't get feedback from most of your players. The ones who do speak up take on outsize importance in the conversation. While they should be heard, always remember that there is a larger proportion of players who are not talking. They give their feedback with their time, engagement, and money.

Bud represents a much smaller group of players. Fewer than Courtney, but more than Korbin. Part of this is due to a very high percentage of Buds in high-player count online PvP games. Buds tend to be very vocal; you will definitely hear from them.

Note: Buds tend to be overrepresented on game dev teams. It's not uncommon for a game dev team to be mostly Buds, which creates a feedback loop. In turn, this can cause the Buds on the team to think that everybody in the world shares the same opinions they do about how much story should be in the game. There is not really a cure for this, as you can never convince someone that they are in an echo chamber or feedback loop. But it is still useful for you to be aware, lest you get sucked into the echo chamber too.

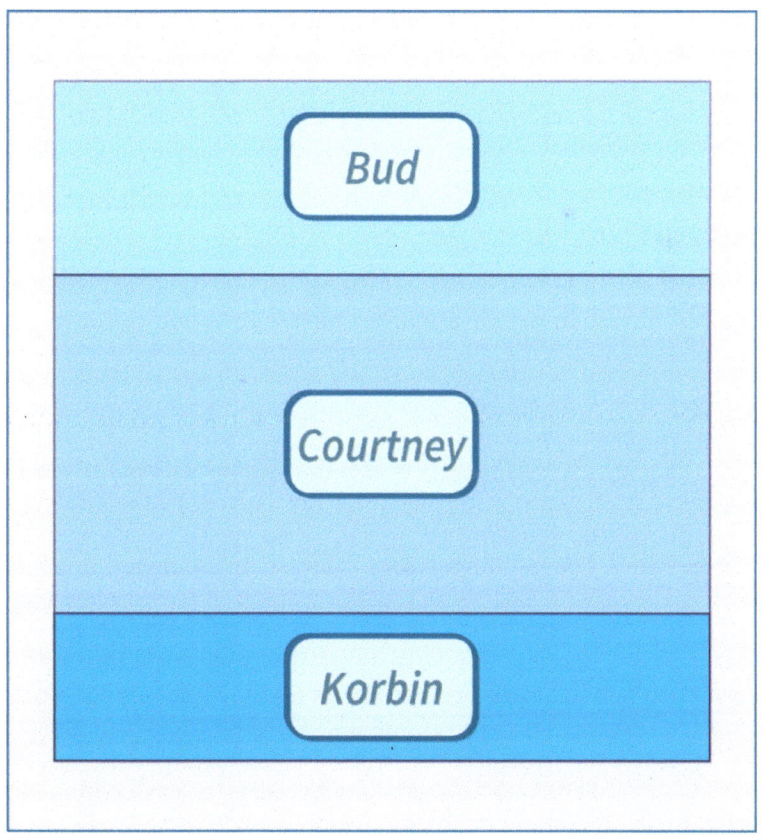

Korbin is the least common player type, but still significant. Korbin is the most vocal, and usually engages with multiple online forums. This can make Korbin's numbers seem greater than they are. And it is true that Korbin's opinions do carry more weight than the numbers suggest. As we said, Korbin is the one who will build the fan wiki, help newcomers understand the IP, and generally contribute to the lore conversation.

It is important to pay attention to what the Korbins in your community are saying. It's easy to take their pulse. They are quick to feel slighted any time "the devs" appear to dismiss their opinions, or even just to not love the IP as deeply as they do. They take silence from the studio or publisher as a sign of neglect. While you and your team must be careful what you say and how you say it, more communication is always better than less with this group.

Korbin can be a great ally, or a terrible enemy. You cannot do everything Korbin demands, or else you end up with an inward-looking IP that is inaccessible to new users, and is built around fanservice. But Korbin can also give you real insight into ways in which the IP might be going in the wrong direction, or even losing the spark that makes it special.

Note: When a game community turns toxic, it is almost always Korbin that has become toxic. But it is important to point out that not all players who become dedicated fans of a game or IP have the potential to turn toxic. In fact, it is only a small percentage of the Korbin group who have this potential. As with so many things in life, the problem is that the toxic types are the loudest and most emphatic, and so are able to ruin a good thing for everybody.

SIDEBAR: TOXIC FANDOM

The topic of toxicity in gaming and among certain fandoms is a huge one, deserving of its own book, and is not something that we can do justice to here. We'd just like to point out that the toxic members of a fandom tend to be a tiny-but-loud percentage, and it is a mistake to get your guard up and be suspicious of all fandom. The vast majority of your players love your game and are glad you're making it.

In fact, they're busy playing your game, not screaming about it online. Even the majority of those who hated it are not toxic. They tried it, they didn't like it, and they moved on.

Sometimes it is difficult to remember the scale. If 300 people in an online space are agreeing with each other that this game is the worst offense to good taste ever submitted to other humans, it can feel overwhelming. Three hundred is a lot of people! And the fact that they're posting online lends a strange authority to their words. And they are all agreeing with each other!

But take a deep breath. If your game sold 1 million copies, then 300 people represents a tiny, statistically irrelevant fraction of your users. We say statistically irrelevant because they are a self-selected group, not a random sampling.

Healthy criticism from anyone is useful, but toxic, hateful critiques serve no purpose other than to leech your joy and motivation, and possibly have a negative effect on your work moving forward.

Ignore it.

How Do You Design for Everybody?

One of the hardest parts of building a game narrative is that you must design your story, characters, and world around all three player types. Bud, Courtney, and Korbin all think that their personal reactions are shared by everybody.

Statements like "Nobody wants that!", "Why would they ever think this is a good idea?", "You don't need to explain, we get it already!", and "It was so confusing, they needed to give us a little more to go on..." could all be addressed by one simple concept: maybe other players feel differently than you? But no one ever believes they are an outlier. Instead, the more likely answer is that the storytellers are just incredibly dumb.

To be fair, an answer can be correct and still be unsatisfying. Nobody will ever think, "I guess this idea works for someone else but not me, so it's a good idea." What players are really saying is: "the choice you made did not suit me and that is all I really care about." And that is a very human reaction.

So you must try to do several contradictory things at once. Below is one way to think about it.

Critical Path and Completionist Playthroughs

While there is no hard-and-fast rule for designing a narrative that appeals to all three player types, there is a rough guideline that can help: Critical Path and Completionist Playthroughs.

The critical path playthrough means everything the player must do to complete the game. Players must defeat the chapter 1 boss to unlock chapter 2, so that boss fight is critical path. Players can also choose to level up their reputation with the townsfolk in the Chapter 1 hub. But if they don't, they can still complete the game, so that's not critical path.

The completionist playthrough is everything in the game. Someone doing a completionist playthrough will not be satisfied with a low reputation score in the chapter 1 town, because the cook in that town sells a dragon ribs recipe that can only be purchased by someone with the requisite reputation score. If you can't make dragon ribs at your campfire, you have not completed all the content in the game.

To make Bud happy, think of the critical path. Bud wants to play the game, and he might choose to spend hours on optional gameplay in order to craft the perfect shield or to achieve the perfect boss fight. But he's only going to engage with the narrative content you put in his way: the critical path. If you force him to watch a cutscene, or if he must puzzle through some story stuff in order to understand a game mechanic, he will. But he won't be happy.

Anytime you want to put some kind of storytelling or world building in the critical path, think of Bud. Does he need to know this? Will his gameplay experience be better for it? Is there a way to make this shorter, punchier, tighter? Can you make it optional side content, but put it in a place where no one will miss it?

Sometimes the answer is no, you cannot. You need everyone to learn this fact in chapter 1 because it is critical in chapter 3, and that means it must be a gate for progress. Players must encounter and learn this to progress the game. Even if you put something directly in the player's path, a certain percentage of players will still miss it if it is not mandatory. And those players will be very confused in chapter 3.

But anything that is mandatory should pass through a rigorous test, and if it is included, it should be tight and punchy. Do it for Bud.

To make Korbin happy, think of the completionist. Korbin is going to read every journal entry, talk to every NPC, and search every drawer. This sounds great, because Korbin will experience the full majesty of your story and world!

But it has drawbacks as well. First, we can go back to one of our basic narrative concepts: Never Be Boring. Even if Korbin is opting-in to read every note you've hidden in the world, you still don't want to waste their time by adding dull filler. They searched every dresser in this abandoned building while cannibals hunted for them—they worked to find this note. They are expecting a rewarding morsel of story, character, or world. And they are right to expect that. Now you must ensure that every bit of content you put in the game—even the one that you have 5 minutes to write before content lock—is worth the effort of finding it.

In addition, Korbin wants the world to make sense. So you must use every narrative means or tool you have to explain seeming inconsistencies in the lore. If you do, they will become a great ally in sharing it with others. If you do not, they will lead the charge of people calling you out for bad or inconsistent lore.

Kerrigan: You were the only one who ever believed in me.

EXAMPLE: *STARCRAFT II: HEART OF THE SWARM*

Jim Raynor was being held prisoner on a Terran ship. Kerrigan arrives to rescue him, and in the end-of-mission cutscene, she returns his gun to him. Most players did not think about or care where she got his gun. Others, if they did think about it, assumed that she found it in a locker where they would have stored Jim's personal effects.

But some testers really did care about it. During an emotionally charged cutscene, all they could think about was "Where'd she get the gun?"

Earlier we discussed understanding the scale of a problem. We suggested that you not put in a solution that 100% of players will see, to solve a problem that 10% of players will have. This felt like one of those situations. However, we realized that Korbin was having a problem with this, and we needed to take it seriously. We added a small "Prisoner Locker" in the final room of the level, which the player must pass through to click on the door to Jim's cell. Players did not need to interact with it, it was just there, and players could notice it or not. But Korbin definitely noticed it. Later, when anyone would go online to complain about where Kerrigan got the gun, Korbin would jump in to point out that there was a locker right outside Jim's cell, where she clearly got the gun. If only the complainer had been attentive enough to notice!

Some of the side lore you put in the game—the note in the dresser, or the subtle environmental storytelling in the optional dungeon—can contribute to the bigger story and world lore. But some might also be entertaining one-off lore. If possible, you should find a way to indicate to Korbin when lore is part of the greater whole and when it is one-off.

If you think of Bud for the critical path, and Korbin for the completionist playthrough, you will likely make Courtney happy. Courtney will go back and forth between charging through the critical path and exploring side content. If you've planned for Bud and Korbin, then Courtney fits in.

When You Must Err in One Direction or the Other

Err on the side of Courtney. Courtney is the largest player type, and also represents the ideological middle ground between Bud and Korbin. This does not mean you should design only for her or that she is your target audience. But when you make decisions in any area, you can err in one direction or another. Err on the side of Courtney.

SIDEBAR: THE CURIOUS CASE OF KORBUD

There is an odd player type that you may encounter every now and then. Korbud is not interested in story or narrative, but feels somehow inconvenienced by any story, including side content.

This is because Korbud also has a completionist streak. When the game presents optional side narrative, which Korbud can easily bypass, he instead groans, rolls his eyes, and sets off to complete it, complaining the whole time.

Like Bud, Korbud seems to be overrepresented on game teams. If you are part of a large enough team, you will work with at least 1 or 2 Korbuds. And you will definitely hear from them often during development.

If you can, try to focus Korbud's thinking on critical path vs completionist. The best you can do for him is to treat him like a Bud, and promise him that you won't make him engage with story unnecessarily. And then reinforce that if he chooses to … that's on him.

A Final Thought on Player Types

One last way to think about our three player types:

1. Bud just wants to understand the big picture. It must be clear, consistent, and exciting.
2. Courtney wants to understand why her actions matter in the world. She can handle some contradictions, so long as it's clear they will be resolved at some point.
3. Korbin wants to know everything, is intrigued by contradictions in the lore, but will also get upset if even the tiniest contradiction is not eventually resolved.

BRANCHING

Later we will look at the structure based on game genre. But branching lives in a category of its own. It's a narrative technique that can show up in a number of other genres: RPG, ARPG, Action Games, and more. Since it is heavily structure-related, it makes sense to discuss it here, independent of game genre.

The basic concept of branching, whether in story structure, dialogue, or anything, is simple:

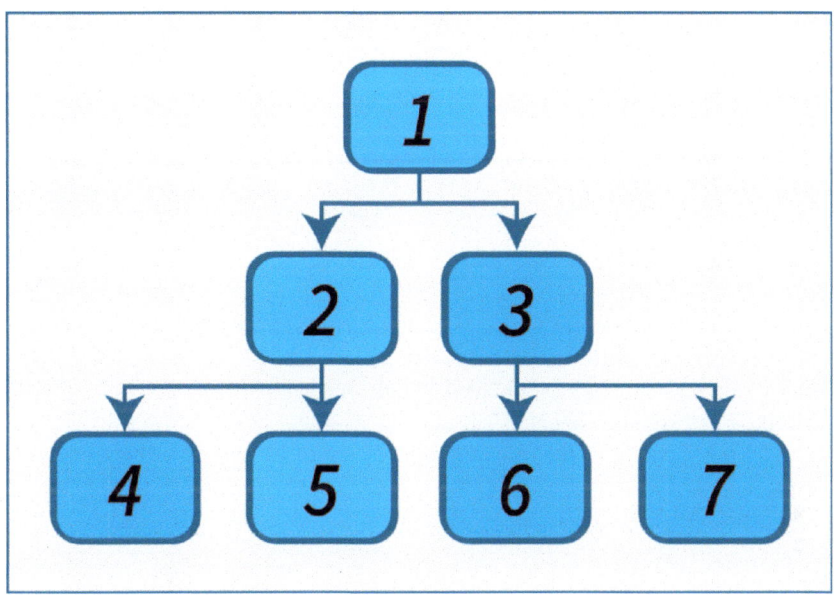

The player makes a choice, and the story follows the path that is a consequence of that choice. Paths not taken are left behind.

Branching is an incredibly powerful tool for game stories. It gives the player a constant sense of interactivity and agency, two of the most potent and sought-after feelings you want to give players. It also adds an immense amount to replayability. Looking at that diagram above, you can see how a player who ended in box 4 might be somewhat curious about box 5, very curious about box 6, and intrigued about box 7.

However, branching has some big drawbacks as well. The key one is bloat:

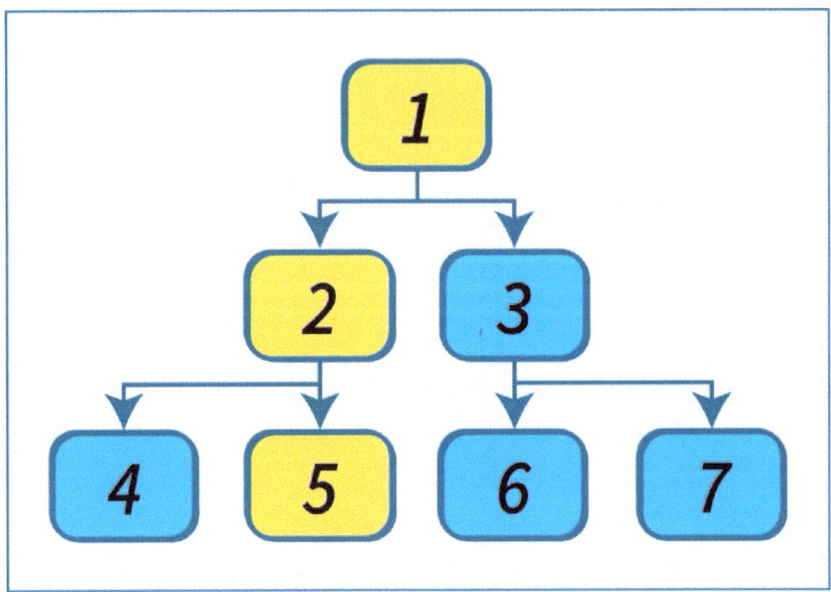

The yellow fields represent a player's choices in the branching structure. Notice that there are four of the seven fields that the player will never see. And that is with two choices. Nobody ever played a game and said, "I had two choices! Wow, I felt like I had so much agency!"

Add 1 more choice to the mix, and now 11 out of 15 will never be seen by the player:

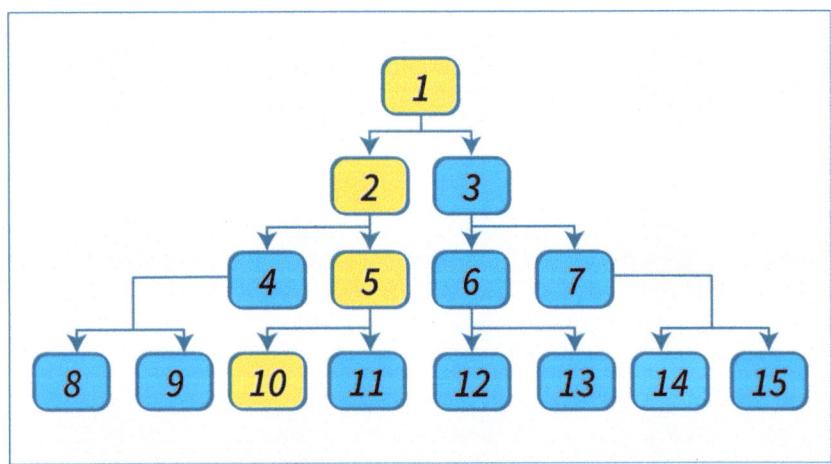

The problem gets worse as the number of choices grows. And of course, this assumes that the player only has two choices at each point. In some structures they may have three, four, or more.

Each of these fields the player doesn't see represent time, effort, and money. On a AAA game, they probably represent multiple art assets, design work, writing, voice over, localization, unique scripting, testing, and build commits with associated bugs. They could also contain cutscenes.

Branching becomes expensive quickly. The problem is not just the omnipresent need for more money. It is that the money does not go as far. In the above example, let's say the budget for this section of the game is $150 dollars. If this section is linear, that means the team can invest $37.5 dollars in each of the four beats the player will experience. If it branches like the above diagram, the team can only invest $10 in each beat.

So, in a linear structure, the player has experienced $150 worth of content. "Wow, that was so cool!" "The way that unique monster died was wild!" "I never thought he'd look at me like that."

In the branching version, they've experienced $40 worth of content. "Cool storytelling." "I liked that I got to choose." "It was pretty good."

Another problem: If you look at the diagrams above, you'll see that if the player makes even one choice that turns out to be not what they wanted and they want to change course, they can't. If they chose box 2 in their first choice, then realize they want to take a path that would lead more toward something like box 14; there is no way for them to course-correct, other than to reload. Asking players to reload due to the structure of your design is a nonstarter.

So you'll eventually end up adding in little "track jumps":

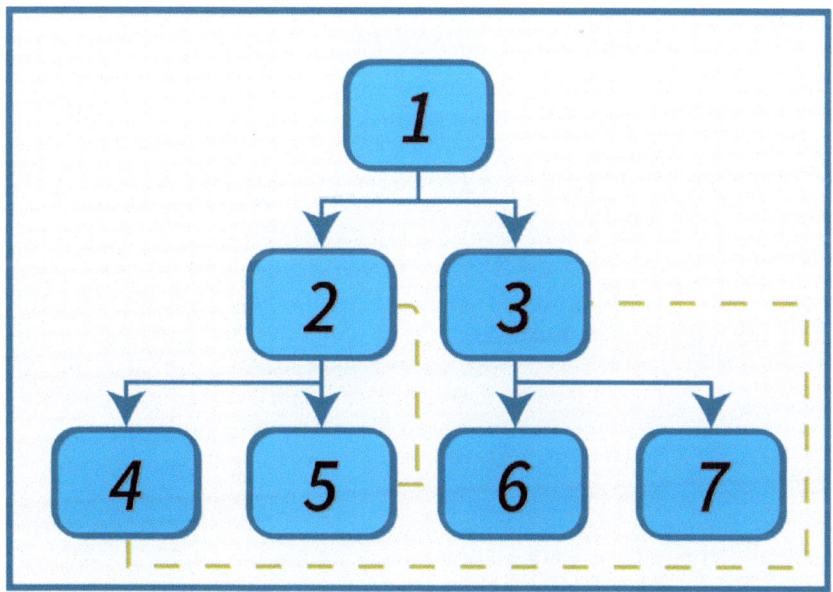

Thus, it will not surprise you to learn, costs more money, more time, and less opportunity in other areas.

None of this is to imply branching is bad. In fact, it's an amazing tool. But you must understand the downsides in order to use it, or to convince your executive producer to use it.

SIDEBAR: FEATURE EXPENSE: AAA VS INDIE

In the early 2000s, most of the dialogue in games did not have voice over. There were virtually no limits on how many lines a character could say. Once all the procedural tools were in place for camera and face effects, the only expenses associated with writing were the writer's salary, the cost of translation, and some limited UI rework to ensure the text of other languages fit in the text box. These are fairly trivial. Yes, we called the writer's salary "trivial." We wish it weren't so!

As time went on, the bar went up. Now dialogue included full-VO, cinematic conversation, and digital acting, including lip sync or face effects. These features all added immeasurably to the experience of talking to a character in the game world. But they also increased the expense of each word.

Now the process included voice actors, voice directors, audio engineers, audio producers, audio programmers, cinematic designers, UX designers, animators, and face-effects specialists. And now localizing into another language included the whole audio pipeline for that other language, as well as revising the face effects.

For example, *Diablo III* had four player classes, and each could be male or female. That meant each time the player character spoke, eight different actors had to be recorded saying the line, in eight different voice over sessions. But *Diablo III* was localized into 12 languages. So in fact, every time the player character spoke, 96 actors had to be called into recording sessions. The game handled dialogue through portraits, so no face effects were required, but you can see how even on the basic scale of VO, the cost was enormous. The player character was reduced to speaking only when necessary.

Suddenly, every word added to the game had a price tag. A writer in the early 2000s could add silly lines that were just there for fun. Or let the player ask any question they might think of. After the arrival of full-VO, strict line limits had to be imposed. Everything was means-tested. Is this line worth it? Does it serve several purposes? Will it introduce confusion which in turn will force us to let the player ask about something?

None of this is to suggest that full-VO is a bad thing. It's simply important to understand that a feature that was once cheap and could be used for many purposes became expensive and how each use had to be justified.

In AAA if a feature is going into the game, it must be highly polished. It must withstand a lot of scrutiny. Gone are the days when someone could stay late at work and slip something wild into the build, just to see if people enjoyed it. Every AAA game you've ever played went through a ruthless process of deciding what could stay and what must go. You simply cannot include a feature in the game that is unpolished.

Comparatively, many Indie teams still have the freedom to experiment and try risky features that might be fun but unpolished. We are not suggesting Indie games don't care about quality: clearly they do. But an Indie dev can say "if it's fun, let's put it in the game, even if the execution will be a bit ragged," in a way that AAA cannot.

Neither structure is inherently better or worse. It's just two very different mindsets. You should decide which one appeals to you more. Ideally, you'll get to try both!

STRATEGIES TO KEEP BRANCHING VIABLE

Less Polish

Establishing a lower level of polish can be invaluable. AAA in general requires a high level of polish, and any feature that is put in the game must meet a high bar. But having a branching structure means accepting that lots of content put in the game will never be seen by a wide variety of players.

An Indie game can handle branching better than most AAA, because the need to polish is not as great. The Stanley Parable can have 19 endings, because each of them can be less polished than an alternate ending in the *God of War* franchise.

Even within AAA, there are different levels of polish. Let's take a side room in a dungeon as an example.

COMPARISON: SIDE ROOM IN A DUNGEON

In *The Last of Us*, if you entered a side room and there were three dressers and a bookcase, and you searched each of them, drawer after drawer, only to find out they were all empty, that the entire room served no purpose, you'd be upset. Last of Us is a curated, polished experience.

But in an *Elder Scrolls* game, if you encountered such a room, you'd search it and move on. Better luck next time! *Elder Scrolls* titles have a high degree of polish, but they have also established a rhythm with players that we would call wide-but-not-deep. Players know they'll get a wide variety of experiences in the game, but they will be uneven experiences, and sometimes shallow.

If your AAA game is going to have branching, you'll want to establish a rhythm with players similar to the one *Elder Scrolls* has, and avoid the rhythm of a Last of Us. You want wide-but-not-deep … or at least not as polished.

Branch in Key Areas

You can create a satisfying branching experience by choosing key moments to give the player a choice. Add weight and drama to those moments, so that the player feels the importance of this choice.

The aftereffects of this choice may cause a divergence in your story for a time, but you'll be able to bring everything back to the spine in a few beats. It looks like the diagram below.

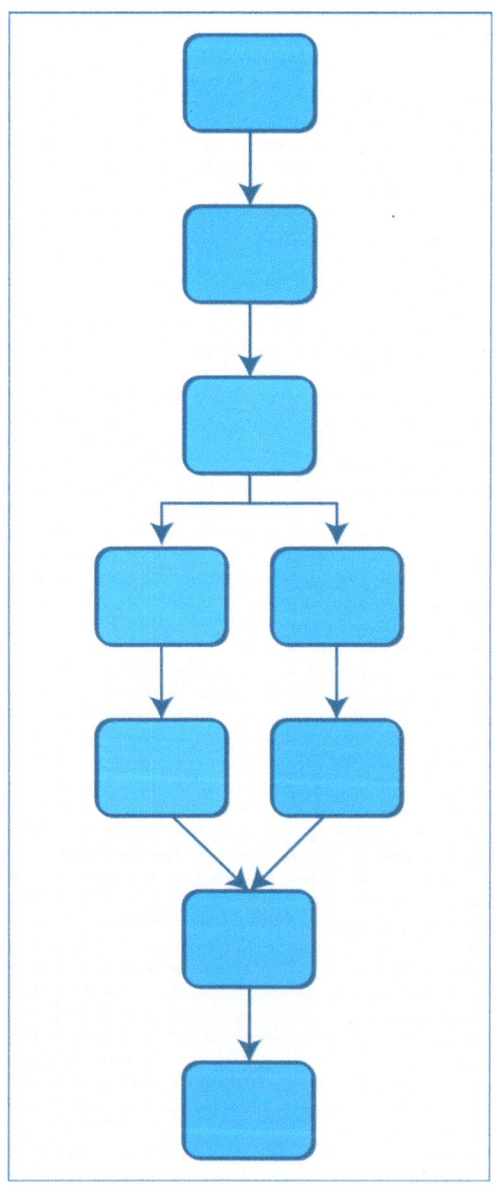

The overall experience is linear, but that key choice will stick with the player.

Telltale games did this quite well. In a typical episode, the player would be faced with a few key choices, and the game would highlight the moment.

After you would make this choice, the game would tell you "NPC X will remember that," which was both ominous and exciting. At the end of an episode, the game would actually list your choices and compare them to other players. All of these features made the choice feel very important.

Fake Choices

This one sounds awful, and if done badly, it absolutely is. If done skillfully, players will not notice. The trick is to give the player many choices, but only a few that matter. The others immediately weave back into the main spine of your story.

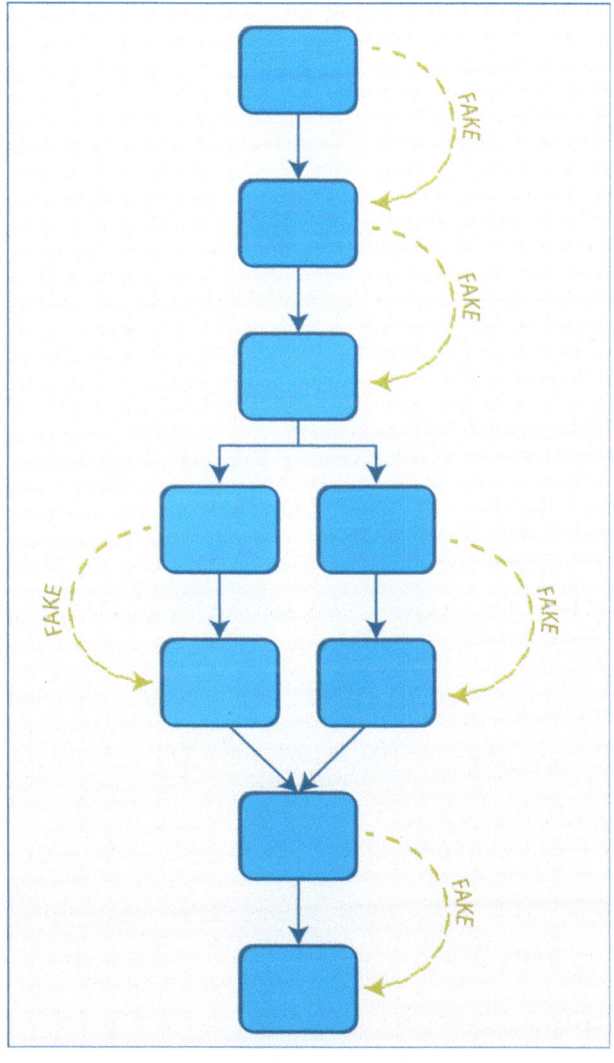

This diagram makes it look tidier than it should be. In truth, you want to intersperse real and fake choices unpredictably, so that players do not sense the pattern.

If you weave the occasional real choice into the narrative, players will sense that their choices do matter, but they won't be able to tell which ones do, so their default approach will be to assume all choices matter.

The key to doing this is that you must never deny or contradict their choice, especially the fake ones.

Let's look at two fake choices, one of which is never contradicted, while the other is.

Good: At the end of a chapter, you must make a powerful choice to save a town, or let it burn. When you choose, there is a bit of text saying "The town burns" or "The town is saved," then the player moves on to the next chapter of the game, and never returns. This is a fake choice in the sense that the player's actions did not make any difference in the game. The player will never come back here and see the prosperous-or-burned-out-town. Nothing has really changed. But the player will remember their choice and feel that it mattered.

Bad: You have been dealing with two factions, playing them off against each other. Here at the end of the chapter, you must choose one to ally with. The leader of the other faction will attack you. You make your choice, and kill the leader of the enemy faction. But then the leader of the faction you allied with goes crazy and attacks you too! This was always a fake choice because the design team created two boss fights and they want you to experience both.

No matter which faction you chose, you were going to fight both bosses. The problem is that players will immediately realize their choice did not matter: the game confirms it. If there is no way around the double boss fight, then try to structure the chapter around which boss to fight first. Make a quest that leads to each boss fight, and allow players to decide the order in which they play the chapter. Do not present the choice as being "which faction do I ally with?"

Finally, you must truly disguise the fake choices. We have played games where the player was offered the chance to take a quest or refuse it. If the player refuses it, the quest giver says something like "Well, I'll just mark it down here in your quest log so you don't forget, in case you change your mind!" It is 100% clear that our choice did not matter, and the game immediately proved that.

If you're going to lie, lie well.

STRUCTURE IN DIFFERENT GENRES OF GAME

Interactive structure varies widely between game genres, so it's a good idea to take a brief look at structures by genre. As always, we are describing the most common shape structures take in each genre. You can certainly come up with examples that defy or contradict what we are saying. But those will be exceptions that prove the rule; we are trying to cover as much ground as we can. Rather than repeat phrases like "most but not all" throughout the following, you should assume that our points are intended to discuss most games in that genre.

The focus here on linear vs open sections of a game structure is to get a sense of where you can get maximum interactivity, and where you benefit from straightforward, linear storytelling.

ADVENTURE AND SHOOTERS

The structure of adventure games tend to be more linear and remarkably similar to film. All of the structure we described earlier with the three-act structure applies.

They are typically a series of missions connected by cutscenes. The cutscenes do hardcore story work, moving things forward, introducing a turn or a new character.

There is some storytelling in the missions. First is the premise/payoff of the mission. Did Lara Croft retrieve the idol? The answer is yes, and that moves the story forward. But action games also tell stories in their missions through environmental means, through collectibles such as notes or audio logs, and through banter between the heroes.

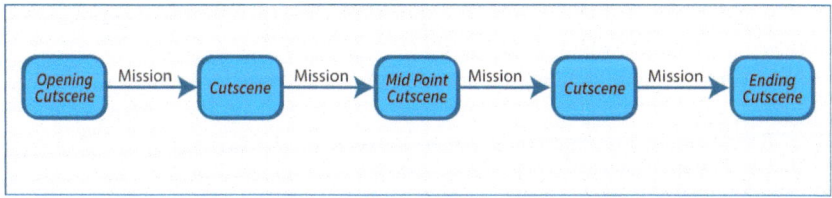

In the above figure, the mission/cutscene combo between the opening and midpoint, and between midpoint and ending, can vary by game; many or few.

An interesting side note about the way story is delivered in this structure: the cutscene at the end of the mission feels like a reward for your hard work. You finished the mission, achieved the goal, defeated the enemies, and now you can sit back and enjoy a cutscene. This tends to help players shift to a passive mindset and make them more amenable to a cutscene than in some other structures.

Shooters such as a *Call of Duty* campaign generally have this structure as well.

RPG

From this point on, diagrams will have a different key. The shapes are not meant to represent cutscenes or missions, or any particular narrative feature. Rather, they represent linear vs open gameplay experiences.

Being heavily story-based, RPGs also have a structure similar to the three-act structure covered earlier. But because they are character based, they also have more open or nonlinear segments.

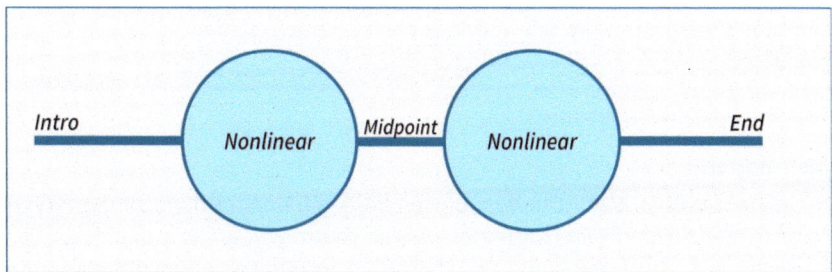

RPGs tend to start with a linear intro, similar to Act 1 in the three-act structure. We meet the protagonists and world, set the stakes and the conflict, and then introduce a major change.

The middle typically has a more open structure, where the player can explore the world, then a critical midpoint changes things, leading to another open section, before the story narrows down to a linear end.

Case Study: *Knights of the Old Republic*

Linear Opening:

You're on a starship that has been boarded by the Sith, and you must fight your way through the ship to an escape pod.

Next you end up on the planet Taris. This is an open section on the microscale: you can choose what order you want to do things. But on the macro-scale, you are still contained: you can't leave Taris. You must recruit certain party members, finish certain quests, and steal a ship. You land at the Jedi academy, where you train to become a Jedi.

Open:

Now you enter the open middle of the game. You have an overall quest to visit four worlds to retrieve the four parts of the starmap. You can visit the worlds in any order, and travel back and forth between them.

Midpoint:

After you have gathered two of the four parts of the starmap, a surprise is forced on you: your ship is captured by the Sith. You must lead a jailbreak to free your party, retrieve your ship, and get out of there. In the course of that surprise mission, you learn a deep and troubling secret that casts your entire experience in a new light.

Open:

After you escape from the Sith, you return to your previous activity: you've still got two worlds to visit in order to complete the star map.

Linear End:

Once you've assembled the starmap, you enter the linear end of the game: you travel to the Star Forge, the source of the antagonist's power, and destroy it.

Those closed, linear sections get the story set up, change the story's direction, and bring the story to a close. The open sections in the middle give the player the chance to breathe, explore the world, level up, explore relationships, and set their own pace.

The Midpoint

The midpoint in an RPG can be a cinematic, a mission, or both. In our KotOR example, the midpoint was a mission, where you free your crew and flee, and a short cutscene, where the secret that changes everything is revealed.

ARPGs

Action RPGs sometimes have a structure similar to RPGs, but they can just as easily have a more linear structure in the mold of Adventure Games/Shooters.

In *Diablo III: Reaper of Souls*, we had a hybrid. The campaign was generally linear, except that a few areas were a bit more open. Perhaps we could call it loose-linear. After the campaign, the game took on something more similar to an open world game.

OPEN WORLD

Open world games have a fairly straightforward structure, which is contained in the name. There are large swaths of the world that are open, able to be explored in any order, with lots of self-directed gameplay, and often mini-games.

The key to the structure is that the world is broken up into regions or zones that unlock in a certain order. In *Grand Theft Auto*, it's neighborhoods. In an *Assassin's Creed* game, it's biomes. There is a short, linear start, then the player is dumped out into a zone, and can really go in any direction from there. But along the way, there will be some critical-path task they must complete.

It might be a quest, or simply to go talk to someone. But completing that task will unlock the next zone. The pattern repeats with each zone. Do as little or as much as you'd like in a given zone, then go unlock the next. In some games, there may be a "gate," i.e., some threshold of power, wealth, or accomplishment that the player must surpass to unlock the next zone. It might be a hard gate, where the game simply says "reach level 30" or "Acquire $1,000" in order to undertake the task or quest that will unlock the next zone. Or it might be a soft gate, in the sense that the unlock action, performing a quest or getting to an NPC to talk, is hard enough that you cannot accomplish it until you have done many other things in the zone and leveled up.

The open world diagram looks like this:

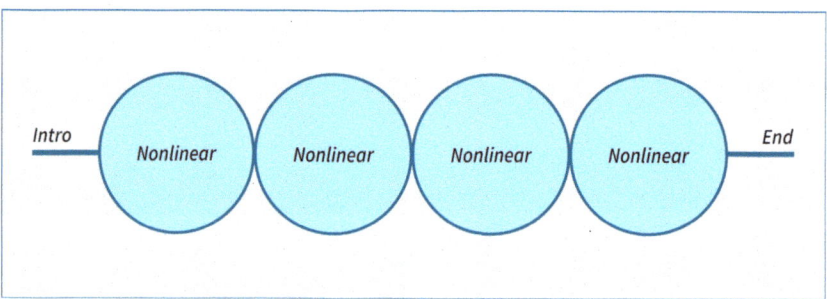

Sometimes the different zones might be connected by a short linear section, like a quest, or a cutscene.

In some games, once the player travels to a new zone, they can never return to the previous one. RPGs do that as well. However, in most open world games, the player can return to any part of the map that they have unlocked.

OTHER GAME GENRES

There are many more genres, but there is no structure that is inherent to them. Battle Royales or MOBAs, for example, have no narrative structure at all: they are purely character-driven from a narrative perspective. Real-Time Strategy games can have a linear structure identical to the Adventure Game/Shooter paradigm. But they can also have something more akin to an RPG.

As you play different games, pay attention to the way the game unfolds. Where is the narrative structure interactive? Where is it linear? How do the pieces fit together?

CHAPTER SUMMARY

In this chapter, we discussed the following topics:

- Ceding authorial control. You can't be in charge if you're going to make the player feel like they're interacting. You must set the stage, fill it with props, and let the player have at it.
- Player Types. There are three different categories of player, in terms of how they consume story. Each has a different expectation and need from story.
  - Bud wants to play the game and doesn't want the story to get in his way.
  - Courtney wants her actions to matter and for the story to make sense, but doesn't want a deep dive into the narrative.
  - Korbin wants to know every last detail, and it better all makes sense.
- Branching. A powerful but expensive technique, with lots of different considerations. It is worth understanding, as it can elevate the narrative of any game where it makes sense to have it.
- Structure in different genres of game.
  - Adventure games and shooters have a linear mission structure connected by cutscenes.
  - RPGs often have open, nonlinear sections connected by tightly defined, linear sections.
  - ARPGs can lean more toward the RPG style, or open world.
  - Open world games are a series nonlinear, wide-open regions that can be explored in any order, but usually require a specific action to unlock the next region.
  - Other Genres. There are many other genres of game, but many of them, such as MOBAs, don't have a narrative structure, or have a structure similar to the ones we've covered.

7 World Building
World Building vs Intellectual Property

IN THIS CHAPTER

- What is the difference between World Building and IP?
- Structures and Systems as an essential of World Building
- History as an essential of World Building
- Stakes in the Ground as an essential of World Building
- World Building in all game aspects

World Building and IP development (Intellectual Property) overlap in many ways. Therefore, this chapter will be somewhat short, since we cover the most of the relevant concepts in the IP section. There are a few things specific to World Building in a game that belong here.

Let's start by discussing the difference between World Building and IP development.

WORLD BUILDING

World Building is more than just developing the setting. It's the process of fleshing out the concepts in the game that contribute to the overall world. In this context, "the world" can mean a small town, a galaxy, another dimension, or the corridors of one character's mind. The boundaries of the world are defined by where the story takes place, where it goes, what is contained within it, and what it references.

Building a world usually means defining something past the edges of the game's story. In the example where the world is a small town, it's important to know what country, culture, geography, and time period that town exists in. All of those factors will influence how you build the town, even if players will never leave that town and explore other areas. Characters may talk about recent laws passed in the capital, or that time they visited another country. Strangers may arrive in the town from elsewhere.

World Building means the physical world, but also everything contained within it. Fleshing out the political structure of a kingdom, or the history of a mercantile guild all qualify as "World Building," despite the fact that they have nothing to do with geography.

The creative efforts you apply to any part of the world in a game, including culture, history, and technology, is World Building.

DOI: 10.1201/9781003624882-10

INTELLECTUAL PROPERTY

Intellectual Property, or IP, simply means anything that is property but is not physical. A car, a house, and a phone are all physical property. Programming code, a company logo, and the story of a novel are all Intellectual Property. If you printed the Disney logo on a banner, you own the material of the banner, but you are stealing Disney's IP by using their logo without permission. Note: If there is one company in the world you should avoid angering about IP, it is Disney.

However, in games, when people talk about IP, they don't mean the full definition. Instead, it is usually interchangeable with the word Franchise. StarCraft is an IP. The code written to power the StarCraft matchmaking system is also IP, as are the internal documents used to plan release cadences. But when people say "the StarCraft IP," they aren't referring to that code. They mean all the things they see in the game.

The characters, locations, concepts, the units, the logo, the music, and more. Everything and anything that has been a part of StarCraft. The concept of a Mutalisk is part of the StarCraft IP. But so is the art. And the design. If you made a game with a creature that was designed just like the StarCraft Mutalisk, in every way, the owner of the StarCraft IP could sue you or send you a cease-and-desist order.

There is a sliding scale of what will trigger a response. In the scenario where you've copied the gameplay design of the Mutalisk, they would likely not bother. But if you copied the art/appearance of the Mutalisk, they would be much more likely to stop you.

The simplest way to think of it is that it's everything contained in a fictional universe, independent of a particular title or medium. *A New Hope* is a movie, *The Mandalorian* is a television show, and *Knights of the Old Republic* is a game. But "Star Wars" is an IP or Franchise.

THE KEY THING ABOUT IP, FOR CREATIVES

For us, IP is something that makes you feel like it belongs to a certain world. When you hear the pop of a Zergling being born, or see oversized shoulder pads on Thrall, or witness a Kratos leap-attack animation, all of those things induce a feeling in you. It's a feeling of familiarity.

Yes, this belongs in the universe of this game that I love.

It will be important to remember this later for our IP section, because you may have to create new ideas that will be included in an IP, and that's a serious responsibility. What if your contribution is not great, and doesn't really fit that feeling? Don't worry—read the IP chapter, and you should be okay.

From this point forward, when we say "IP," we mean the creative definition of the word. We are not talking about the code or documents owned by a company or individual. We are talking about that creative feeling. Something that fits into a bigger world.

KEY DIFFERENCES BETWEEN WORLD BUILDING AND IP

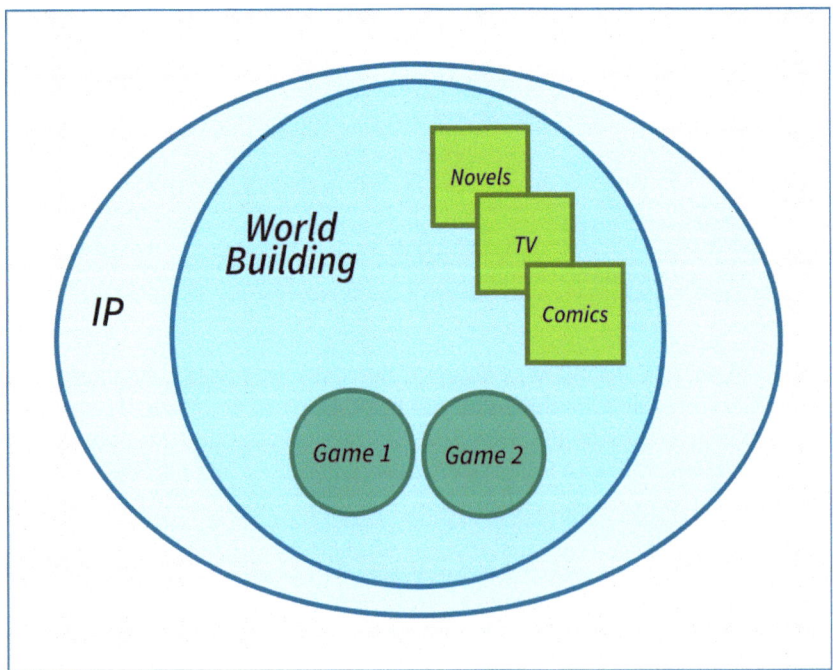

You may notice there is an area that is IP but not World Building. What is that about?

We mentioned earlier that there are parts of IP like programming code, or internal documents, that are not World Building, and that is part of the reason for that in the diagram.

But there is another way to look at that area. World Building is done in a title, like a novel that is based on Popular Game X. Sometimes really big IPs declare something non-canon. Now the World Building in that book? No longer a part of the World Building for Game X. It's still technically part of the IP, in the sense that the company still owns the concepts in that novel. But it's no longer part of the World Building. So it gets to live in the cold outer ring of our IP diagram, with the programming code and the internal documents.

For you in your day-to-day work, however, the biggest difference between World Building and IP is simple: immediacy.

World Building is what you are doing because the game needs it. Do a write up of this zone, or name that magic system.

IP is how you think about the bigger picture: Where does this IP need to grow into? How do I keep room for it to grow? How do I keep it fresh? How do I keep it consistent?

ESSENTIALS OF WORLD BUILDING

World Building can be daunting, whether you are starting with a brand-new world and a blank page, or contributing to a large, vibrant game world. Where to begin?

Unsurprisingly, most narrative developers go right to a narrative mindset. "Well, there was a big kingdom, and then that dissolved, and now there's all these little kingdoms living in the aftermath, competing with each other..."

And while that kind of historical build-up is necessary, it should not be the first step.

STRUCTURE AND SYSTEMS

What systems and cycles made the world into what it is today? Drought, famine, war, and plague have all come and gone cyclically in human history, and so most worlds should show their effects.

And this is true of any setting, from historical or fantasy to contemporary or science fiction. In 2019, many people would have argued that worldwide plague was not a part of the human experience any more, but by 2020, we had all learned the truth: that system is still with us.

Whether you are building a river valley, a dimension, or a galaxy, there will be systems that have helped develop that location. Some of these systems can be based on the sciences, such as geography or astrophysics. In fact, some very much should be based on sciences, to better ground your world.

But you can also create new systems, like magic or a new field of technology, that will influence the state of the world. It is vital that you think through these systems and make sure they are internally consistent, before you begin to consider how they have influenced your world.

Once you have defined major systems and cycles that would impact the world, you will need to think about how those would interact with each other.

Heavy rain seasons in an otherwise dry desert create runoff, which in turn creates flash floods. How would flash flooding have influenced the agricultural practices of a tribe that lives in the dry desert? How would those agricultural practices have affected that tribe's toolmaking, and how would that toolmaking have affected their weapon technology? How would periodic flooding in an arid region affect their mythologies and religions?

HISTORICAL EXAMPLE

Two early western civilizations show the influence geography can have on culture.

Ancient Egypt sprang up around a single river system in an arid environment, with a regular, reliable flooding season. It had natural boundaries on some of its borders, making it easier to defend. It was one of the most stable, lasting, and inward-looking civilizations in history.

Mesopotamia was a chaotic region, with a double river system that was unpredictable in its flooding, creating a lush but dangerous landscape. It was in a bad neighborhood: any civilization that sprang up was likely to be invaded by barbarians very quickly. In fact, Mesopotamia is a region, not a civilization, because the civilization in the area was constantly changing. Cities like Babylon were sacked over and over. Sumerians, Akkadians, Assyrians, Medes, and many others came to prominence, only to fall and be replaced.

Both cultures produced amazing works of art and culture. Everything about their works, from the pyramids and hieroglyphs of Egypt, to Hammurabi's Code and Epic of Gilgamesh in Mesopotamia, display very different energies.

One is stable while the other is chaotic. One is inward-looking, while the other is expansionist. One is ordered, while the other is wild.

SIDEBAR: AN ORGANIC PROCESS

Everything we discuss in this chapter sounds like a linear, step-by-step process, but of course it is not so simple. It is unlikely that you could start building an IP by thinking about geography, with nothing else defined.

World Building truly means adding small pieces together until you have a greater whole, seeing how the pieces change the whole, then going back and changing some of the other pieces to fit the new greater whole. It's a process of moving back and forth along multiple axes.

It is quite natural to start at the beginning and then follow the trail of something—say time, or history. But it is also normal to reverse engineer things as well. Two civilizations that have been at war for millennia? How did that start? How did it continue until it became unstoppable? Go back in time and lay the foundations. But also, where is it going? How does it eventually end?

HISTORY

Now you can begin to build the narratives about civilizations, cultures, families, and individuals. Try to understand the context that would have influenced them, as well as how they would have influenced their time and place.

The best guide for building the history of a world is to have read lots of histories. The universe of human experience is wide, deep, and wildly unpredictable. People will often dismiss something as "unlikely" in fiction that is far tamer than things that have happened in real human history.

Some creators use historical periods as a guide or inspiration for the setup to their world. While this can be useful, be careful not to draw from one source as it can become obvious. Another danger is that history, despite the careful work of historians, is still written by the victors and can be one-sided, meaning that if you base a world off of a particular history, you might create something lopsided.

Read lots of history. But read it widely—across many historical periods, geographical locales, and cultures. This discipline will give you a grounded view of what is possible and how things work.

STAKES IN THE GROUND

Even if you have something of a blank slate, there will likely be a few things that you know at the very start, so begin with those.

Game Genre: This is often the first defining feature of a game, and it impacts the kind of stories that can be told in that genre. When an IP outgrows a particular title, many more stories can be considered. But at the start, the genre affects the storytelling.

EXAMPLE: *WARCRAFT*

Warcraft was originally an RTS, and was well suited for telling stories about wars between civilizations. It was not able to tell the story of a romance. As the IP evolved to *Warcraft 2, 3, Frozen Throne, World of Warcraft*, and beyond, the manner and types of stories that could be told in the Warcraft universe had expanded a great deal.

World Size: If you are telling a story that takes place in a small village, your world has one kind of possibility space. If it takes place in an interstellar civilization, your story has another kind of possibility space. There are certain kinds of stories that fit into certain sizes of world.

For example, a small medieval village is probably not the best world for a story about a group of locals who are conquered by an invading alien species, who gain possession of some of the alien tech, reverse-engineer it, and use that to build weapons with which to drive off the alien invaders. Of course, there could be an awkward way to accomplish that, but it is not a good fit. It is good to know the proper scale of your world and what kind of stories reside there most comfortably.

But is the opposite case true? Could you tell a very small, personal story, of the type that would fit in a medieval village, in a bigger setting? For instance, could you not use the setting of an interstellar empire to tell the story of an apprentice blacksmith who is secretly in love with his master's daughter and so enters the annual sword competition to prove his worth? Just switch "blacksmith" to "amorer" and "sword" to "blaster," and set it near the spaceport on the capital planet?

You could. But at some point, if the science fiction setting isn't an intrinsic part of the game world, it becomes a weird background element. Setting is not window dressing; it must resonate with the rest of the world.

That is the conceptual case for understanding the world size of your game. But there is a concrete aspect as well. Eventually, your world can grow beyond the boundary of the first title. But within that first title, there is an absolute limit to how many places and what distances the player will be able to travel, so it is important to understand those limits as you conceptualize the world.

There is also a temporal element. Some IPs are anchored in time, telling stories and focusing on characters centered around a particular month, year, or decade. Other IPs can jump around centuries at a time. This particular lens can always be widened later, but it's important to decide at the start how anchored to a specific time your IP will be.

EXAMPLE: *STARCRAFT*

The *StarCraft* universe spans millions of years. An epic time scale. Yet the events of *StarCraft I* and *StarCraft II* take place over the course of just a few years. The IP is incredibly wide, but the World Building of the StarCraft games is quite fixed in time ... for now.

Fiction Genre: Even at the start of the process, you likely already know if this is a medieval fantasy, science fiction, spy, or other type of game. Knowing that fiction genre will also plant some stakes in the ground for you. This is another point that may seem obvious: *Well of course a medieval fantasy game will be set in a magic kingdom. It wouldn't be set on Jupiter or New York City!*

But if you think about it deeply, you'll find more information contained in the fiction genre than you might have expected. For instance, most genres have norms and conventions. And many of those contribute to World Building. You can use the conventions of the genre to quickly get some stakes in the ground with your World Building. It will be easy to sell them to the team because they are familiar.

And if you want to defy or break the conventions of your fiction genre, this is still a good way to start. Once you've made some progress, you can come back, look at those conventions, and start subverting them.

OTHER TYPES OF GAME WRITING

A narrative designer does many types of writing that have nothing to do with dialogue or voice-over. Item names and descriptions, ability names, point-of-interest descriptions, menus, tooltips, Skill trees, and more.

TOOLTIPS, QUEST LOGS, AND SUCH

For the most functional types of writing, the basic rules apply. Concision, clarity, and appropriate tone are the three keys. This part of the job is not high art.

It's difficult to give more detailed guidance on these types of writing, because each game has its own aesthetics and rules. The team or game you are working on will define the style that makes sense. Whatever rules they have should be considered ironclad. This kind of writing is precise.

If they haven't created rules and it falls to you, consider the game's needs.

What Kind of Combat Does the Game Have?

A turn- or round-based RPG like *Baldur's Gate 3* or *Persona 5* tends to have complex, detailed combat and abilities. Is the rogue in the right zone to do backstab damage? How will different abilities combo? How many rounds will this debuff last? For that kind of combat, you'll probably want detailed, comprehensive tooltips. If they become a bit longer than you'd like, that's okay. The player is under no time constraint, and can pause the game while they read it.

An ARPG like *God of War*, or a PvP game like *Overwatch* requires tooltips that can be quickly scanned, while the game is active. This means different color text to indicate different information, or graphic icons to represent a particular game feature. Ice damage, burning effect, hunger, broken gear, or anything similar that can be conveyed in an icon should be. This makes tooltips more quickly readable in combat.

Tone

Does the game have a particular tone that needs to be captured in the tooltips? Again, the requirement here is clarity and concision. But games with a strong tone may accept the tradeoff in order to reinforce their tone.

EXAMPLE: *HELLDIVERS II*

The "Training Manual Tips" in *Helldivers II* contain such gems as:

> Don't forget to take breaks! That is, if you want to be remembered as a coward.

Tone is not a requirement for tooltips, but you should take every chance to imbue your game with the tone of your world.

Tokens

Be aware that many tooltip systems will use tokens. This means that you insert a variable into the text string, which can be updated from a central database.

For example, you would not write,

"Inflicts 34 fire damage per second for 10 seconds."

You would instead write,

"Inflicts [X] [FI] per second for [Y] seconds."

This way when design changes the amount of damage fire damage does, or for how many seconds, they can update the database, and wherever these tokens exist, they will update with the correct number. And they will change it many times. In this example the [FI] token is so that the icon will appear in the text string, since the text editor probably does not support pasting the fire icon into a text field. And if art updates the icon, it should update automatically as well.

JOURNALS, FLAVOR TEXT, AND SUCH

This type of writing is still functional, but there is more room for expression.

Flavor Text

Flavor text is highly situational. It can be attached to a variety of different features, and that will change things like style and length.

For example, item description, at its baseline, fits in the previous category of highly functional text. It should just describe the item in the most straightforward manner possible. But if your game has flavor text attached to item descriptions, then the standards for flavor text would overrule the standards for item descriptions.

Flavor text serves two main purposes. The first is simply to entertain. Good flavor text makes whatever it is attached to more memorable. The second is to add World Building to a game that may not have room for it in many places.

The best flavor text follows one of three conventions:

- World Building. Rather than tell us a story, tell us something about a far-away land or famous hero. Not their story, just an interesting fact about them.

- Tone. Simply add a short phrase or sentence that adds to the tone of the game, the world, and whatever the flavor text is attached to.
- Story or character. This is the hardest to do. Some narrative developers try too hard to tell a story in the flavor text, with the result that it feels forced and calls attention to itself.

The best approach for the third convention is to create something short and evocative which hints at a greater story without trying to tell it.

Case Study: *Diablo III: Reaper of Souls*

Diablo III: Reaper of Souls introduced legendary potions. As legendary items, they all came with some sort of flavor text. Players usually grind or craft to get legendary items, and some fun flavor text is part of their reward.

Nine of these potions got flavor text that implies a story without telling it. Each bit of flavor text adds a new development in the story of Jentulf the apothecary. Some of them imply a logical order, while others are timeline agnostic. The point is that each is discrete and doesn't require much outside knowledge. None of them tell a story, they just give us a sense of a character in an environment. But that sense is hopefully entertaining, without being burdensome.

Here is the flavor text for these eight potions:

"I don't know how it works, but it's safe to say that I am the finest apothecary of our age." —Royal Apothecary Jentulf, in his speech to the Society of Apothecaries.

"It heals you, it helps you resist damage, and it cures warts!" —Royal Apothecary Jentulf, presenting his newest creation to the king.

"Well, I had to test it on someone, didn't I? You're all just jealous!" —Royal Apothecary Jentulf at his trial, just before sentencing.

"When you are losing a fight, healing is no help, as you'll just lose that health in turn. No, what you need is a potion that gives you energy. And I know how to make that potion!" —Prisoner Jentulf, in a letter to the King pleading for early release.

"If I learned one thing from my years in the dungeons it's this: fear is a great motivator. We all need some fear in our lives!" —Royal Apothecary Jentulf at his reinstatement ceremony.

"Some of you claimed I lost the touch during my sojourn in the King's dungeon. To you I say, this potion amplifies healing and puts the lie to your feckless assertions! Yes, I'm back, lackies!" —Royal Apothecary Jentulf in his weekly address to the Society of Apothecaries.

"Does Your Majesty know what would serve his armies better than mere healing? Healing combined with more healing!" —Royal Apothecary Jentulf, advising His Majesty in council.

When Royal Apothecary Jentulf said "If only there were a way to lessen the need for healing," Royal Blacksmith Akmmenn replied "I have an idea."

"In my workshop, when one sees liquid in a bottle, logic dictates that it is something beneficial. But bottle logic is wrong! My genius has transcended the beneficial. Now, I ride the waves of chaos. Chaos!" —Royal Apothecary Jentulf, in his final letter to the Society of Apothecaries, before his disappearance.

Each of these bits of text imply a bigger story around Jentulf, but don't spell it out.

The last example in the above list came with the requirement that the writer use the phrase "bottle logic" in the text. This was the name of a brewery who had created a custom beer for Blizzard at one of its annual BlizzCon conventions.

It was fairly tricky for Brian to include the words "bottle logic" in the flavor text of a fantasy game, and what you see above was his solution.

Journals

Many RPGs have some kind of quest journal. Unlike a quest log, which is a bare-bones description of what must be done, the journal provides a lot of context. If a player stops playing a big sprawling RPG for a few weeks and then comes back to it, they may have forgotten the context around a particular quest. In a narrative heavy game, context is everything.

EXAMPLE: QUEST LOGS VS QUEST JOURNALS

A quest log may have an entry such as follows:

"Return to Horvald."

A quest journal would more likely have an entry such as follows:

"You've secured the money that Chivy owed to Horvald. Chivy was unhappy about the interaction, but his bruises will heal with time. Now you can return the gold to Horvald, so that he and his friends can finally put on that play they've been dreaming about."

If a player logs back in and sees they have a gold pouch in their inventory, but has no memory of why, this short bit of text in the log will give them several pieces of information:

- The pouch belongs to Horvald, and the next step is to return it to him.
- Horvald wants to use the money to put on a play. If the player returns the pouch to Horvald and gets a new quest to go rough up a reluctant playwright, they will now know why.
- Chivy is likely unhappy with the player, and if the player talks to them at some later date, they will now understand Chivy's attitude.

However, these kind of journal entries immediately pose a new question: how much context to include? It is quite easy to start writing very long entries, including too much information. This is where your discipline as a writer comes into play. You must determine the absolute minimum amount of context to get the player up to speed on the quest, and include only that.

There are a few stylistic issues to consider with journals.

In theory, these are written by the protagonist of the RPG, so it would make sense to write them in the first person. Yet RPGs are entirely about role play and identity, and a first-person quest journal may accidentally give the wrong note to the player.

Contradicting the player's identity in an RPG is a cardinal sin.

EXAMPLE

In our earlier example where the player roughed up Chivy for some money, a first-person journal entry may say something like this:

"I had to explain a few things to Chivy before he coughed up the gold. The bruises will heal soon."

But maybe the player felt awful about beating up Chivy, and the glib tone of the journal entry will feel wrong.

If the entry is written in second person:

"Chivy was unhappy about the interaction, but his bruises will heal with time."

The player will feel that the glib tone is the game's tone, not their own opinion about the interaction.

If you use second person, you avoid those possible inconsistencies. On the other hand, it opens up some strange questions: Who is writing these entries? Why are they addressed to me?

However, most players have played games where this is the norm, and are well past asking those kind of questions.

There is no universal right answer to this type of question. It depends on the tone and feel of the game.

In-Jokes or Easter Eggs

Some games include in-jokes or easter eggs as a nod to some community of players in some way or other. This would be too fourth-wall and immersion breaking in some games, and completely acceptable in others. It really depends on the IP.

If you are planning to add an in-joke or easter egg to flavor text, it's useful to remember this core rule: the in-joke is only acceptable if someone who is not clued in can read it without knowing there is an in-joke there.

If a player who is not clued in reads your flavor text in-joke and thinks "Huh, that was weird. What was that all about?" you've hurt their play experience.

They should be able to read it and think that it all made sense, even if it was not memorable.

Those in the know will have a very different experience. Your job is to make sure that both outcomes work.

Here is some flavor text from *Diablo III: Reaper of Souls*:

This fragment of a gem, called a chip, was discovered in an underground vault by old man Boyarsky, who fashioned it into the beautiful gem it is today. It damages those who would damage its owner, and once inserted into a socket, it will never fall out.

It contains four direct references to the fallout IP, and they are pretty obvious. But there is nothing in the text that would be unclear or confusing if the reader did not know anything about Fallout.

CONCLUSION

There are many other aspects to World Building, such as tone and feel. But those aspects fit comfortably within the IP discussion as well, so we will dive into them more deeply in the IP section of the book.

CHAPTER SUMMARY

In this chapter, we discussed the following topics:

- World Building vs Intellectual Property. There is a lot of overlap between these two topics, but some differences as well.
- What is World Building? The process of fleshing out the concepts in the game that contribute to the overall world. It is not specific to geography.
- Essentials of World Building.
  - Structure and Systems. Try to understand what systems contributed to make your game world what it is, from the gravitational effects of a multiple moon system, to famine, to magic systems.
  - History. With systems in place, you can build narratives around the history of your world.
  - Stakes in the ground. Identify what parts of your game world are defined and can't change. This might be due to game genre, world size, fiction genre, or some other factor. Once you understand those, you can proceed with everything else.

Section 3

Characters

Once we have a handle on storytelling in games, it's time to discuss the most important aspect of any storytelling: Characters. This section comes later in the book because it builds on what has come before.

DOI: 10.1201/9781003624882-11

8 Where to Start

- Different methods of making a character
- How to introduce a character into the story
- Testing out your characters in different scenes
- Assigning the label of Protagonist or Antagonist for main characters

Characters are the most important part of any narrative endeavor. People connect with characters more than any other element. When players discuss their favorite story, they always talk about a character they love or hate. They never say "Wow, what a plot!" On occasion, they may reference a scene they loved, but even then the emotional weight and excitement of the scene is built upon the foundation of the characters involved.

Understanding how to develop and present characters is one of the most important skills a narrative professional can attain.

There's a lot to cover, so, let's get to it!

WORK FROM WHAT IS KNOWN

It has never happened in video game history that an executive producer or game director approached a narrative developer and said, "Hey, can you create a character? We don't know anything about them, who they are, what they look like, what they do, or what their purpose is in the game. Just come up with a character!"

There is always something. This might be just a simple sentence, to a fully textured, finished model with a name. In *Mass Effect 2*, the character Samara began with only two data points:

- She is an Asari who will not sleep with the player.
- She is a Mystic Warrior. (Whatever that means.)

From those two points, art, narrative, and design had to realize the character.

When developing a character, an important first step is to gather everything that you know about the character. If the character is already part of an intellectual property (IP) and has appeared in released games, that might be quite a lot.

But even when it is as bare bones as the Samara example above, you can begin to piece together facts, and then make intuitive—or counterintuitive—jumps.

DOI: 10.1201/9781003624882-12

APPEARANCE AND ABILITIES

If art has begun work on the character, then we can glean some basics from that.

- Age
- Gender
- Weight
- Socioeconomic class. Are their clothes expensive? Worn out? Are they wearing the uniform of a mechanic?
- History. Do they have scars?
- Attitude. Do they look aggressive? Shy? Cocky? Sneaky?

If this is a character that will be involved in gameplay, then the design will also have some insight for you.

What are their abilities? If they are a sniper, we know they spent a lot of time practicing at the range, and that they have taken the time to master the use of a very precise weapon.

On the other hand, if they wield a shotgun and are able to load it by throwing two bullets up in the air, opening the shotgun, and holding it so the bullets fall into the chamber, we know that they are agile and fast—but also that this may be something they do at the local bar after a few beers, to impress their friends. We know they like up-close-and-personal combat, and that they like explosions.

ARCHETYPES

Archetypes are a useful tool for conceiving of a character or revising one who is not working well. They are also a much larger topic in other fields, such as psychiatry and philosophy. We will be focused only on how they are useful in game narrative, and nothing else. If you would like to research archetypes on your own, the psychiatrist Carl Jung is probably a good place to start, as his work on archetypes has been widely influential.

For us, an archetype is a way to categorize characters. You take a set of related ideas and make them the basis for a character type. Like any tool, there are hazards involved, so we will dive into the good and bad of archetypes.

EXAMPLE: THE KNIGHT

This is a warrior who has a code and follows it strictly. They are not necessarily good. In D&D Alignment terms, they can be lawful good or lawful evil. The code may be moral and ethical, it may be evil, or it may not even fall on the good/evil spectrum. What makes the archetype of the knight is that they follow this code and try to enforce its structures on the world around them. "Live and let live" is not a part of the Knight archetype. There may be other archetypes where a character adheres to a code but doesn't care if the world around them does, but that is not the Knight.

From the foundation of a character who strictly follows a code, you can start to build a character. However, the archetype should not be limiting. It tells you a few key things about a character, and you may be tempted to extrapolate those key attributes into other ideas, and thus limit yourself.

It may be tempting to say:

- She is a Knight, so she definitely doesn't have a ballet recital next week.
- He is the Evil Overlord, and therefore he definitely does not cook Sunday dinner for his family.
- He is the Leader, so he never has self-doubt.

Do not try to extrapolate the core of the idea to other areas. All you will do is limit your thinking.

A Knight can be a gourmet cook. Or a ballet dancer. Or an alcoholic. Or a thief. What the Knight character can never do is casually fail to live up to her code. She cannot put her code on hold for a day while she takes some action that violates it. A character who does that is interesting, but they are not the Knight archetype. They are something else.

Changing an Archetype

If our Knight decided to give up on her code to achieve some critical goal, couldn't this just mean that she is evolving into a new archetype? Sure, that is possible, and no rule or tool is inviolable. So if it feels necessary to do that, then you should proceed. But do it with caution. On some level, a Knight who gives up her code when expedient was never truly a Knight, because that code and adherence to it are at the core of the Knight.

The audience may be impressed and awestruck at the power of the story beat where the Knight does this. But some part of their brain will also file away the fact that the character was never what they thought it was. A little bit of trust will be lost.

As discussed elsewhere, trust can be lost in small measures, and it can be regained. But trust is the most valuable currency a storyteller has. Spend it wisely.

How to Use Archetypes

From the above example, you can start to understand that the Knight archetype gives us a starting point with a character, from which we can build outward.

You can take what is known about a character, find an archetype that seems to reinforce that, and springboard into developing more qualities about the character. It is important to remember the word "springboard." That's all the archetype is, a starting point.

Think of it as something that gets you 85% of the way to realizing a compelling character. The last 15%, the part that archetypes won't help you with, is where the real work gets done. That last 15% of effort is what makes the character shine. It makes them compelling and real and memorable.

So why use an archetype at all? Because that 15% is built upon the foundation of the 85%. If you stop at the 85% point and just rely on the archetype to render the character, you will have created a stereotype or a caricature. It's just a forgettable sketch of a character, which players have seen many times before.

Find an archetype that builds off of "what is known," use that to springboard to a bigger idea of a character, and then roll up your sleeves and turn this idea into a unique, interesting, and compelling character.

A Second Way to Use Archetypes

As with most of the tools we discuss in this book, archetypes can be used at the start, or near the end of a creative process. Or both!

If you've already created a character and integrated them into a story, but they just don't seem to be working, you have got to find a way to revise them. Maybe playtesters don't find them compelling. Maybe they just don't seem to fit the role they must perform. Maybe they just feel off.

When the source of the problem is unclear, it can be hard to propose solutions. That's when you can enter diagnostic mode and try using some kind of objective criteria to measure your character against. In that situation, you can try applying an archetype to the character you've already created. Does the character have some set of core attributes that fit together in a coherent way? What drives them?

If you're having trouble finding a good archetype for the character in their current form, it may indicate that some part of the character's core is adrift. You can try going back to basics: take what you know about the character from their role in the game, find an archetype to base them on, and rebuild from there.

No one likes throwing out a bunch of work and starting over, but it is a common occurrence in game development in general, and narrative in particular. Archetypes can be a good tool to accelerate that process.

Where Is the List of Archetypes?

Archetypes have evocative names: The Archer, The Hermit, The Pirate, The Hanged Man. Now if you could just find a list of what each means, you'd be all set, right? There are a number of resources online where an individual or organization has shared their list of archetypes with definition. You should review those, as there is a lot of helpful information there.

But the reality is that there is no official, perfect set of archetypes. Each narrative person must define their own version of what a particular archetype is or means. The point is not to use someone else's definition to make your work better. The point is to organize your own thinking.

When we say "the Archer," a bunch of associations leap to mind for us:

- Fast
- Precise
- Agile
- Smart-ass

- Fragile
- Optimistic
- Reckless.

Some of those words seem intuitive to an archer. Precise feels like an easy connection. Others have almost no concrete connection. Why would an archer be more or less smartass than, say, a swordsman? Why would they be optimistic?

The answer is that those are just the ideas that the archetype conjures for us. Perhaps we've played online games where the ranged characters were generally controlled by smart-ass players and the association just seeped into us.

Obviously, that association may not exist for you, so if we define the Archer with the above qualities, it may not be helpful to you. The power of archetypes then is to find out what associations you have with the evocative name.

CREATE AN ARCHETYPE

Write "the Archer" on a sheet of paper and then list a bunch of qualities that leap to mind for you. They don't have to mean anything to anyone else. You're mapping out something that will guide your understanding of a character under the surface.

The guiding force of the archetype will impose some kind of coherence and unity on the character, but it is behind the scenes. If the team playtests a quest where they meet a character who you've decided is the Archer, and none of them know that this character is based on the archetype of the Archer, that is fine. In fact it would be a little odd if they did, considering that this is actually your Archer archetype.

So you've written this list of qualities. Hopefully, some of them don't naturally fit with the others. That's good! As you assemble them all into one idea of a character, you've got some unity, some disunity, some coherence, and some dissonance.

Congratulations, you've just created an archetype.

The evocative name of an archetype is a part of the magic. It creates connections in your mind. As a shortcut, you can put "the" in front of a wide variety of words, and do the same exercise that we did above with "the Archer," and now you're building your own library of archetypes.

Here are some examples:

- The Thief
- The Assassin
- The Architect
- The Influencer
- The Liar
- The Nurse
- The Lover
- The Hanged Man
- The Pirate

- The Giant
- The Beggar
- The Vampire
- The Hater
- The Socialite
- The Hermit
- The Monster
- The Saint
- The Trickster
- The Priest
- The Wizard
- The Sorcerer
- The Mentor
- The Rogue
- The Difficult Man
- The Ghost
- The Elder
- The Wanderer
- The Madman
- The Soldier
- The Knight
- The Apostate
- The Betrayer
- The Chosen
- The Freak
- The Savant
- The Sinner
- The Sniper
- The Saboteur
- The Provocateur
- The Tower
- The Rebel
- The Escapist
- The Poet
- The Dancer
- The Convict
- The Gymnast
- The Gravedigger
- The Robot
- The Magi

There are many more.

It is important to remember: there is no right or wrong way to translate these words into an archetype. You don't need to render judgment on the characters. It's more of a free association for you: what does this word conjure in your mind?

SIMILAR ARCHETYPES

Some archetypes listed above may sound very similar, and if they feel that way to you, then it's probably not important to distinguish them. After all, you can keep making more and more archetypes.

However, it can be useful to map out how two seemingly similar archetypes are different. Understanding the subtleties of this can help you render two characters who may seem similar, yet will present as very different to the player.

So let's take two archetypes: the Trickster and the Rogue.

Both seem to share a lot of qualities:

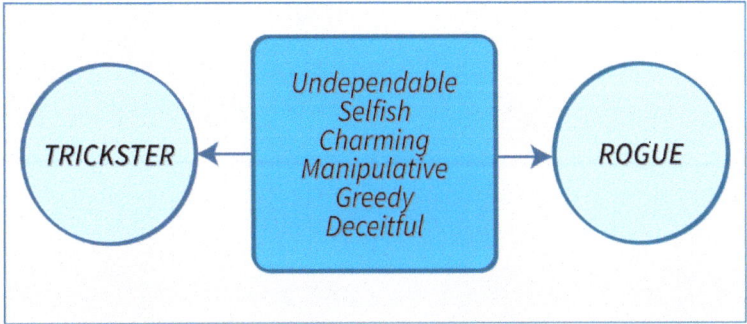

Given this much overlap, won't these two feel essentially the same to players? In truth, these two archetypes are very different and will feel very different to players, so it's important to understand how they are different.

A famous Rogue character is Varric from *Dragon Age*. A famous Trickster character is the Joker from the *Batman* series.

Despite having overlapping qualities, these two archetypes have fundamental differences, as seen here.

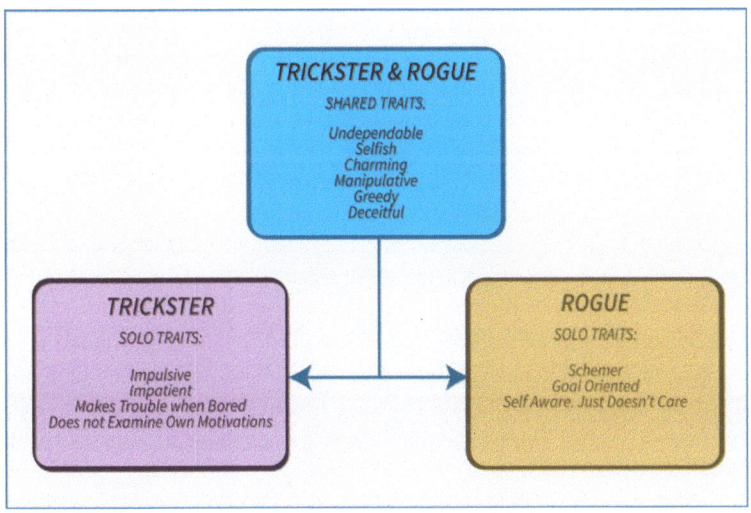

A Well-Presented Trickster

Heath Ledger's Joker in the 2008 Batman film *The Dark Knight* is a particularly powerful representation of the Trickster archetype.

The character is violent and highly capable, but those qualities attach to a wide variety of archetypes. The character is also playful, unpredictable, and lies constantly. Those qualities are much more specific to a Trickster, but can still be attributed to other archetypes.

But the film goes well beyond the basic trickster qualities. Another character famously describes the Joker by saying "Some men just want to watch the world burn." And this line begins to hint at the truly chaotic nature of the Joker.

Throughout the film, the character is surprising and compelling. How do we know this is due to a strong portrayal of the Trickster archetype?

Because there is a scene where the Joker explains himself, the only time he is clear and coherent about himself. And in that scene, he describes the fundamental qualities of a Trickster. He says the following things:

> "Do I really look like a guy with a plan? You know what I am? I'm a dog chasing cars. I wouldn't know what to do with one if I caught it. I just do things. The mob has plans. The cops have plans. Gordon's got plans. Y'know? They're schemers. Schemers trying to control their little worlds. I'm not a schemer. I try to show the schemers how pathetic their attempts to control things really are."
> "You know what I noticed? Nobody panics when things go according to plan, even if the plan is horrifying."
> "Introduce a little anarchy. Upset the established order. And everything becomes chaos. I'm an agent of chaos. And you the thing about chaos? It's fair."

As he says this last line, he hands Harvey Dent a loaded gun and points it at his own head. Harvey Dent hates the Joker and has every reason to kill him. Yet the Trickster is willing to leave his fate to the whim of chaos.

To be clear, this portrayal of the Joker is not exceptional because the character explains himself. It's incredible because of the way it uses the Trickster archetype, as well as the great performance. The reason we dwell on this scene is because for those of us who study narrative, having a well-rendered character describe their own archetype is a revealing, awesome moment.

Don't Be Literal

Don't let the specificity of the archetype names confuse you. If you are mapping an archetype to a character in your game who is a literal archer, they don't need to be the Archer archetype. Likewise, if you've mapped out a character's archetype as "the Brawler" before their gameplay role has been decided, they don't need to be a frontline melee character.

An archer character could easily be a Brawler archetype, and a frontline melee character could be some other archetype such as "the Poet."

ATTITUDE

An early step when developing a character is to choose an overall attitude. Just as with archetypes, this can be dangerous if you make it all there is to your character, but so long as you realize it's a surface quality, an overall attitude can be helpful.

Think of the attitude like the paint on a house. It's the first thing you see, and it has a big impact on your first impression. But it doesn't really tell you what is inside that house. So, attitude is a great way to get to know a character quickly, but not deeply.

Still, it's a powerful tool. Pick an attitude—cocky, earnest, apathetic, hopeful, shy, gloomy, mean. You instantly get an idea of a character! You just have to build past that, so that the character is more than that.

The attitude can spring from an archetype you've chosen, or the archetype can spring from an attitude you've chosen. Or they can be independent of each other!

INTRODUCING A CHARACTER

The way a character is introduced will have a huge impact on how the player regards that character. This is true of NPCs, but also true of the player character. The introduction is an opportunity, which you should not miss. It is also a danger, which you should avoid.

The screenwriter Blake Snyder said in his ubiquitous book *Save the Cat* that when we first meet the protagonist, they should perform some small act of goodness, such as rescuing a cat stuck up in a tree. Even if our protagonist is an unlikable antihero, this small act gets the viewer on their side emotionally, so that they can carry the audience forward with them.

This is a small technique, but a useful one. Even if you plan for the player to thoroughly dislike the player character from the start, you do need to find some way to make them emotionally accessible. This does not mean making them likable. Simply that you must give players a way to connect with them and thus follow them into the game and story.

The highly accomplished screenwriter Aaron Sorkin has his protagonists fail at something very soon after we meet them. Seeing how a character reacts to failure is hugely revealing, and it provides momentum to the story.

This is also a useful technique. Like any tool, it should not be used indiscriminately and does not fit every situation. However, when possible, it can highlight the character's personality and put them in a dramatic situation. Both techniques are incredibly useful elements in a character's introduction.

If a character is important enough to have a specific introduction, whether NPC or Player Character, you should spend time thinking about a situation that will highlight whatever is compelling about that character.

In the first *Halo*, when a UNSC ship is attacked and boarded, the crew thaws a warrior who was cryogenically frozen: Master Chief. This is the character's introduction. It is simple, straightforward, and high-octane ... just like Master Chief.

In the opening of The Last of Us, we meet Joel on the night that the apocalypse begins. We control him through the first moments of horror and fear. We see his daughter die, not to an infected, but to a human bullet. When we meet him again, several game years later, we understand the weight hanging over him.

When we first encounter Sylvanas Windrunner in the *Warcraft* universe, she has led an attack against the Lich King who defeats her and twists her soul into a banshee to fight for his side. We later witness Sylvanas free herself of his enslavement when the spell on her weakens. When she returns, she rallies the other freed undead who are now outcasts from humanity. This gives us a deep insight into her strength and capability as well as her antipathy toward humans.

When we first meet Liara in *Mass Effect*, she has been caught in a Prothean energy field while hiding from invading Geth. This reveals a number of things about her at once. She is an archaeologist, who was studying ancient, mystical technology. She is resourceful, in that she was able to devise a plan that saved her from the marauding Geth. And she is a bit naive, and allowed herself to be trapped in an embarrassing situation, even if it was one that saved her life.

Let's create an example of our own: perhaps you meet Clyde, an NPC who will later join your gang, in an old west setting. You find him in a saloon, and he is caught cheating at a hand of poker. He has to bluff his way out of the situation, using a waitress as a shield.

From this you know that Clyde is a cheater, but he is not a very good cheater. You know that he is not afraid to use an innocent civilian as a shield. But you also see that he is crafty and a quick thinker. Later when you track him down, you will have a common point of discussion: he will remember you as the observer who did not help him, and you can remind him that you were the observer who did not shoot him.

Use the Environment

The environment should not just be a backdrop. The location and the state of the location tell us about the character.

In *Mass Effect 2*, we meet Jack "the Convict" in a prison ship. By itself, that tells us something, but environmental storytelling goes beyond that.

While most prisoners are kept in cells, Jack is kept in cryo-stasis, indicating that she is considered far more dangerous than the average prisoner.

There is another step beyond this, however. When the player arrives on the ship, they must move through the ship toward the back to get to Jack. Along the way, players see an orderly, tightly controlled prison. When players reach Jack and unfreeze her, she escapes her shackles and goes on a rampage through the ship. Now the player is pursuing her, going back through parts of the ship they've already passed through. But now the orderly environment is destroyed, with wrecked walls and bulkheads, and dead guards strewn everywhere.

Jack has actually changed the environment around her. This not only shows her power, but it also hints at her inner turmoil. She is changing her exterior environment to reflect her inner self.

Environmental storytelling is powerful!

SIDEBAR: BACKSTORY IS NOT YOUR FRIEND

Don't try to use backstory as the foundation of a character. Some narrative folks come up with long, involved backstories to try and motivate or explain things about their character. There's nothing wrong with a deep, powerful backstory—this can help you build a complex, nuanced, memorable character.

But it won't help the player understand this character. It is useful for getting the player to the starting line. "Oh, that's the woman who grew up with no feet, then could finally afford cybernetic replacements after she won the lottery. Cool!" But that's it—it just helps the player identify the character.

Players won't care about this at the deepest level, because backstory is intellectual—they *know* something happened. To make them *feel* it and care, they have to experience it themselves.

So if they spend early levels with slow movement, but they win a lottery and get cool enhancements that let them move at a normal or faster pace, they'll feel that connection to the character and her struggles.

If the player does not experience it in the game, it's not real.

MORE THAN APPEARANCE AND ABILITIES

Earlier, we said to work from what is known about a character. This is true, but you must be careful not to stop there. Many narrative developers build the entire character around the appearance and abilities. They might add a few details here and there, but the core of the character is those two things. Unfortunately, that leaves those characters feeling incomplete in a fundamental way.

In the example of the sniper, you might think that they are super precise in all aspects of their life, very careful and always watching. The first problem with pursuing that idea is that it is exactly what every other narrative developer has done with sniper characters. The bigger problem, though, is that it's such an obvious idea for the sniper that it just makes them a boring character. Now imagine a sniper who is always forgetting to pay her rent, is always having fights with her partner—when she even remembers that she has a partner. A sniper who gets sloppy drunk and has a bad sense of direction. But put a sniper rifle in her hand, and she turns into a professional. Much more memorable than the precise sniper.

We are all more than our abilities and more than our appearance. Take yourself for example: you are a talented storyteller. But does that mean someone can define you by that? You never read history, debate philosophy, or watch trashy TV shows? You must have a favorite type of food. Maybe a life partner who doesn't play or care about game stories?

And you are certainly more than your appearance. Sure, we can learn some things about you from your appearance—did you forget to brush your hair? Are your clothes carefully ironed? But that's also not the sum total of who you are. Someone with unbrushed hair may have spent their morning getting a child ready for school. Someone with carefully ironed clothes may have just come from a job interview.

If we are all more than our appearance and abilities, then our characters can be too! Use those things as one data point among many for a character.

BACKSTORY

At this point, you have enough to start thinking about the character's backstory. But remember, this is still an additive, creative process. Don't try to construct a backstory that simply explains all the other things you've decided about the character. As you write their backstory, keep creating. Surprise yourself. Write things that don't fit with what you already know—it's okay, you can go back and change those previous steps afterwards.

And remember: backstory is very useful in helping you contextualize and understand the character. It is useful in helping the team understand a character who is currently not in the game. But ultimately, the backstory does not impact the player's opinion of a character as much as we narrative developers like to think. The player will experience this character in the game, and that will contribute to almost all of their opinions.

DIALOGUE

Here it's a good idea to stop and write a few lines of dialogue, as that can be very revealing. The character is still forming, and you don't fully know who they are, so the lines may change, but it's a good way to start to get to know the character.

Here are some lines we've written for different characters in the past—it's just a few words, but gives a sense of them:

> *I like people. They are strange and sometimes try to kill you. But I like them the same.*
> *Don't be shy. I promise, you'll have the time of your life.*
> *Don't worry! The heat-death of the universe will solve everything.*
> *If fate made plans for me, it must have been drunk.*
> *Two kinds of people. Those that have seen it and done it, and all the rest.*

The goal with these lines is just to get more of a sense of the character.

Case Study: Finding the Perfect Line: Jack, from *Mass Effect 2*

WARNING: STRONG LANGUAGE, GENDERED INSULT

Sometimes a line of dialogue can go a long way toward defining a character. This is useful not just to order your own thinking, but the line can be a tool to communicate to the rest of the team, and ultimately to players. If the team hates the line, then it means they are not aligned with you on the character. If they love the line, you're all on the same page about who the character is.

In *Mass Effect 2*, the player character, Shepard, goes on a mission to find a dangerous criminal, Jack, and get her to join the squad. At the end of that mission, Shepard confronts Jack in the shuttle bay of a ship that is falling apart and about to implode.

Jack asks, *What the hell do you want?*

And Shepard, as they often do in *Mass Effect* games, replies with a reassuring, steady confidence: *You're in a bad situation, and I'm here to get you out.*

In most other interactions in the *Mass Effect* universe, NPCs respond to this kind of line with gratitude and relief. And that makes total sense—part of the fantasy of playing as Shepard is having social confidence and authority.

But Jack responds: *Shit, you sound like a pussy.*

This line does not define the entire character of Jack, but it makes a strong statement about who she is and how she wants to present herself to the world.

When it first came up at a review, it was polarizing. Many on the team felt that strong language had no place in *Mass Effect 2*, despite the game's Mature rating. Brian was asked to write the rest of Jack's lines for the entire game without swearing. He did so to the best of his ability. After the entire first pass of Jack writing was in place, everyone felt like something was missing. It became apparent that Jack was a character who needed to swear, and Brian was allowed to rewrite her to bring swearing into her vocabulary.

More importantly, however, that line made a certain percent of colleagues hate Jack. *How dare she talk to me that way! I'm Shepard, and I'm trying to save her!*

But another group of colleagues instantly recognized that this made her unique and interesting. And if she'd been a shallow character who was trying to be edgy just by swearing, the enthusiasm of this second group would likely have worn off. But the line was a peek into who she really was.

The polarization of the team was actually useful. It forced conversations about who this character is, and ultimately, those who saw Jack as an intriguing, difficult, but ultimately worthy companion were able to persuade those who wanted a "toned down" character.

When the game came out, players had similarly polarized reactions to the line, which made her an instantly powerful character.

SIDEBAR: MALICIOUS COMPLIANCE

In the previous case study, we mentioned that Brian followed the direction to write Jack in *Mass Effect 2* without swearing, knowing it was wrong. This practice could be described as malicious compliance, but that is not quite correct. It's more akin to good-faith-malicious compliance.

The difference is this:

Malicious compliance means to follow bad direction to the letter, with this mindset: "This is so dumb, and I'll give them exactly what they are asking for, and they will be confronted with how dumb it is!"

In most disciplines, this is fine. If your boss tells you to use a hard-to-read font in the presentation, then you should do exactly that, and when people complain, you can look at your boss.

In creative fields, it's trickier. There are hundreds of ways to approach a creative problem, and if your primary goal is to show your boss that they were wrong, you'll end up shortchanging the effort in a way that undermines your own goals.

This takes two forms:

First, you may think it's clear that the work suffered from bad
    direction, but to others it will likely appear you just did a bad job.
Second, you will not have actually demonstrated that the direction is
    bad, only that you didn't like it.

In a creative discipline, your malicious compliance effort must be good-faith. That is to say, you must embrace the direction and do everything in your power to make it work. If you've gone above and beyond to make it work, and it still fails because the core direction was wrong, that will become apparent to all. At least, in a healthy creative culture it will.

Once it becomes clear, you can speak up with the solution that you'd wanted to implement at the start, or ideally that solution will finally be obvious to others. Is it frustrating to have to do it wrong the first time, knowing it's wrong? Absolutely, but getting everyone on the same page is usually one of the most frustrating and labor-intensive parts of any collaborative endeavor. You'd probably end up doing that work one way or another, and hopefully earn some trust in the process.

CONTRADICTION

Do the contradiction! Take what you know about the character—including their backstory—and find something that doesn't fit. The poet who grew up in the streets, fighting for survival, and is now famous throughout the land for his poetry … but he likes to sit in bed at night and read trashy romance novels. The scientist who hates experimentation. The criminal who anonymously donates all his money to charity.

Find that one quality that just doesn't fit. This is really important for the character.

However, don't just impose a contradiction onto an otherwise complete character, or it will feel artificial and insincere. Instead, try to find a natural contradiction through exploration.

A SCENE

Finally, with all of this, try putting the character in a short scene with another character you know or are working on. Maybe they're having an argument. It could be anything from which restaurant to go to for dinner all the way to the best way to save the earth. It doesn't really matter—just that they think differently and are arguing. This will help you really start to see the character.

It's like taking a car for a test drive. It's the only way to really see how it performs!

PROTAGONIST AND ANTAGONIST TYPES

What follows is a generalization of hero and villain types. Like all generalizations, it doesn't stand up to close scrutiny: every character is and should be unique. Each should defy easy categorization.

However, starting with general categories is just a tool to help you build the basic foundation of a character, much like an archetype or attitude. The work you do after that is what makes them unique.

In addition, this kind of categorization is useful for critiquing a character you've already created. You can compare your character to similar characters from fiction you admire. How is your character better than the other character? How are they worse? Most importantly, how are they different?

There is a lot of overlap with archetypes here, but after we examine the types, we will explain the key differences.

PROTAGONISTS

Paladin: The most common hero type. This character knows what's right and is determined to do it. If they have any doubts, they have them under control. The simpler version of this character has always been this way. A more complex iteration is one who has been through many experiences and has arrived at their world view. In either case, the character can be counted on to know what is right and to do the right thing.

EXAMPLE: JEAN-LUC PICARD, *STAR TREK*

We occasionally see glimpses of his past, and he is clearly a very experienced captain at the time of his first appearance in the *Star Trek* universe. But we quickly come to understand that he adheres to an overriding, but nuanced and thoughtful code of both personal and professional conduct.

That he will always do what he understands to be the right thing, even if it comes at personal or professional cost. That he will never accept choosing between two evils, he will keep searching for the path that veers to the right way of doing things. But he's not a cardboard character: his opponents would describe him as a crafty, wiley, and even deceptive enemy.

Pragmatist: This character believes in the cause, but is willing to bend or even break some of the rules in service to the goal. This is not quite the "Ends Justify the Means" character, as that archetype has a distinct lack of morality.

Rather, the pragmatist is a more mild version of that. They do have red lines and moral limits. But they do not fall into dogmatic beliefs around a set of principles. They want to achieve their goals and are willing to think outside the box, ignore accepted norms, and break from the orthodoxy.

EXAMPLE: JIN SAKAI, *GHOST OF TSUSHIMA*

Trained in the Bushido code of the Samurai, he realizes that he cannot defeat the Mongol invaders by following the code. He must be practical and do things that no honorable samurai would do. Nonetheless, he retains his morality and ethics. He will do what he must to win, within the bounds of being a good person, but not a good samurai.

Conflicted: This is a hero unsure of their cause. Or if they are sure of their cause, they may be conflicted about the means they must pursue to further their cause. In either case, the hero is fighting themselves on some level while also fighting their enemy.

EXAMPLE: SHEPARD, *MASS EFFECT*

Shepard is sure of their cause in trying to prepare the galaxy to face the reapers. But in *Mass Effect 2*, Shepard's only way to pursue that goal is to work for Cerberus, a terrorist organization, and they spend the entire game suspicious and conflicted about it.

Innocent: The innocent is naive and simplistic. Yet they still navigate their way through a story as the protagonist. Often, they are protected by an invisible shield of innocence, and their bright view of the world can infect those around them.

EXAMPLE: *FORREST GUMP*

He is an innocent, and a dynamic protagonist.

Redeemed: A protagonist who has a dark past. They've made questionable choices in their past and may even have been the villain of another story. There are tales where the protagonist becomes redeemed during the story—that's a redemption arc. But a redeemed protagonist is simply one who is already redeemed, and their villainy is in their past. However, it may just be backstory, or their past acts may catch up with them during the story.

EXAMPLE: JOHN MARSTON, *RED DEAD REDEMPTION*

He was an outlaw and did many terrible things. By the time we meet him, he's just a man trying to save his family and live a quiet life. But the world won't let him walk away.

Rebel: One who has left the fold. They were once part of the organization, but now they are on the outside and determined to burn down the institution they once served.

EXAMPLE: JC DENTON, *DEUS EX*

He begins the game working for the UN; then discovers that it is part of a conspiracy, and is thrown in a jail cell. He escapes and then brings down the forces who imprisoned him.

Antihero: This kind of protagonist is not a hero, but they are still the main character of their story. They behave in ways that no conventional hero would, whether it's a smaller matter of sending non-heroic signals, or in larger ways, such as taking morally questionable actions. The antihero role is based more on the emotional reaction of players to a character than the character's moral compass. Critically, the antihero is not heroic, but still fills the role of the hero in a story. In other words, they are still opposing the antagonists and seeking the outcome most players would deem best, even if for the wrong reasons. If players feel intrigue, interest, insight, empathy, or sympathy for a character who is not behaving in a classically "heroic" way, then you've got yourself an antihero.

EXAMPLE: *DEADPOOL*

A superhero who subverts all expectations of what a hero is or should be. He is petty, whiny, and painfully self-aware/referential. He makes many morally questionable choices. Yet he is engaging and fun to watch, if only to see how he'll mess up next. Critically though, he does fulfill the role of protagonist or main character in his stories.

There are some characters that are commonly referred to as antiheroes, but are not. Walter White from *Breaking Bad* and Tony Soprano from *The Sopranos* are not antiheroes. They are the protagonists of their story and are the main characters. But they do not fill the role of hero in their stories.

ANTAGONISTS

True Believer: The bad version of the Paladin. They are not acting for personal gain or aggrandizement. The True Believer has a cause, and they will do anything to further it. The cause may be good, but their interpretation of it is bad. Or the cause itself may be corrupt. In either case, they will not be dissuaded.

EXAMPLE: THANOS, *THE AVENGERS*

He believes that what he is doing is right, and he will not stop until he has accomplished it.

The Cad: This character knows that what they are doing is wrong, but they just don't care. If they have a belief system, it is some version of "might makes right" or "If it benefits me, then it is good." Cads tend to be pretty flat villains, but can be enjoyable for all that.

EXAMPLE: HANDSOME JACK, *BORDERLANDS 2*

He's in it for himself and he isn't trying to hide it.

Sympathetic: This villain has a point. They may have learned the wrong lesson or taken the point too far, but there is a kernel of truth at the core of their beliefs. We can understand what drives them, even if we can see that their ultimate goals will cause more harm than good.

EXAMPLE: KILLMONGER, *BLACK PANTHER*

He is fixated on the injustice that has been done to people who look like him in the last few centuries. He's seen the harm done by colonialism. And he is right about all that. Unfortunately, his solution is to do more harm to other people. He essentially falls into the trap of believing you should play the same game as the oppressors, just play it better.

Realist: The bad version of the pragmatist. This character believes that the ends justify the means. Their ultimate goal may be bad and selfish, or it may actually be for the betterment of all of society. But they have in some sense lost their way because they do not recognize any limit to what actions are acceptable to achieve their goals. Note that they are not truly a realist. That's just how this type describes themselves, as a justification.

EXAMPLE: FRANK UNDERWOOD, *HOUSE OF CARDS*

He's animated by operational success. If it works, do it.

The Apostate: This antagonist just wants to destroy the established order, even if that will cause more pain and suffering than the system they seek to destroy. They are the bad version of the rebel.

EXAMPLE: TYLER DURDEN, *FIGHT CLUB*

He just wants to tear it all down, and is driven by nothing deeper. If you think that Tyler Durden is in some way a protagonist or an antihero, reread the book or rewatch the film.

Nihilist: This is a character who believes in nothing. There is no guiding principle or overarching belief. They believe that nothing matters and everyone else's morality systems are useless and made up. In fact, that is their only deeply held conviction.

EXAMPLE: ANTON CHIGURH, *NO COUNTRY FOR OLD MEN*

He's been correctly described as a psychopath, but psychopathy is a root cause, nihilism is the result. Chigurh does not believe in a cause or in anything greater than himself. Even his coin flip mechanic is simply a way to order his thoughts and actions. As one of his victims tells him, "The coin don't have no say. It's just you." In the end, there is nothing inside him.

There is some overlap with the archetypes we discussed earlier. The difference is that archetypes are agnostic of a character's role in a story. They are pure character foundations.

These types, on the other hand, are intrinsically tied to the character's role. The archetype is who the character is. The type is what the character does—and why they do those things.

Knowing that the Joker is a trickster archetype helps you conceive of him as a character. But when you work out a plot, just attributing all his actions to being a trickster is unsatisfying. However, if you understand that his motivations and actions spring from nihilism, it serves to support his role in the story more deeply.

Finally, there is also some overlap between the types. To keep on with the Joker example, you could make the case that he is actually a True Believer, it's just that what he believes in is chaos. That's an accurate argument and is a testament to the depth and conception of that character. Well-rendered characters will defy easy categorization; they spread across several categories.

The category is a tool to get started with a character; it is not the end result.

CHAPTER SUMMARY

In this chapter, we discussed the following topics:

- Work from what is known. When you start developing a character, there are certain things you will already know. It might be their appearance or gameplay abilities. It might be their role in the story, or just their attitude. It might be something else entirely, but begin by defining what is known.
- Archetypes. As you develop the character, consider what archetype they may fall into. The archetype is just a starting point. You'll have to develop the character further, but it gets you into the general area and helps in selling the character to the team.
- Define an attitude. It's one of the fastest ways to communicate something about a character, even if it's one of the shallowest.
- Introducing a character. There are a number of important considerations when you introduce a character. If they are a player character, you must make them emotionally accessible to the player. If you can, try to construct a compelling and revealing situation for the player to meet a character. Use the environment where we meet the character as well.
- More than appearance and abilities. Those are starting points for a character, but there is more to everyone than their appearance and abilities. A character who isn't developed further will feel incomplete.
- Map out a backstory. This is a useful tool to add context to a character, but remember that it is not as powerful for players as most narrative developers think it is. If it didn't happen in the game, it's not real to most players.
- Write some dialogue. When the character is starting to take shape, writing a few lines can help you think about their voice. These lines may never be used in the game, but they help you conceive of the character more fully.
- Contradiction. Great characters have internal contradictions. Try to come to this naturally, through exploration, rather than just tacking a contradiction onto an otherwise complete character.
- Write a scene. Putting your character in a situation is like taking a car out for a test drive. It's the only way to really know how it performs!
- Protagonist and Antagonist types. Another way to think about your main characters and their roles. Like any tool, it's not always the right one for the job, but sometimes it can be of immense help.

9 Characters from the Outside

IN THIS CHAPTER

- Building a character from the outside-in
- Making character tiers to define importance and roles
- Why diversity is important

The previous chapter had to do with building a character from the inside out. And that is the correct place to start: build a foundation internally, until you arrive at a strong external rendering of a character.

But we must never forget that game characters are always viewed from the outside. They are not characters in a novel; the player can never get in their head.

So, we must understand our characters from an external perspective as well.

CHARACTER TIERS

For the rest of this chapter, let's break characters down into tiers to more easily refer to their importance in the story.

These tiers have been created for this book and are not used outside of it. If you walk into a story meeting and say you'd like to discuss the Tier 3 characters, you will likely get a lot of blank looks. That said, if you can make Tier 3 happen, go for it.

Tier 1: The protagonist and the antagonist. If it is an ensemble narrative, where there is truly no singular protagonist, then each member of the ensemble is Tier 1.

TIER 1 EXAMPLES

Master Chief in *Halo*; Darth Malak in *Star Wars: Knights of the Old Republic*.

Tier 2: Sidekicks, friends, lovers, family, chapter bosses, quest givers. These are characters who are important to the story, and appear in many scenes, even if they are not in every scene. They often have some kind of relationship to the protagonist or antagonist.

TIER 2 EXAMPLES

Cortana in *Halo*; Bloody Baron in *The Witcher 3*, Saruman in *Lord of the Rings*.

Tier 3: Characters who have some impact on the story in a specific part, but are not present throughout. Here for a good time, but not a long time.

TIER 3 EXAMPLES

Quest givers in *World of Warcraft* for a one-off quest; Rost in *Horizon Zero Dawn* (Aloy's adoptive father).

Tier 4: Named characters with little to no impact on the story. These might be merchants who have a little bit of flavor dialogue, or a townsperson with whom the player can have an amusing exchange. They are important enough to have a name and likely voice over, and so must have an attitude, but are not vital to the overall experience.

TIER 4 EXAMPLES

Any merchant in any game. Any NPC who is stationed in a location to answer questions or give information.

NOTE ABOUT DEPTH AND TIERS

One would assume that Tier 1 characters would have the most depth, and Tier 4 the least. While that is normally true, it is quite common for Tier 2 characters to have the most depth. This is because in some games, Tier 1 characters are left a bit blank so that players can fill in the blanks with their own ideas.

EXAMPLE: *MASS EFFECT*

The player can define Shepard through their actions, but Shepard's development as a character is necessarily pretty thin. Meanwhile, most of the squadmates who join Shepard have very highly developed personalities and backstories.

SIDEBAR: THE CURSE OF KNOWLEDGE

Make a habit of stepping back and regarding your work from the outside as if you were a player encountering it for the first time. If you succeed at this, you will see it in a new light. This applies to characters, but it is also true of all narrative endeavors.

You are burdened by the curse of knowledge: you know what a particular narrative element is supposed to be, and so you forget that players will not know this.

The easiest way to understand this is from a real example. A colleague of ours created a scientist character, and he wanted her to play against type. She was a researcher, but she should be cool and funny and open-minded. He knew that she had three doctorates, and had published a number of books. But he thought she should also speak openly about her sexual tastes and interests, making jokes and be self-deprecating.

Our colleague did not have sleazy or lascivious intent: he felt it would be a breath-of-fresh air for a learned character to be guileless and open on subjects about which most people are guarded.

Conceptually, this was a good plan. But it fell apart because all the character beats about her academic accomplishment were in his head. Yes, players were aware of her academic background. But the practical effect was that there was a woman in a lab coat who just wouldn't stop talking about her sex life, and making jokes about herself. It did not feel like a new take on a scientist; it felt like it was simply written by someone who did not take women scientists seriously. This was not the case, but perception is reality.

Another narrative designer had to come in and revise the character. While this example is extreme, any narrative professional, from rookie to veteran, can fall prey to the curse of knowledge. You must periodically step back, forget what you know about something, and just look at it from the outside.

WHAT A CHARACTER NEEDS TO BE

Characters have roles and occupy different functions, and we will get to all of that soon. But to start, let's establish some high-level attributes that characters should have. We are viewing the character from the outside, the same way that players will encounter and understand the characters.

A CHARACTER NEEDS TO BE IMPORTANT

Each Tier 1 and 2 character should feel like they could be the protagonist of an important movie or novel. It could be an action thriller, a heartwarming drama, or a crushing tragedy. Perhaps it's a wacky comedy, or a deeply emotional exploration of the challenges of poverty.

But each should have a story profound enough, compelling enough, and entertaining enough to warrant making a movie or novel around. Approach the story of each as if you were writing a pitch for a novel or film about this character.

This approach may seem over-blown. After all, Tier 2 characters are just that: secondary. But it is all too common for characters to become diminished over the course of putting a story together. They become nothing more than the sum of their scenes.

It's better to aim high with them, and if they diminish over the course of development, you still end up with a strong, distinct character.

Think of side or secondary characters who have stolen the show, despite having much less time in the game. This is usually the result of a strong attitude, a great performance, and a narrative developer who has fleshed that character out.

You can also remember that, as we discuss later, you should develop a character in far greater depth and breadth than players will see.

A Character Needs to Be Compelling

This one sounds obvious, but you'd be surprised how easy it is to fall into boring.

This often comes from a desire on the part of the storyteller to make their characters "Likable." Likability is where characters go to die.

It's an old cliche that love and hate are two sides of the same coin. Like many cliches, it has a grain of truth to it. Love and Hate exist in the same category of emotion: a strong, passion-filled reaction to a character.

The emotion of "like" is often mistaken as somehow a lesser version of the same category as "love," like a weaker form of love. But "like" is actually a completely different category, unrelated to love:

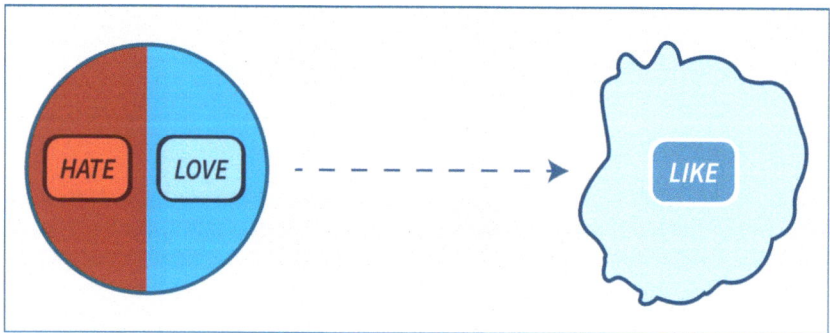

If players love a character, they can grow to hate them. If they hate them, they can grow to love them. And if the needle moves in either direction, the feeling will be even stronger than it was before.

Either reaction is powerful because it means players are highly engaged and invested in what happens to the character next. The desire to see a hated character get their comeuppance is just as strong as wanting to see a beloved character get their well-deserved rewards.

Like, on the other hand, is a dead-end, a closed system. If a player likes a character, they will find them inoffensive and think "they're fine." And that is the end of it. Short of a massive plot twist that changes the entire identity of the character, it's over. If that character turns out to have been the evil mastermind behind the massacre of the protagonist's village or some other huge change, then players will reassess. But in general, a well-liked character will stay just that.

For Tiers 1 and 2, that is deadly. For Tiers 3 and 4, it's perfectly fine.

It is far better to create a hated character than a well-liked one. One could sum up this section with the phrase "Go Big or Go Home" about character creation.

Case Study: Jack, *Mass Effect 2*

When Brian started to write her, many people on the team approached him to say "I hate her." Which he thought was great, because there were characters on the squad who got the reaction "Yeah, he's okay, I like him." Those characters are largely forgotten today. Yet 15 years after release, Jack still gets strong reactions, and they come in three varieties:

- I love Jack!
- I hate Jack!
- At first I hated Jack, but now I love her!

These are all powerful reactions, and are all closely related to each other. The third one is the most powerful. A player who has gone from hating a character to loving them will be a lifelong fan of that character.

Likable Protagonists

As referenced earlier, protagonists are often less interesting than the side characters who support them. This can be intentional, as with Master Chief in *Halo* or Shepard in *Mass Effect*.

In those cases, the protagonist has not fallen into the likability trap. Instead they are less developed so that they can be whatever players project onto them.

But in other cases, the protagonist is less interesting than side characters by accident. The wacky sidekick can be fun and humorous. The smoldering-eyed romantic interest can be intense and flirty. Yet developers often shrink back from giving the protagonist strong or vibrant qualities. This is done for fear of offending some segment of players.

Ironically, when developers create a character without worrying about turning off some segment of players, as when they create a sidekick, they make characters that are much more widely loved. There are notes below to deal with this problem, but the important point here is to keep an eye on your protagonist.

If you plan to make the protagonist a blank slate on purpose, that's a solid plan. But if you want the protagonist to be a distinct character, just as they would be in a novel or movie, you must ensure you develop them like one.

Make them vibrant and distinct. If a player hates the protagonist, then perhaps your story is not meant for that player.

A Character Needs to Be Skilled

We are drawn to characters who are good at something, preferably their main vocation. Unless your game is a slapstick comedy of errors, you will want principal characters to be highly skilled in some area. This applies to protagonists, antagonists, party members, and minions—anyone worthy of a name.

All of us find people of great skill interesting. There was an entire genre of television shows built around antisocial, misanthropic antiheroes whose one redeeming quality was that they were good, or the best, or always right. But that lone trait was, for at least a decade of American prestige television, enough to keep people watching.

Case Study: *House, M.D.*

Dr. House is rude, sexist, a drug addict, and seems to delight in inflicting mental torture and fear onto his subordinates, each of whom is an accomplished doctor in their own right. He is always happy to sneeringly tell patients they are stupid, foolish, dishonest, or any other insightful criticism he may have.

But he's always right. He's right about the medical condition that is the central mystery of each episode, and he is right about the flaws of others that he points out.

House is not a nice character, and over the course of the show, his general hostility becomes trying. However, it's telling that simply by having mastery of his calling, he was able to lead one of the top-rated shows on television for eight seasons.

You may point out that a principal character, with lots of screen time to shine, is one sort of example. But even secondary characters who are skilled will keep our attention.

Case Study: Omar Little, *The Wire*

Some would dispute that he is a secondary character, because he loomed so large over the show. But by any measure of screen time, episode count, line count, anything, he was in fact a secondary character. Yet many people, including former US President Barack Obama, hold Omar up as their favorite character from the show.

There were a few reasons that he stood out. He adhered to a code that few other criminals did. He spoke truth to power. He was openly gay in a world that was violently homophobic.

But the core of Omar's appeal was always that he was the best at what he did. He was a step ahead of the police and the drug gangs he made a habit of robbing. He was always studying, watching, and making notes. He was infamous on the streets of Baltimore.

The storytellers conveyed that with very little screen time and it worked, proving that people are drawn to proficiency, competence, skill, and mastery.

A CHARACTER NEEDS TO HAVE TAKEN DAMAGE

Depending on how deep or fun a character is, their backstory might be extensive or shallow. Regardless, it's important to test your characters in their backstory. That is to say, their starting point and their endpoint should be miles apart, due to conflict.

Shy introvert with agoraphobia? Ends up being the mayor. Rich scion? Ends up as queen of the beggars.

We've used external situations like wealth and introversion because they make for easy examples. But to be clear, a character's journey doesn't always need to result in a strong change in circumstance.

Ebenezer Scrooge is a wealthy businessman at the start of his story. He's also a wealthy businessman at the end of his story. Externally, nothing changed. But his start and end points in the story are far apart: he's a new man.

Use conflict to move a character far away from their start point. It is through conflict that we take a character with a basic premise and test them. "I'm rich!" becomes "I've lost everything. Who am I now?" That testing, and the change it introduces in a character, lead them to their end point. The end point, of course, is our narrative's starting point, since we are discussing backstory here. That endpoint is who they are on day 1 of the game.

Case Study: Scrooge

He became a new man because the ghost of Christmas future terrified him. He saw everything he valued called into question. Every operating assumption in his life was proven wrong. In the end, he saw that he was on a course to have the worst ending possible: dying alone and being forgotten.

Charles Dickens put him through the wringer.

A character's journey might be a welcome change for them, or a tragic one, but it should be the result of who they are, who they are becoming, and how they have dealt with the conflict that came their way.

Perhaps the wealthy woman who lost it all gained immense wisdom and would not trade that for all the gold in the world. Or maybe she misses her silks every day. Even fun or shallow characters can still go through the wringer.

Case Study: Tychus Findlay, *StarCraft II*

What follows is an abbreviated biography of Tychus Findlay.

He ran away from home at 12. Fought in the Guild Wars on the side of the Confederacy, and when his commander put his squad in extreme danger unnecessarily, Tychus punched him. He was demoted and served hard-labor at a military correctional facility. He was singled out for abuse by the guards. Tychus managed to kill one of the guards without catching the blame.

Eventually he was released and deployed to a new fort. He fought against the Kel-Morians, beating one opponent to death with a rifle. Later he led a raid on one of their internment camps. When he found out his commander was planning to steal captured equipment and sell it on the black market, Tychus planned a job-within-a-job, to steal the stolen gear.

But the entire thing went sideways, many people were killed, and Tychus had to flee into the unknown with his friend Jim Raynor. The Confederacy convicted him of manslaughter in absentia.

Tychus lived for a time as an outlaw, robbing convoys and trains. During this time he had many adventures, and was regularly chased, beaten, and threatened. He was also betrayed by many people, although never by his friend Raynor.

When Tychus and Raynor found themselves trapped and surrounded by police officers, Tychus took them all on so that Raynor could escape. He was captured, beaten, and consigned to a terrible prison.

Later he was fitted with a marine suit that was designed to kill him if he disobeyed orders.

That is the backstory of Tychus Findlay up to the point where he first appears in *StarCraft II: Wings of Liberty*.

Tychus was a quasi-comic relief character, and so a full biography would gloss over some of the points we highlight here.

This fun, brash character still took a lot of damage to become the character he is when we meet him.

What's the Worst That Could Happen?

When constructing a character's backstory, one way to ensure that they've taken damage is to ask at every key junction: what is the worst thing that could happen?

Then have that thing happen. What is important to them at any particular moment? What happens if they lose that thing? Or it turns on them? Now you can figure out how to beat them up. And you want to beat them up.

A CHARACTER NEEDS TO BE EXTERNAL

To make the point of this entire chapter a bit more explicit, we need to find a way to externalize the parts of the character that would be internal in a novel. Games are a visual medium. We can't go inside a character's head and see their deepest fears and hopes, so those things must become external.

In *Black Swan*, Lily is an external manifestation of Nina Sayers's internal anxiety and ambition.

The worst way to make the internal into external is to have voice over: the player character or protagonist simply tells players what they are thinking. "And so I would work with Magus Grinklefort for now ... but I would not trust her."

The second worst way to make the internal into external is to give the protagonist a sidekick or foil. This character will ask questions or disagree with the protagonist, requiring the protagonist to share their inner thoughts. It leads to dialogue exchanges like so:

Protagonist: "Let's get going."
Sidekick: "Shouldn't we wait here for the scouts to return?"
Protagonist: "The scouts are already dead. And we will be too, if we don't move."

Having a sidekick is not inherently bad. A fun or interesting character engaging with your protagonist to highlight or contrast certain qualities can be useful. However, the reason we classify it as the second worst approach is that it holds two traps.

The first trap is that the sidekick can quickly become more interesting than your protagonist. We've spoken about this problem elsewhere, and it is always a danger with sidekicks.

The second, and more insidious trap is that having an omnipresent character designed to pull internal thoughts and feelings out of your protagonist quickly becomes a crutch that prevents you from finding a way to externalize a concept.

If a concept is important enough that it must be conveyed to the player, then find a way to let us see it. Yes, this is the old "Show don't tell" rule.

In our example above, we could have the protagonist hurriedly pack up the camp and set out.

Then as the player navigates the level, we find the scouts, lying dead in a ditch. It's environmental storytelling: visual and external.

You Can't Externalize Everything!

You may say: we can't realize everything in the world. Maybe we don't have time to create a little scene with the dead scouts. But a short dialogue exchange could have done the job for us.

This is true, but the first question to ask is: if the concept is not worth realizing beyond dialogue, is it important enough to tell the player about it at all?

Occasionally, the answer to this question is yes. More often, it is no.

A CHARACTER NEEDS TO BE SPECIFIC

Three different characters, placed in the same situation, should have three different reactions. Even if the situation called for the same physical action in each case, their personal reaction would be very different.

EXAMPLE: A SINKING SHIP

Imagine a sinking ship. The only way off is to get to a lifeboat, so any character in that situation would take the same action: get to the lifeboat. But their reactions would vary a great deal. Master Chief from *Halo* would react one way, Trevor from *GTA V* would react another, and Mario would react a third way.

Ask yourself, "how would my character react and how is it different from other characters?" How a character reacts to conflict and stressful situations is a key part of who they are—and a key part of how they end up where they do in life.

It should be unique to them.

Interestingly, the same exact idea applies to their dialogue: anyone can say "I'm sorry." How would your character say "I'm sorry?"

EXAMPLE: WAYS TO SAY SORRY

- "I'm sorry you feel that way."
- "Okay, but hear me out."
- "I fucked up. Big time."
- "I am literally the most despicable being to have ever lived on this planet. Stalin? Genghis? Ain't got nothing on me. The. Worst."
- "You look tired." They hand you a cup of tea.
- "I would like to formally offer you my sincere apologies. I will never, through action or inaction, allow it to happen again."
- "Wanna get drunk and start some trouble?"

The list could go on forever. Every character in your first and second tiers should have a way of reacting that is unique to them.

SIDEBAR: PLAYING AGAINST TYPE

Writers always want to find a new and fresh way to present familiar material, and so it is quite common to try and play against type.

Are you writing a bare knuckle brawler? Maybe he loves to read sonnets, and cries easily. A meek accountant who puts up with bullying from her boss? She's definitely in a fight club. A criminal with a code of ethics. A vegan zombie. The list goes on.

Playing against type can be a powerful tool, but like most powerful tools, it requires care in how it is used. Often developers come on strong with the against-type approach immediately. "Look how cool this character is! She's a nun who robs museums at night!"

The problem is that if you don't establish the baseline of the type itself, then you are not really playing against a type. You're just playing a type. A museum-thief nun who doesn't feel like a nun is just a museum thief. You are only playing against type if you first establish the type. It's not enough to say she's a nun or he's a zombie. You must show us this, establish it, and make us believe it.

Start with that, and then once the type is firmly believable, you can play against type.

This entire topic may seem very similar to the "Curse of Knowledge" point. But that is an error committed by a writer who has forgotten how players will perceive their character from the outside. This is an error where a writer has forgotten that a character must have a basic context in order to be contrasted against it.

THE DEEP-TO-FUN SPECTRUM

Some of your characters can have deep and complex motivations, backstories, emotional journeys, and ambitions. Others can absolutely be engaging and entertaining, with a personality that pops, but not a lot of depth.

This is the Deep-to-Fun Spectrum. Another term for this could be the Powerful to Compelling Spectrum.

At first this may seem confusing. Depth and Fun are not opposites of each other. That would be Shallow and Boring, respectively. But this spectrum is not meant to represent opposites. Rather, these are both aspirations— something you want a character to be. But they exist at some distance from each other.

You could have a character that has some of each, so they are not mutually exclusive. But, as represented in the figure, the two aspirations are far enough away from each other that as you add more of one, you have less of the other.

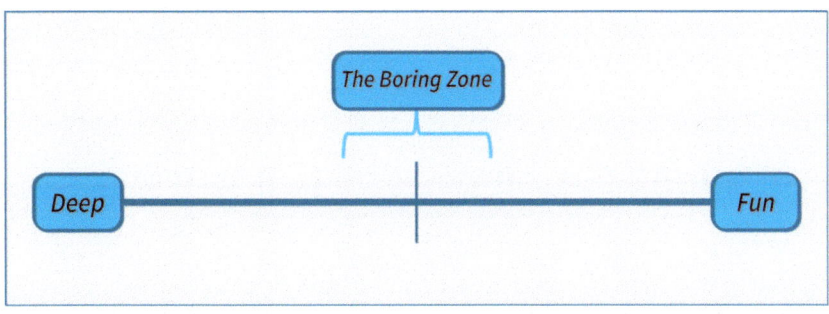

Deep

Advantages: Deep characters can sustain long term engagement. Their stories can play out over a long period and can find new angles to explore the character's depths, renewing themselves. Once players are interested in a deep character, they will generally want to follow them for a long time.

Disadvantages: Deep characters are harder to get to know and like. They grow on players slowly. Also, players are sometimes not in the headspace for deep and profound stories. Somedays you just want to laugh or be amazed.

Fun

Advantages: Fun characters "pop." This means that players can get strong feelings about them very quickly. "That woman is a badass!" "That guy is funny!" Those strong feelings can pull players in not just to the character, but to the game and IP. Later, if players are not in the mood for deep, profound storytelling, they can come back to these characters for a laugh or some amazement.

Disadvantages: Fun characters can't hold one's interest for long. There's a reason that comedies on American TV are 22 minutes, and dramas are 45 or more minutes. Players can be pulled in by fun characters, but it is deep characters that will catch on to them and keep them interested in an IP.

Your Lineup on the Spectrum

Your game will have a cast of characters. If it's an RPG like *Baldur's Gate*, it will have one sort of lineup. If it's a PvP Hero Shooter, like *Overwatch*, it will have a different sort of lineup—but either way, you will need to define your characters in part by where they stand in relation to other characters.

You do this to ensure that your characters are not all similar to each other, and also to ensure that they share enough attributes that they feel like they live in the same universe.

When you map your lineup on the deep-to-fun spectrum, you should find some space between them. But you should also find that they cluster toward either edge of the spectrum. There is a "deadzone" in the middle, where characters are boring. An interesting character could exist near the dead zone, but don't create any that live in it! They'll be eminently forgettable.

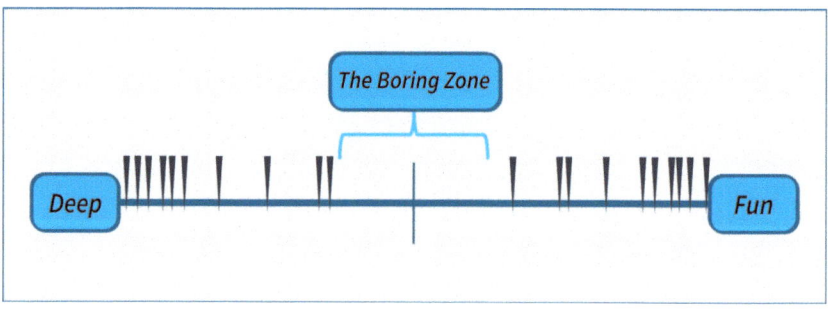

MOVEMENT ON THE SPECTRUM

When you create a character, it's good to know where they fall on the deep-to-fun spectrum. But characters are not static. They change over time, and this is particularly true in a live IP. It is quite common for a character to be introduced as a fun, in-your-face attitude-type character, and eventually, they get a special backstory or they go through some traumatic event that reveals or creates a hidden depth in them.

It's possible for a character to go the other way, but that is rare, and seems to be usually unintentional.

Case Study: Joey, *Friends*

In the first season, Joey was somewhat dim witted and sweet. Not deep by any means, but a character in full. By the final season, he had evolved to such a simple state that it feels like someone must tie his shoes for him each morning.

This is not a criticism. That may have been where the character needed to go as the show and the ensemble progressed.

DIVERSITY AND STEREOTYPES

Our world is diverse, and getting more so by the day. The necessity of having diversity in your character lineup is simply a reflection of the world in which we live. In any contemporary, future, or alternate, having a cast that is mono-racial/gender/orientation draws attention to itself simply through its lack.

Even historical or medieval fantasy should have a wealth of diversity.

EXAMPLE: MEDIEVAL EUROPE

Any place in Europe that had a Roman garrison during the Imperial years would almost certainly have drawn a variety of ethnicities and skin tones to the region for quite some time. Soldiers, camp followers, and merchants from the Middle East or Africa would have spent time there, and mixed with the local population. It was quite common for soldiers from one side of the Empire to settle down where they were stationed, It would not have been as monolithic as one might assume.

In fact, the variation in racial type in Europe would have been more diverse in Medieval times than during, say, the Enlightenment, as it was temporally closer to the height of the Roman Empire. As time goes on, any other racial types in the main population would become more deeply blended.

Aside from the need to reflect a more diverse world, stories are just better with a diverse cast. It immediately lends variation and interest to the group while also giving a wide variety of players the chance to see characters that they can identify with represented in a game.

It also adds durability. If you go back and watch old American movies from the 1940s or 50s, where most of the cast were good looking white men, you may have trouble telling them apart. This one wears a black suit. That one wears his hair in a pompadour. The fact is, they're all pretty similar.

Yet audiences at the time would not have had any trouble telling them apart, because they were plugged into context clues that made sense for their time. But we have lost those clues in subsequent generations. In the same way, when we look at a cast lineup today, we see lots of clues that indicate the difference in our characters. But if you are lucky enough to work on a timeless game, future generations may not have those same clues. Cast diversity will make your lineup more durable over time.

THE CHALLENGE

As storytellers, we focus on ensuring our cast makes sense for the story. The challenge that diversity can present us is that you and your team must be able to correctly represent a variety of people, and that diversity may not be reflected in your team. You may be called on to write characters who have a very different identity from yourself.

And that's okay. Even though the best-case scenario is writing a character who authentically comes from a writer who shares the identity with the character, there will be times when that will not be possible. Sometimes it's budget where you are unable to secure funding for a writing contract for someone representative, sometimes it will be time constraints, and sometimes it will be locale if you cannot hire someone from out of country. In any of these cases, it is still better to try and have a diverse cast than to just limit the cast to what has been done before. Making a cast monocultured robs the game of the value of diversity described above.

Instead, you must find a way to represent a wide variety of characters as well as you can. Here are a few tips:

All characters are people first. With the occasional exception of aliens, most characters you write are made of the same building blocks as any other. Their lived experience as their particular identity is a filter that can have a huge impact on them. But it's still a filter overlaying the same fundamentals.

On an even deeper level, you should be careful not to write them as primarily their surface-level identity. A blind woman is not primarily a blind woman. Being blind, and a woman, is a huge part of her experience, but it's not who she really is. If you were writing a blind character, and built everything around their blindness, they would not feel authentic at all. And would be a pretty shallow character!

If you can, find a subject matter expert. This means talking to a person who shares an identity with the character. Try to understand their lived experience. This is a delicate point though, so be careful. Nobody wants to be treated like the representative of all people who share their identity. On top of that, discussions of identity and lived experience can lead to some uncomfortable questions and discussions. That discomfort is a good sign that you are learning, but it is vital to ensure you have the person's trust, and that you respect their feelings.

A suggestion is to engage on the topic by asking about other representations of that person's identity in games, movies, television, or books. What felt authentic, and why? What felt wrong, and why? What are mistakes that seem to appear every time that identity is presented? How can that be avoided?

In certain cases, a project can hire a consultant for a specific type. One game we worked on had a Native-American character, and we were able to hire a consultant who was a member of a tribe that was closely related to the character's tribe. For a small fee, she was willing to review our work, and the art team's work, to give critical feedback. You'd obviously want to make sure your consultant's credentials are accurate, but one real benefit of the consultant route is that the discussions and questions don't have to be awkward: the entire relationship is premised on the fact that you don't know what you're doing and this person is here to help you understand.

Barring a subject matter expert, scour the internet or libraries for any information you can get, including criticisms or essays on how other characters with that identity were received. Obviously, the internet is full of people who are confidently wrong, so you'll have to develop a filter for what you read.

Finally, if your project can afford it, the games industry has a consultant role called "sensitivity reader." These are different from an identity-specific consultant like the Native-American tribesperson mentioned above, in that they are paid to review all the material in the game and can call out offensive, incorrect, or stereotyped information across a wide variety of topics. As with any kind of paid consultant, there is a variety of skill and experience levels out there, so do your research.

Another benefit of any kind of paid consultant is that it is easier to get the team to accommodate the consultant's feedback. If you tell the artists the tattoo they put on the character is offensive and wrong, they may not want to listen. But if you tell the art director that the consultant, an expert, said the same thing, and remind them that the studio paid this person money for their feedback, the chances of getting the offending tattoo changed are much greater.

SIDEBAR: ARE GAMES POLITICAL?

There has been a lot of debate recently about political stances in games. Should developers insert their political viewpoint into a game? Some argue that there is a moral imperative to do so, and that it is an attempt to include players who have traditionally been excluded. Others say it's an artificial addition that breaks immersion and makes traditional players feel excluded.

Our focus here is the craft of storytelling, so we are going to point out three key things to consider as a storyteller in games.

First: Please understand that any form of creative expression is political. If you tell a story, there is a political element to it. You may not mean or want a political dimension—but it is there. If you don't pay any attention to it, then the politics of it will be by default. There are thousands of stories of authors discovering their work has been associated with some political view they never intended or wanted.

A few major IPs, such as *The Hunger Games*, have turned out to be a Rorschach test, in the sense that most readers believed the story affirmed their own political worldview, even when their views differed from each other, and those of the author.

This is not to say that you must have a political angle or bent to your story. That is entirely your decision. We simply mean that if you think "I'm not political and I'm abstaining from all of that!" you are fooling yourself, because your players will bring themselves to the experience, and that includes politics.

Again, feel free to consciously avoid political issues or stances in your game; just be aware that there is some element of it attached to your game regardless.

Second: Any message or viewpoint the storyteller wants to deal with in the story should be layered into the experience seamlessly. Imagine you were watching a crime drama. At the end, the police catch the bad guy, and one of them looks into the camera and says, "Remember: crime doesn't pay!" You'd be cringing, right? Not because you are pro-crime and disagree with the message. Rather, you understand that if a story tries to preach a message, it takes fatal damage.

Whatever viewpoint the storyteller has must be embedded into the story and characters, so that it feels like an intrinsic part of the experience. The goal would be for players to finish the game without being hit over the head by the philosophical question at issue, but afterward, they would realize there are some deep questions here for them to consider. That is an indication that any message or philosophical point is well layered into the experience. Not invisible by any means, just a harmonious part of the whole. This is the same standard we apply to anything else. Music, sound effects, UI, palette, and animations—every element of the game—must fit into the cohesive whole.

Third: If you want to consciously add some political viewpoint to the story, our recommendation for the best way to do it is as follows:

Examine your viewpoint. Express it as a philosophy. Next, consider the opposite viewpoint—the one that is in total opposition to yours. Then, and this is the hard part: try to consider that viewpoint at its highest aspiration. Forget the reactionaries, the hot takes, and the online cranks. Put all that aside, think of that argument in the best light you can. What is it really saying? Why do some otherwise rational people believe this? Now express that as a philosophy.

Now you've got two antithetical philosophies. Rather than just message all of us about what you think is right or best, put these two into conflict. Let the avatars of each duke it out in your story. Show the consequences of both. Show the best and worst of both. If your viewpoint is as powerful as you think it is, it should shine.

In our opinion—and this is purely opinion—this is the right way to grapple with strong political viewpoints. But it only works if you take the opposing idea at its highest aspiration. Otherwise, you're just stacking the deck in favor of your argument, which will lead to a story that feels preachy and hollow.

In the scenario we mentioned earlier where a player finishes the game, then realizes there are deep questions to consider, this approach may lead to discussion among a group of friends. Through debate and discussion, they can refine their thoughts, and if they come to share your view, their beliefs will be much stronger for having gone through this process. Obviously, we are talking about a group of friends discussing things in real life. No one ever achieved anything by arguing on the internet.

CHAPTER SUMMARY

In this chapter, we discussed the following topics:

- Character Tiers. To facilitate the character discussion in the rest of this chapter, we established tiers for the characters.
  - Tier 1: Protagonist and antagonist.
  - Tier 2: Sidekicks, friends, family, chapter bosses.
  - Tier 3: Characters with some impact, but limited involvement.
  - Tier 4: Background characters such as merchants.
- What a character needs to be. This is a way to think about characters in terms of how they are perceived from the outside.
  - Important.
  - Interesting.
  - Damaged.
  - External.
  - Specific.
- The deep-to-fun spectrum. Figure out where your character falls on this spectrum. You can also map the entire character lineup to the spectrum to make sure they're not all in the same place.
- Diversity and stereotypes. Find a way to have lots of variation in your character lineup, do your research, and be respectful.

10 Characters in a Story

IN THIS CHAPTER

- Evolving characters through character arcs
- Listening to your characters
- Why characters change

Everything we've discussed about characters thus far involves constructing the character, from the outside and the inside. But it's time to discuss putting that character into the story.

The two processes, building the character and putting them into the story, are not truly distinct, separate actions. We are discussing them that way for clarity, but in fact you work on them together, as they each affect the other. Like so much of narrative, it's an organic process of back-and-forth. When you change the character, the way they interact with the story changes. When the character interacts with the story, who they are as a character changes.

CHARACTER ARCS

Everyone in film and games knows about "Character Arcs," but most people simply mean it to refer to the fact that a character changes by the end of the story. It is actually a more interesting and complex process.

Your characters should undergo changes if they are part of a story with a beginning, middle, and end. Experience changes us, and it will change characters as well.

CHARACTER ARCS BY TIER

Tier 1 and 2 characters should have character arcs. As the story progresses, they change and grow. Both tiers should have equally meaningful arcs. Obviously the player character, unless they are the blank-slate style, should be changed by the events of the story. Aside from the direct effects of the story, it would also make sense that your character would grow and change as they acquire new abilities and become more sure of themselves due to accomplishment.

In an RPG context, think of it that a level 1 warrior killing rats in the basement will likely be somewhat different when she has become a max level warrior/paladin dual class who killed the God of Plagues.

But don't neglect those around the player character. The change in these characters is what the player will notice the most. Their arcs will give them

DOI: 10.1201/9781003624882-14

texture and keep them interesting. They will also be a crystal-clear reflection of all the things the characters have gone through.

Tier 3 characters can certainly experience some kind of change, but it is more likely to be a simple on/off, binary state change. The widow who asked you to hunt down her husband's killers? She was despairing when you met her, but now she is content. The instructor who trained the player character to hold a sword as a child? He was alive during the prologue, but after the castle is sacked in chapter 1, he's now dead.

Tier 4 characters should not have any change at all. If a Tier 4 character is going through some kind of change, they are not a Tier 4 character.

PUTTING THE ARC IN CHARACTER ARC

People do not change or grow in a straight line. As they go through different events and meet new people, they begin to internalize the experiences, and over time the product of those experiences bubbles up, mixing with other experiences.

Change comes in zigs and zags, and can be halting, with backsliding.

The practical effect of all this is that as you plan out how a character changes and grows over the course of your story, don't think of it like addition. It's not $1+1=2$. It's a circuitous process, where characters move in one direction, then in another, in fits and starts. This intuitively feels real to most players and keeps the character interesting and surprising.

Here's a very simple example:

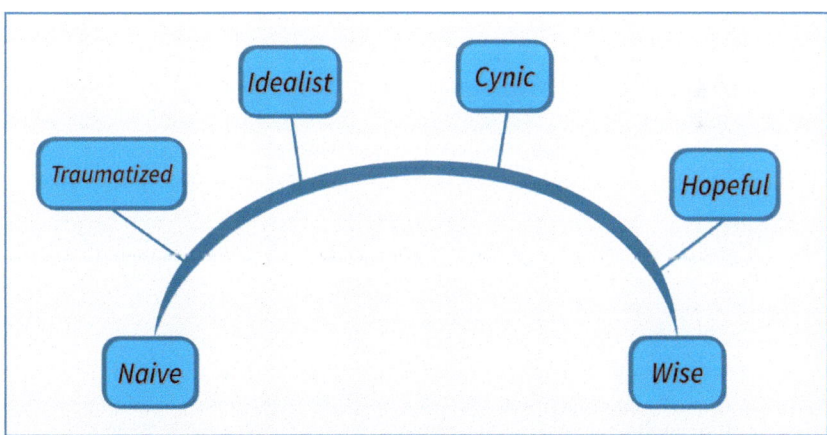

Our character begins the story as a sheltered innocent, naive about how the world really works. As the plot gets underway, they go out into the world and discover that it is not a very nice place. There is injustice and cruelty.

In their innocent state, this revelation traumatizes them. They will need some time to process all of this—often the first step in growth is the hardest.

When they have finally processed the trauma, the strength of their naive background reasserts itself in a new form: now they know the world is not what they thought it was, but they still believe that there is a way that the world "should be."

The fact that it isn't that way doesn't mean one should despair; it means one should roll up their sleeves and get to work making the world better. They've become an idealist.

But bad things continue to happen. Only now, instead of happening to others, they happen to our character. Experiencing cruelty and darkness first hand, they stop believing in a better world and realize it's time to grow up.

They put idealism behind them and develop a thick, protective outer shell: cynicism. They understand the world to be a bad place, and if you expect the worst, you can never be disappointed.

From this low-expectations vantage point, the character can hang out and remain unchanged for quite some time. But eventually they begin to notice things that don't quite match their grim worldview, e.g., new growth in the spring, young people fighting for a better future, and an old love who inspires them. Hope awakens inside the character, and they begin to believe that change is possible.

Their cynicism turns to hope, but a more profound hope than their earlier idealism, because now they've seen the worst the world has to offer. They can also hang out in the state of hope for a long time. But as they experience more, learn more, and absorb more, that hope will eventually mature into wisdom.

The way this character moves through different phases demonstrates why it's an arc and not a straight line.

Imagine if we tried to make this character move in a straight line. It would go from "Naive" to "Wise," and that simply doesn't make sense. If your story is deep enough to portray true character growth, even the character arc above may be too straightforward. But the above can serve as an example of the minimum acceptable steps of a character arc.

Case Study: Scrooge

Earlier we used Scrooge as an example of a character that had been put through the wringer. He is also the perfect example of a character arc.

At the start of the story, Scrooge is closed off, bitter, mean, and happy to be alone. He finds warmth, human connection, and love frivolous.

If that character had gone to bed on Christmas Eve and been visited by the Ghost of Christmas Yet to Come, who had shown him how others celebrated his death, the bitter Scrooge would likely have dismissed it as unimportant. Who cares what people think about you after you're dead?

He would likely have felt that way because he has already severed all connection with others.

However, Scrooge experiences four visitations, which move his psyche through an arc in very short order.

First, he is visited by the ghost of Jacob Marley, his old business partner. Seeing the chained ghost of someone he knows induces an understandable terror in him. The terror shoves him out of his hardened fortress of bitterness.

Next, he is visited by the Ghost of Christmas Past. With his mind being opened by terror, Scrooge is open to going along for the ride, and settles down as the ghost shows him his own past. It reminds him that like any human, he once craved and had love and connection. Seeing his own past moves Scrooge from terror to a state of sadness and nostalgia.

Next, he is visited by the Ghost of Christmas Present. Now that he is sad and nostalgic, his mind is able to make the next leap. This ghost shows him the lives of others. How even if they lack his wealth, they are rich in human warmth and connection. And he perceives how that connection also opens them up to great pain and loss, but how it is worth it nonetheless. This experience moves him from sadness and nostalgia to craving human warmth and connection.

It would seem his arc is complete at that moment: he has relearned the importance of connection and kindness. But his arc is not truly complete: such a feeling could still fade over time. He's been reminded of it, but the lesson has not truly been brought home.

Finally, he is visited by the Ghost of Christmas Yet to Come, who is immediately unsettling. Scrooge is quickly brought from craving human connection to a feeling of ominous dread. And indeed, this ghost shows him the fate we discussed earlier: the few people who think of him at all are glad he is gone.

It is only because Scrooge moved through a range of emotions, from terror to sadness, from sadness to craving connection, that the final lesson induces despair in him, in a way that it would not have if he'd been exposed only to that.

When Scrooge awakens, his despair is transformed into optimism and hope: the final lesson is not inevitable. He still has time, and can regain his humanity through warmth and compassion. This lesson would also not have been possible without all the steps that came before.

LISTEN TO YOUR CHARACTERS

When you first conceive of a character, and their role in the story, you will make a variety of plans for them. As the character begins to move through the story, some of those plans may not make sense any more.

It's tempting to try and force the character into the choices and paths you previously defined. No one likes throwing away work. But it can hurt a character's development immeasurably if you don't let them take shape and start talking back to you. It becomes an organic process of your plans for the character vs the character's own choices.

There is a positive reason to listen to your characters as well. It provides an opportunity to come up with something better.

Case Study: Jack, *Mass Effect 2*

The player travels to a prison ship to recruit Jack, a convict. The mission goes sideways, the guards turn on the player character, and Jack escapes. Now the player must spend the entire mission chasing through a prison ship, which is falling apart, to chase down Jack and try to get her to join them.

In Brian's original plan for the mission, the player catches up to her in the docking bay, explains that they have a ship, and can extract her before the prison ship falls into the heart of a star. Seems pretty straightforward.

But as Jack's character development progressed, it became clear that she trusts no one and is very capable. It was hard to imagine her meekly getting on a stranger's ship, where she would be completely at their mercy. She would be more likely to try and find her own way off of the ship.

Brian really wanted her to get on that ship. When you catch up to her, the mission is over. There is no more gameplay, and the storytelling that introduces Jack to the player has already been done. But Jack was not cooperating. It simply didn't feel right for her to get on the ship.

Instead, there was a short scene where Jack negotiates with the player for the terms of her joining the crew—all while the ship crumbles around them. This negotiation revealed the hatred she held for Cerberus, the player's employer, and showed how capable, stubborn, and mistrustful she is.

It was more work, and a frustrating process, but in the end, Jack's introduction was the better for it. Players came away from the experience with a powerful sense of Jack and her priorities.

DO YOUR CHARACTERS TALK TO YOU?

Some writers say that as their characters evolve, they begin "speaking" to the writer, refusing to do certain things. Other writers say that's ridiculous, and their characters never argue with them.

We think that it's a meaningless argument. The concept is the same either way: as a character gets fleshed out and starts moving through the story, certain actions and attitudes that made sense in the planning stage no longer make sense.

If you want to frame that as the character speaking to you, or frame it as you adapting, go for it! Just make sure you pay attention to how your character fits into the story.

THREE REASONS

There are three reasons a character changes: Conflict, Other Characters, or Time.

CONFLICT

As the story unfolds, the characters go through conflict. It could be a massive space battle, a quiet struggle with depression and anxiety, a relationship break up, a tussle to get a cat to take medicine, or any of a hundred other scenarios. The point is that something is happening that the character does not want. They make plans to deal with that something, and those plans are thwarted, or cause a new problem.

Facing conflict changes a person. You can understand that simply by thinking back on your own life. It causes growth, reflection, and new understanding. It causes you to make mistakes, which become lessons. It drives you to learn new skills and gain new insights. This is equally true of characters in a story. The storyteller can direct their growth through the conflicts that they face. You curate what lessons they learn and how they internalize those lessons.

Remember, not all growth is good. Characters can internalize trauma, develop metaphorical scar tissue, or simply learn the wrong lessons. In military theory, "fighting the last war" refers to the tendency of militaries to use tactics and methods that were useful in an earlier war, which are not appropriate for the current situation.

As your characters go through trials and tribulations, as they suffer setbacks, always be thinking about how this will affect them. Think of it as opportunities for your characters to develop.

OTHER CHARACTERS

We are all influenced by those around us. Teachers, parents, and mentors are obvious influences. But in reality, everyone we come into regular contact with has some effect on us. We may like something about them and unconsciously try to emulate that. Or we may want them to like us, so we act in a way that we think they will like. But it can also be negative. We may begin to hate something that they do or say, so we become grumpy with anyone who does that. Or we may see others as a cautionary tale, and do everything in our power to avoid becoming like them.

The same is true of our characters. In any group dynamic, the characters will begin to influence each other. The synthesis of all these influences could be thought of as the group's culture.

EXAMPLE: *THE GOOD PLACE*

This show is four seasons of characters gradually influencing each other. While it doesn't make for a tidy example that we can summarize here, it is such a powerful example that it's worth watching if you haven't, and rewatching if you have.

One very useful aspect of characters influencing each other is that introducing a new character to the story can spur or consolidate major changes going on with another character, or even the whole group.

TIME

Time heals some wounds, or allows others to fester. Lessons learned long ago take root and become foundational, or are forgotten, allowing a reset. You've seen this in others, and in yourself, whether you are young or old.

Never forget that time is one of the tools in your toolbox for changing a character. If a character has just gone through a stressful event, you don't need to show the fallout from it immediately. They may be processing for a time. It's actually a more elegant approach to have the trauma come up at a later date.

You can use time in very obvious ways, by jumping forward 20 years in your game story. But you can also use time in much more subtle and effective ways by simply pacing out how characters react, process, and internalize different events.

GAMES THAT END VS LIVE GAMES

In a traditional story, characters start in a certain spot, personality-wise, then grow and change over the course of the story, going through their arc, until they have become someone new by the end. If there is a sequel, they start off as the character who they were at the end of the previous story. Or, if enough time has passed, they may have grown even further.

But what about live games? A hero-based brawler like *Overwatch*, can continue for years. Yet the characters involved must remain fairly static. If you evolve a character too much, then you may fracture your community. Many players will have fallen in love with the hero through repeated experiences playing them. They're not looking for change; they want the hero that they love to stay the same. Because change would happen independently of an in-game story, it's not the natural flow of a normal character arc.

So how do you maintain characters and tell stories when they can't change?

The answer is that you do it very gradually, and you take advantage of depth. That is to say, the player will have a deeper experience with a character they really like. They'll have played that character many times, and heard all of their voice over lines again and again. This leads to a sensitivity to the smallest of changes.

A good model here is film vs television. A film is a discrete story with a beginning, middle, and end. As such, the character arc in a film works very much like that of an RPG, adventure game, or other non-live game.

Television shows must chart a character's growth and changes over the course of many seasons. In fact, many shows, such as sitcoms, don't want a character to change at all, because the show will later go to syndication and the episodes will play out-of-order, so the character must always be recognizably the same. Other shows have an overarching story that leads to gradual change over time. But even then, a character can't change drastically in the course of one season, or else an eight-season show would end up with eight different characters.

So it's a matter of pacing out the changes. Let new experiences stew inside the character. Let them process, and backslide, and go through similar experiences that reinforce the direction they are already moving. But keep your eye on the big picture and how to best chart the character's growth over years.

CANON VS NON-CANON

Some game universes have the concept of canon stories vs non-canon stories. There is not much to say on this topic. A non-canon story is a stand-alone. It's the narrative equivalent of junk food: a quick sugar high, then nothing.

"Those two mortal enemies went on a date!"

"The antagonist from the first game got away with everything and now runs a small consignment shop in Manhattan!"

"The protagonist and her partner never met each other years ago, who are they today?"

They can be fun experiments, but they don't build toward anything, and in some way, they damage the core character building of your canon characters, because they remind the player that these are not real people. They seem like parts of a simulation that can be rewound and played differently.

If you ever have the option to incorporate non-canonical stories into your universe, we'd urge you to resist the temptation. That said, such decisions are often made at a high level in publishing, so the best we can say is that if you are working on an IP with canon/non-canon storytelling, try to reserve your most powerful beats for the canon story. It's the real one.

CHAPTER SUMMARY

In this chapter,, we discussed the following topics:

- Character Arcs. Characters don't change in a straight line. Understand how they evolve.
- Listen to your characters. Actions and reactions that made sense in the planning stage may no longer apply as the character moves through the story.
- Three reasons. There are three reasons a character changes.
  - Conflict.
  - Other characters.
  - Time.
- Characters in games that end vs live games. The way you conceive of a character is quite different in these two formats.
- Canon vs Non-canon. Some game universes categorize certain stories as canon, and others as non-canon. This should influence how you think about the character as well.

Section 4

Dialogue and Voice Over

Writing dialogue for Voice Over, and shepherding your writing through the VO process, are two of the most important and ubiquitous tasks a game narrative professional engages in during the early and middle parts of their career. It truly pays off to understand this stuff.

DOI: 10.1201/9781003624882-15

11 Writing Dialogue for VO

IN THIS CHAPTER

- Rules for writing good VO
- Guidelines on what to do and what not to do
- Why it is important to read your lines out loud

This chapter is focused on competence, not high art. The below points won't add that extra something to your dialogue that will make you a great dialogue writer. Rather, they are designed to keep you from being a bad one.

If you learn the rules in this chapter, your dialogue writing won't suck. If that seems like a low bar, consider how much terrible writing you've encountered in games.

If you want to learn the trick to great dialogue, you won't learn it in a book. That's because there is no trick. It is the product of many years of observation. You can certainly learn it, in fact it's easy, but it takes a long time and focus. Fortunately, if you're interested in writing, you've probably already started.

It's as easy as listening to the way people talk, i.e., the words they use to express their thoughts, and the subtext it betrays. Notice the way they order their thoughts. Pay attention to the way they react in the moment during a conversation, when they're on the defense or the attack. Listen all the time. Analyze. The world is full of examples of dialogue, right there for the taking. As you gain a greater library of knowledge about the way people talk and the subtext involved, you will develop the skills that will make you a great writer of dialogue.

SIDEBAR: THE IMPORTANCE OF VO DIALOGUE

As writers gain more experience and ship more games, they begin to realize that dialogue is not the most important aspect of game writing. Characters, structure, conflict, and many other elements have a bigger impact on the narrative than the words that characters choose.

Yet dialogue is extremely important in two ways. First, it is one of the strongest elements a player experiences, conveying a character's personality. Much like the paint job on a car, it is ultimately unimportant to the performance, but powerful in terms of first impressions.

The second is that it is one of the primary ways we evaluate writing candidates and junior writers. When we hire a junior writer, we are hopeful

DOI: 10.1201/9781003624882-16

that they will grow into a great storyteller someday, be a vital part of the team, and handle themselves well in meetings and conflict situations. We can look for clues that they will go on to create vibrant, surprising characters, and will develop incredible world building skills in the future. But there is no assurance any of that will happen.

Their dialogue, on the other hand, we can judge immediately—is it at a level where they can start next Monday? Will it require lots of feedback? Will they be a drain on the team while their dialogue skills get up to speed? Is there another candidate with better dialogue writing skills?

Writing dialogue and tooltips are a sizable portion of a junior writer's work, and they need to excel at both.

OUR FOCUS ON VOICE OVER

Most games have dialogue of some kind, conveyed either in purely text form, or lines that are recorded into voice over. The former allows for deeper concepts, is cheaper, and is generally found in Indie titles. The latter is more impactful, expensive, requires more tech, and is generally found in AAA titles.

We're going to focus on writing dialogue for voice over, because it is the more demanding approach. If you write dialogue that is suitable for voice over, it will still work as text-only. But the converse is not always true: dialogue suitable for text-only may not work in voice over.

Learn to write dialogue that works in voice over, and you'll have the ability to write in any format. If you find yourself working on a game with text-only dialogue, you can experiment and learn what other things are possible, confident in the knowledge that you've got the basics covered.

RHYTHM

Lines that are meant for VO should have a rhythm to them. Read your lines aloud and see if you can find a pattern like the following:

Long. Short. Short: *I don't care what you think! Never did, never will.*
Short. Short. Long: *Stop! I don't want this. I never wanted any of this, Jordan.*
Short. Short. Short: *Really? Ya think? Better not…*
Short. Long: *I hate that guy. But he's the only mechanic we've got.*
Long. Short: That guy's got a real problem, y'know? Diarrhea of the mouth.

If you read each of the example lines aloud, you'll realize that you can naturally add a rhythm and tempo to them.

RHYTHM AND DOUBLE LINES

When you have two or more lines, you must ensure the second line moves things forward.

Often, we end up with lines like this:

I hate that guy. He's a real shitbird.

There is a flavor and rhythm to the two lines, but the second line does not progress anything. It just adds to what is already there.

The second line must either escalate from the first or change direction.
Escalation:

I hate that guy. Honestly, I'd kill his whole family if I could.

Direction change:

I hate that guy. But I wouldn't kick him out of bed.

Note that changing direction means a line that is still hooked into the previous line. But you should not introduce a whole new idea in the second line.
New Idea:

I hate that guy. But I do want to buy flowers for his mom.

HUMOR

Humorous voice over is incredibly difficult. First, it's cultural, so it likely will not work in foreign markets. Second, it requires tight timing, meaning that the writer, the voice actor, and the audio designer must all deliver pitch perfect work.

However, humor is also powerful, and if you can deliver on it, then it is worth trying.

The key to writing humorous voice over lines is to remember that you are not trying to be funny. You are trying to set the stage for the voice actor to be funny.

These lines:

When you're wearing this much armor, you'd better hope you don't get an itch on your backside … ohhh no.
Someday I shall defeat evil, wherever it hides! What'll I do then, I wonder?

Are not inherently funny. If you read them in a flat tone, they sound confusing rather than humorous. But they give the voice actor the opportunity to bring humor to them.

If someone says to you "The line you wrote wasn't that great, but the actor really made it work!", then you should know that first, they are wrong, and second, you did a great job.

GUIDELINES

Here are some straightforward guidelines for writing dialogue. Note that while some of the "bad" examples below might work well in print, they are bad for voice over dialogue. If you read certain lines in a novel, you would immediately grasp them—no problem. Some of these "Bad" examples could be considered good writing in other media.

What makes them bad for our purposes is that we are writing for voice over, and the rules for spoken words are different. Also, we are applying all the rules discussed above that are specific to games: brevity, clarity, and style.

DON'TS: AVOID THESE

Characters announce their emotions

If you write dialogue for text-only, you may have gotten used to including emotions in the words, as there is no other way to let players know how a character is feeling. But when the dialogue is going to be recorded with voice over, including emotion is redundant and clunky.

Bad: *Why did you do that? I'm so angry!*

The actor will read this line sounding angry, so the inclusion of I'm so angry! Will be too much.

Good: *Why did you do that?*

There are more subtle instances of this as well:

Bad: *I failed the test and lost my favorite pen. I wish I was dead.*
Good: *I failed the test and lost my favorite pen.*

The actor's read will convey *I wish I was dead* without it needing to be included in the words.

You may think this note is obvious, but if you pay attention and read your lines aloud, you'll discover this happening in your work more than you think.

Only in the most intimate situations do people talk directly about their feelings.

I was hurt that you missed my graduation.
You left me and went off on your adventure. I felt so alone.
When I saw you, my heart raced, and I felt … I don't even have the words for it.

These lines are powerful because it is so rare for a character to directly reference their feelings. Be careful not to overuse them.

Announcing an Intention

Imagine a character who hears a doorbell, then announces: *I'm going to answer the door.*

If they then walk to the door and open it, you'd think that was pretty dumb, and you'd be right. There is little need for a character to announce their actions.

Yet writers often have lines like *I'm going to kill you!* Or *I will get back at you for this!*

The rare occasion where it makes sense for a character to announce their intention is when it will be defeated or has a twist.

So, if Rhonda says: *I'm going to the store, be back in five.*

Then steps out the door and is never seen again, that line added to the mystery and was useful.

Complex Constructions

The eye/brain is able to track complex construction better than the ear/brain. Lines written to be read on the page can indulge in complexity that lines spoken aloud cannot.

> Bad: *With great enthusiasm we took to the streets, and not for a short time, to proclaim our hatred of the government.*
> Good: *We took to the streets to proclaim our hatred of the government, for as long as necessary.*
> Bad: *Do you not think that I wouldn't have called if he hadn't disappeared?*
> Good: *I would have called if he'd disappeared.*

In the bad version, the writer probably intended the "Do you not think" to convey disdain. But as we discussed in the previous section, an actor can put the disdain in the read.

Information Summary

Don't try to summarize information in dialogue. If you start a line with "though" or "although," you're probably summarizing.

> Bad: *Though we are strong and sure, our doom will come.*
> Good: *We are strong and sure, but our doom will come.*
> Or if your character is fancier:
> Good: *We are strong and sure, yet our doom approaches.*
> Bad: *Although we are at the top of our class, we are made to feel like losers at every opportunity.*
> Good: *We are at the top of our class, yet we are made to feel like losers at every opportunity.*

Plot Summary

Lines that try to summarize the plot occur when the writer has some exposition to get out and wishes to avoid it, so they try to gloss over it quickly and get on to the meat of the line.

Examples:

> *Now that Julnar is free, we can begin plans for the revolution.*
> *With Alexia having been safely married off, my thoughts can now turn to Harold's future.*

In the first example, the player already knows the information, but the writer wants to summarize it because there are NPCs who don't know it yet, so it seems like it must be stated. Otherwise, someone will ask, "how did that NPC know Julnar is free?" The writer is aware that it is deadly boring to repeat information the player already knows, so is attempting to summarize quickly.

But this is a terrible idea—no one talks this way, and the stilted, unnatural dialogue will simply call attention to the clunkiness of what is happening.

In games, NPCs often seem to know things that they shouldn't—as soon as the player discovers it, everyone in their inner circle knows it. The idea is that the player character told the others during "downtime" or "offscreen."

In fact, when the player knows something, they rarely devote much thought to whether or not an NPC would know it as well. The only time this question will occur to the player is if an enemy conveniently knows something that they have no reason to know.

If the player frees Julnar, then returns to base and the janitor says, "good job freeing Julnar"; players likely won't think about it.

However, if they had an argument with their romantic partner last night in bed, and the next day the antagonist taunts them about it, they'll wonder how the antagonist knows about it.

Ending Words with "ing."

Ing robs a line of its power and velocity.

Bad: *We've been looking all over for you!*
Good: *We've looked all over for you!*
Bad: *I've been having terrible nightmares.*
Good: *I have terrible nightmares.*
Bad: *This isn't over. I still must face Morwan, and I'm not planning on losing.*
Good: *This isn't over. I will face Morwan, and I do not plan to lose.*

Interrupt the Flow

With the rare exception of a character who has a particular verbal tic, don't insert a subclause into the middle of a bigger clause. Rather, put it at the beginning or the end.

Bad: *I will triumph with—and I think you know this—the most trivial of effort.*
Good: *I think you know that I will triumph with the most trivial of effort.*
Or
Good: *I will triumph with the most trivial of effort. I think you know this.*

Break Up Word Pairings

Certain words naturally go together, and you should keep them together.

Bad: *We struck Bertrand and all his band down.*
Good: *We struck down Bertrand and all his band.*

Bad: *We have to clean this mess up!*
Good: *We have to clean up this mess!*

Temporal Jumping

Try to arrange your ideas in a temporally sequential flow.

Bad: *I walked into the Walmart knowing that Juniper would be there in an hour, to discuss the events of last night.*
Good: *Something went down last night, and I went to discuss it with Juniper at the Walmart, knowing she'd be there in another hour.*

This is another example where the bad version works just fine in print. But it is harder to make sense of it in voice over.

Long Sentences

It is always better to break a long line into two or three short simple ones. This is true for the sake of your players, but also for the sake of the actors, allowing them to put more performance into a shorter line.

Bad: *I did not know why he was bothering about this, but I surely wished he would stop, as I had no interest in the topic and would really have preferred to move on.*
Good: *Why was he bothering about this? I wanted him to stop so we could move on.*

Note that many games have a character limit on individual lines, usually for UI reasons, but it's a useful constraint creatively as well. In *Mass Effect 2*, no single line of dialogue exceeded 120 characters. If a character had to say something longer than that, two lines would be strung together. This forced writers to be concise and gave the voice actors the space to focus on one line at a time.

Alliteration

Writers sometimes use alliteration as a crutch to appear clever, or ironically clever. Sadly, it fools no one.

If you are going to use alliteration, then pair it with a strong rhythm. But better yet, avoid it.

Word Repetition

We tend to repeat words a lot, using certain words as one of the words in a sentence, which is made up of words. And when those words get spoken aloud and you hear the same words over and over again, you really notice those words. So, try to avoid those words and do not use those words when choosing words for your line of dialogue. Also, words.

The above line may seem silly, but you'll be shocked when you read your dialogue aloud at how often you fall prey to this.

Tacking Words on the End of a Line

Bad: *I shall stand against the dread overlord! And his minions.*
Try to incorporate the added bit into the bigger sentence:
Good: *I shall stand against the dread overlord and his minions!*
Or cut it:
Good: *I shall stand against the dread overlord!*

The chances are excellent that fighting the dread overlord also means fighting his minions, and you probably don't need to delineate that.

Repetition of an Idea

Bad:

Haley: *I cannot stand for this! I will not stand for it!*
Bruno: *You have no choice!*
Haley: *I do have a choice—and I choose not to stand for it!*

There is some subtlety and evolution of the thinking/conflict in this exchange. But most players will never see it—and indeed the voice actors won't see it, and as a result won't be able to sell the line properly.

Players and voice actors are not obtuse or stupid. Instead, this is one of those situations where the subtlety and nuance of the line exists in the writer's head. It's really not there in the line—you, the writer, see much more than is there.

We all must learn to distinguish between this and true subtlety. Not that we've got much room for that either.

Good:

Haley: *I will not stand for this!*
Bruno: *You have no choice.*
Haley: *I have made my decision.*

This example escalates the tension because Character A has shut down the discussion at the end, rather than just repeating his position from the beginning.

Note that this guideline may seem similar to the earlier section "Rhythm and Double Lines," but that section was focused on making sure a second line moved the conversation forward, whereas this guideline is about finding and cutting any repeated information in your lines, which can happen anywhere.

Haplology

Words that end in the same sound as the start of the next word, so they blend into one word. Note that Haplology can also mean contracting two words into one, like "going to" into "gonna."
Examples:

Safe from.
Were recently.

Good actors can make these constructions work. But if the actor is working to make your construction play, it's likely subtracting from their performance. Fix all of these things in the writing—your job! —so they can give you a great performance—their job.

Complex Word Combinations or Bad Mouthfeel

Bad: *Which sigil is correct?*
Many actors work hard on their enunciation and can deliver lines such as this just fine, but not all, and it's important to be aware that you're doing this.
Good: *Which of these is correct?*
Good: *Which of these sigils is correct?*

It is hard to define what constitutes complex word combinations or bad mouth-feel … but if you read all your lines out loud, you'll know the bad ones, because you'll stumble over them.

Half-formed or Interrupted Thoughts

Sometimes a character forms half a thought, then trails off in horror, or is interrupted by another character. These are useful tools and can add some interesting drama or conflict, but first, you must decide if the truncated line is meant to convey anything or not.

We've seen numerous examples in games where a character only gets half a thought out and the writers clearly intended that we would take meaning from it, but there was not enough context. If you want the player to take meaning, you must decide which words are necessary to get across the thought. It's not about having a complete thought, just finding the necessary keywords.

Example: We want to say "Jintarre has the amulet, and he's going to use it to kill us all."

Bad:

Jintarre...
Or
That amulet...

The writer is assuming that the player's context will be enough to piece it together, especially with some great VO, delivered full of dread. Less is generally more, and we admire the writer's attempt to be economical, but a single word is rarely enough.

Good:

If Jintarre comes at us with the amulet...

We've changed the construction of the line a bit, without changing the meaning. Most importantly, we've put the keywords in there—"Jintarre," "amulet," and "comes at us."

The character doesn't need to finish this thought—they can trail off or be interrupted, and the player will still take their meaning.

One way to gauge if you have enough meaning in a line is if another character could complete the thought easily.

So, in our bad examples: *Jintarre...*

An NPC seeking to finish the thought would have to say: *He's got the amulet and if he comes after us, we're dead.*

Of the other bad example: *That amulet...*

An NPC would have to say: *Is strong enough to kill us, and now Jintarre has it.*

But in the good example: *If Jintarre comes at us with the amulet...*

The NPC seeking to finish the thought could just say: *We're dead.*

Stating the Null

It is rarely useful to have a character explain what they *didn't* think or know or feel. Writers often try this in an attempt to be subtle, or to write defensively. It is always better to simply state what the character is feeling.

Bad: *I thought I would be mad at him, but in the moment of his betrayal, I found myself filled with pity.*
Good: *At the moment he betrayed me, I felt only pity for him.*

The player can probably deduce that a character expecting betrayal also expected to be angry. Since the character didn't feel it in a meaningful way, and it had no impact on the story, there is no reason to present it.

Bad: *Normally I would have known about a midnight meeting of the Shark's Club. But this one flew under the radar.*
Good: *I didn't know about this midnight meeting of the shark's club.*

The statement itself implies that not knowing is an abnormal circumstance.
If that's too subtle, you could add "and that's strange," at the end.

Ellipsis

Real conversation is filled with silent ellipses, as we lurch from one topic to another without transition or segue. This is because as we talk to someone, our mind runs ahead of the conversation on different tracks.

But our dialogue must be constructed and must flow well. So, we cannot rely on ellipses to connect topics. Rather, we must provide transitions.

Bad: *Killed my whole family … never looked back … I'm a monster.*
Good: *I killed my whole family, and never looked back. Do you understand? I'm a monster.*
Bad: *I thought I'd come to grips with his flaws … but now this … I just don't know anymore … is it even worth it?*
Good: *Just when I thought I'd come to grips with his flaws, he does something like this. I don't even know if it's worth it anymore.*

You may notice that the lines with transitions in them are longer than the lines with ellipses. Yet we are always telling you to make your lines shorter and more economical. Well, writing is about balancing competing priorities. Look at it this way: if writing was easy, it wouldn't be rewarding, right?

SIDEBAR: NATURALISTIC DIALOG

Some games have highly stylized dialogue, while others strive for dialogue that sounds totally natural. If you're aiming for the latter, it can be tempting to mimic the way they actually speak, as if you've recorded a transcript. The truth is that human conversations are wildly free flowing, with people jumping from topic to topic, following the thread of an invisible subtext and a nearly invisible context. The result can be an incoherent jumble of topics, sudden shifts, and lots of "Uh," "Ah," "Cool," "Yeah," and "Y'know?" segues.

This transcript:

Hey, yeah, I'm thinking and this is just whatever, y'know? I'm thinking uh that you … you … You want uh to get some ah, what do ya … for later, I mean, like, Thai?

When written as dialogue should be:

Hey, want to get some Thai for dinner?

Good natural dialogue is not a transcript. Rather, it feels authentic to the player. The word "natural" does not refer to how accurate it is in copying the way people talk. Instead, it refers to how players feel about it.

You must write constructed dialogue that feels natural but isn't. Game dialogue must be economical, sharp, full of conflict and character. So, we can try to capture that natural feel without capturing the inherent chaos.

The rules above and below will help you write natural sounding dialogue that is still tight.

Dos: Try These

Hang a Lantern on It

When you must have a line that repeats something the player knows, or is awkward, celebrate it. Rather than try to sneak it into another line, feature the repetition.

In the earlier example where the writer tried to stuff some information into a line:

Now that Julnar is free, we can begin plans for the revolution.

They could have instead had the character announce it. This will give the actor something to work with, a chance to make the line sound and feel good.

I have freed Julnar! Now we can begin plans for the revolution.

Find Conflict in It

If a character must say something the player already knows, see if you can add some conflict to it.

Player: *I freed Julnar.*
NPC: *You what?*
Player: *You heard me.*
NPC: *Are you trying to get us all killed?*
Player: *Now we can begin the revolution.*

One Topic per Line

When you can, limit each line to one idea. This allows you to make each line a clear, single statement that can conflict with what came before, and which the following line can conflict with. If you're changing topics, it may be a sign that you have two different conversations going on and should break them into two conversations.

Sometimes you must cover two topics in one conversation, and that's when you want to think with transitions.

Transitions

Rather than have a character just switch topics midline, you usually want to find a natural way to transition the topic of a conversation. The easiest way to transition topics is to introduce a new character to the conversation.

Example:

Harper: We're screwed if we don't get these seals in place before nightfall.
Jason: I know. But we can't rush the installation.
             Jimbo staggers up, gin bottle in hand.
Jimbo: Hey everybody—it's ma birthday! Happy birthday to me!
Harper: Happy birthday, you old souse.
Jason: We'll come to your party after we get the seals in place. Is your sister going to be there?

Another way is to have one character want to discuss that topic from the start:

Harper: We're screwed if we don't get these seals in place before nightfall.

Jason: I know, but
Harper: Hand me the next seal.
Jason: It's Jimbo's birthday, and I promised his sister I'd be there!

This way, the new topic doesn't come out of nowhere. Rather, Jason wanted to discuss it all along, but Harper was overriding him.

Yet another way is to introduce a prop that leads to a new topic.

Gus: … in conclusion, you have one week to make this right.
Buster: Yep, got it. Is that all? Can I go now?

Gus opens the drawer of his desk, takes something out, and sets it carefully on the desk between them. It's an old hunting knife with dark red stains on the blade.

Buster: Where … where did you get that?

Connect Lines through Word Order

If a character is responding to something someone said in a previous line, make sure the previous line ends with that beat or phrase.

Good:

> *We'll find your money later. Now pay attention!*
> *I can't, I'm arguing on the internet!*

Bad:

> *Pay attention! We'll find your money later.*
> *I can't, I'm arguing on the internet!*

Players will still be able to make the connection, but at least some portion of their attention is spent on connecting concepts that your dialogue disconnected.

Once you keep this in mind, you will be shocked at how often your natural structuring of a line inserts a different idea between the core concept of the two lines, as in the bad example.

End Important Lines on a Keyword

Just as with the previous note, the word you end on has more power and importance than other words in the line. In the previous note, it was relevant to connecting lines. But the end word also has a resonance on its own.

This note does not apply to all lines. For the sake of rhythm, variation, and freshness, you will need to be flexible in constructing your lines. But for important lines, consider the power of ending on a keyword.

Good:

> *With torches and fear, we began our journey into the earth, and darkness.*
> *With torches and fear, we began our journey into the cave, ever downward.*
> *We began our journey into the earth, possessing only torches and fear.*

Bad:

With torches and fear, we began our journey.
With torches and fear, we began our journey down into the cave system.
We began our journey into the earth, possessing only fear and torches.

Read Your Lines Aloud

You've heard this many times, while reading this chapter even. Yet many professionals stop doing it for fear of looking foolish, or perhaps because they've "outgrown" it. But even the most experienced writer will benefit from doing this.

You'll solve 90% of issues this way. Even better—have someone else do it. Ask another writer to open your file and read it aloud while you listen. Someone who doesn't know the rhythm and subtext of your lines will likely read them in the worst possible way, and that's what you want. It will help you hear what's wrong with them.

Hearing your lines read in a wooden, deadpan voice not only helps you identify problems, but also helps you understand how many of your teammates will read your dialogue before offering a critique. Most of your intention will be lost, and that may cause their critique to lead you astray.

CONCLUSION

Learn these rules, and your dialogue will be sturdy and workable. If you can impose these rules and instill a strong character voice into each line, your dialogue will begin to truly shine. Later we will discuss conversations, their flow and structure. Combining the guidelines from this chapter with the knowledge from the conversation chapter will bring your writing to the next level.

Frankly, if you can do that, you'll already be ahead of many professional game writers.

CHAPTER SUMMARY

In this chapter, we discussed the following topics:

- We focus on writing dialogue for voice over rather than text-only, as that is the more demanding discipline.
- Rhythm. Learn to think of your dialogue as having a rhythm to it.
- Humor. Writing humor for voice over means not trying to be funny. Instead, it means writing lines that will let the voice actor be funny.
- Guidelines. We list some "Don'ts" and some "Dos."
- Read your lines aloud. Advice that everybody hears, and nobody does.

12 Barks

IN THIS CHAPTER

- The purpose of Barks
- Line variation and clarity when writing barks
- How not to get bored with lines

One of the earliest and most common tasks a writer in games performs is writing barks. These are a set of lines that characters will say during gameplay, triggered by some external stimuli, usually combat-related.

If a player initiates a conversation or cutscene, and the character begins speaking, these are not barks, they are lines. If a character picks up an audio-log and voice over begins to play, that is also not a bark, it's still a line.

But if a character runs out of ammunition and automatically yells "reloading!" while the reload animation plays, that is a bark. If the character gets healed and automatically says "Thank you," that is also a bark.

Barks exist in almost any game with voice over. Single player and multiplayer. PvP and PvE. RPG, Open World, Adventure, RTS.

A character's bark script can consist of a dozen lines or hundreds. In AAA games, it is usually the latter. There are dozens of categories, and many categories will have three, four, five, or more variants.

SAMPLE CATEGORIES

- Taking sniper fire
- Reloading
- Throwing a grenade
- Stepped on a mine
- Detected a mine
- Resurrected
- Healed
- Used ability
- Used ultimate ability
- Used potion
- Out of mana
- Mana restored
- Found a good item
- Tried to use an ability on cooldown

DOI: 10.1201/9781003624882-17

- Won the match
- Lost the match
- Scored a headshot
- Character idle.

There are many more categories. Each game and team will develop its own template. The template is dependent on the game type. A single-player open-world game like Far Cry will come up with a very different template than a PvP game like League of Legends.

For example, if you were writing barks for a guard NPC in an open world game, they might have several categories of barks having to do with stealth.

SAMPLE CATEGORIES

- Suspicious. The guard thought they heard something.
- Minor alert. The guard thought they saw the player sneaking around.
- Searching. The guard is alerted and actively searching for the player.
- Call for help. The guard found the player!
- Giving up. The guard didn't find the player and is returning to their normal patrol route.

When the criteria for one of these barks is met, for example if the guard's perception AI detected a hint of the player, the guard says a line, either to themselves or to the other guards.

Meanwhile, the barks for a hero character in a PvP game are more likely to use categories like the ones we listed earlier—reloading, grenade, used potion, etc., things the player would do during combat.

BARKS PURPOSE

Barks serve three basic purposes:

- To give the player auditory feedback. If the player used a potion in the middle of an intense fight, and they hear their character say something about using a potion, they'll know it worked, even if they didn't see the animation. Likewise, if they hear the guard say "Hm, thought I heard something, but I guess I was wrong," they'll know the AI guards are no longer searching for them.
- To give other players feedback. In a PvP setting, if your character is reloading, they will not be able to shoot for several seconds. Your teammates need to know that you are out of the fight for a short time, and hearing an automated bark alerts them to this without you having to do anything.

- To convey character. Every single time a character talks, it's a chance to convey their personality, even if it is just due to the sound of the actor's voice.

Items 1 and 2 on the above list are mechanical in nature. Only Item 3 is artistic. This means that your barks must serve their mechanical purpose first and foremost.

A bark that is clunky but conveys its message is better than the most artful but unclear bark.

LINE VARIATION

The reason a category of bark may have multiple variations is that many barks play over and over. If the same line played each time your character reloaded their gun, you'd hear it four times per minute in a 10-minute PvP match. You would quickly become sick of it.

So a typical bark template might have four variations for "Reloading!"

VARIATION EXAMPLES

- *Reloading!*
- *New Mag!*
- *Fillin' up!*
- *One in the chamber, ten in the mag!*

Now when the reloading category is called, the game can play the next line in the sequence, or choose one randomly, depending on how it is scripted.

This presents a challenge to writers because you must find interesting, artful ways to say the same thing over and over. And over. And over.

CLARITY

In other parts of this book, we state that clarity is not the highest aspiration of writing, that in fact some ambiguity is desirable. That is true elsewhere. For barks, clarity is absolutely the first priority, and ambiguity is the enemy.

Here are some problems writers often encounter:

SIMILAR TO ANOTHER CATEGORY

In the above "reloading" example, if you had to add a fifth line, you might want to say something like:

"I need more rounds!"

But that line would be unclear, because it might sound to your teammates like you are saying that you are out of ammunition and unable to reload. Indeed, "out of ammo" might even be another category in the bark script.

Context in the Writer's Head

When you're writing a bark, you're staring at the category, and so you'll create a bark that makes sense with the proper context. But the player will experience it without that context, and it won't make any sense.

EXAMPLE

Taking Sniper Fire: "Somebody's out there!"

On the page, this makes total sense. The hero just took some sniper fire and reacted appropriately.

Surely the player will understand what's going on?

But the player is in a chaotic environment. They just stepped on a mine, ran out of ammo, and got punched by a nearby enemy. There is a timer counting down to the end of the match, and it's almost at zero. A teammate just died.

The bark is to tell them:

"You are taking fire from a sniper. So you may think you're in cover, but you are exposed, and you need to move immediately."

If the player hears "Somebody's out there!" in the chaotic environment we mentioned earlier, it won't mean anything to them. You must write every bark with the knowledge that it will be heard without any context.

Writer Boredom

By the time you are writing your third or fourth character, you'll feel like you've come up with everything possible. It's over, you've got nothing left.

There are a few obvious solutions you can take right away: ask to see barks scripts that have been written by other writers. Simply seeing the thought process of other writers can widen your thinking. If you don't have access to other barks scripts, just go play another game in the same genre as yours and listen to the barks for inspiration. A variety of PvP games have their full character barks available on YouTube or other video-sharing platforms.

Here is one piece of solid advice we can offer: don't be afraid to repeat yourself. Many writers will use the line "Reloading!" on their first script. Then with each subsequent script, they will think they can't use that line because they don't want to repeat themselves.

But remember, this is a different character. The voice saying the line will be a different voice, with a different performance.

In general, it is good to try something new and avoid repeating yourself. But remember that the first and second priorities of barks are clarity and mechanical accuracy. That's why you can fill out the first two or three variants of a category with the most straightforward line. After the third one is where you start to need to get creative again and find a character specific way of saying things.

The lines you want to be sure never to repeat are the ones that are distinct to a character.

EXAMPLE

Biff the Merc and Gustav the Surgeon can both say:
Grenade!
But while another grenade line for Biff may be:
Grenade to your face!
It wouldn't make sense for Gustav to say that.

COMFORTABLE OR IRRITATING?

Barks play over and over. If a player has a favorite character in a PvP game, they may hear that character's barks thousands of times over the course of a couple of weeks. If the barks are too generic, they will be forgettable, and so will the character.

But if the barks are too distinct, they can also become irritating. A distinct bark calls attention to itself, and if we hear that bark over and over, we will notice it each time.

You'll have to find a happy middle ground. Fun, interesting lines that are not too distinct. Note that you can write a few very distinct lines if the bark scripting in your game has a way to weight the randomization. Then you can set those lines to play rarely, so that it's like a treat, or an easter egg.

CONCLUSION

Most writers start off their career writing lots of barks. And while it is grunt work, and can be mind-numbing at times, it is also quite hard, so think of it as a baptism of fire. If you've written thousands of barks on a game, you know you've arrived and you now share some trauma and accomplishment with most other game writers.

Be clever, characterful, and delightful. Easy, right?

CHAPTER SUMMARY

In this chapter, we discussed the following topics:

- The purpose of barks. A quick explanation of what they're used for. To give the player audio feedback of their actions or situation. To give other players on the player's team audio feedback. To convey character.
- Line variations. Barks have multiple variations of lines with the same function because barks repeat often.
- Clarity. For barks, clarity is the top priority.

13 Conversations

With barks and soundsets, writing a great line is crucial. But you will need to write conversations as well.

SURFACE, SUBTEXT, AND CHARACTER

Earlier, we discussed the stakes of a story, and how there are external, internal, and philosophical stakes. Conversations are similar in that a conversation is usually about one thing on the surface, something else below, and a third, fundamental thing at the core.

This surface topic is the external stakes. It's vital to keep the conversation focused on one main topic. Witty asides or quips are fine, if they suit the tone, but overall, you must stay on point in a conversation.

A conversation also has subtext. This is what the characters really want to discuss, even if they don't know it themselves. It is like the internal stakes. It can be part of a continuing conflict or exploration between the characters, or something unique to this conversation. It will never be stated explicitly, but it is very much at work under the surface.

At the core, conversations have something similar to the philosophical stakes. The characters in a conversation each have their own philosophy or worldview, and these philosophies are in conflict during the conversation.

STRUCTURE

The structure of a conversation is very much like the structure of a story or scene. A beginning, middle, end. Rising tension. Reversals. Resolution.

You should structure the external, surface topic of your conversation in a similar manner to your story. Introduce the topic, present a counterpoint, escalate the stakes, and finally achieve a resolution to the topic.

However, you should also be thinking about subtext in terms of structure as well. For the conversation to feel complete, the subtext must work around a structure, even if it is never made explicit.

If you take everything you've learned about structure elsewhere in this book and apply it to the surface and subtext of your discussion, you will have the basis

DOI: 10.1201/9781003624882-18

for a conversation. However, this advice may still feel a bit vague unless you have a framework to apply it all to.

That framework is the thing that all conversations are about: power.

POWER IN A CONVERSATION

In a dramatic context, a conversation is two people trying to convince each other of something. Sometimes it's overt, such as two politicos arguing their views in a coffee shop. Sometimes it's veiled, but still fairly transparent, such as two teenagers talking in a mall, one trying to subtly convince the other that he/she is cool enough to be worth dating, and the other trying to subtly convince the first that he/she should never ask them out because it'll be awkward when the answer is no.

Often it is more subtle still. Two friends talking in a park may simply be trying to convince each other that they're both still good friends when they've felt the fires cooling. Or a businesswoman may be trying to convince her colleagues that she's very nice, while they're trying to convince her to quit.

Often this subtext is deep and subtle, and you won't always be able to get to it. But it's there, and if you're on the lookout for it, you may hear traces of it.

THE DYNAMICS

Inevitably, one person is in a greater position of power. That dynamic may change during the conversation, or even change several times. But at any given moment, someone has more power.

This is usually tied to the subtext, whatever it is they are trying to convince each other of. In our example of the two teenagers in the mall, they have asymmetrical goals.

EXAMPLE: TWO TEENAGERS AT THE MALL

Mike wants Ashley to like him. Ashley wants Mike to not ask her out. The one with the power in that scenario is Mike. At first glance, you'd assume it is Ashley, because Mike wants something from Ashley and she has the power to give it or not—her affection. But if Ashley is hoping that Mike will not ask her out, it follows that Ashley has no agency at that moment. She is simply hoping Mike won't do something. Mike has the power to decide if he is going to take the plunge and ask her out or not. He has the power to move the conversation in a safe or dangerous direction.

Of course, if Mike ignores all the warning signs and asks Ashley out, the power immediately shifts.

When you listen to a conversation, pay attention to what people say, but more importantly, what they really want. Sometimes you can find this by what they don't say. And if you can identify what they really want, then pay attention to who has the power. Do the words and tone of the person with less power sound different from the one with more power? How does the power dynamic affect everything else?

One clue is that the person with less power in the conversation tends to be the more articulate, thoughtful one. They have more to gain, and more to lose, so they will command a greater range of language, and bring more firepower to bear in making their point.

FLOW

A conversation flow needs conflict and escalation. You may want it to serve other purposes, such as exposition or characterization, but it must have conflict and escalation to be compelling.

CONVERSATION FLOW

Character 1: Premise
Character 2: Conflict
Character 1: Rebuttal, escalation
Character 2: Conflict, resolution
Optional: Character 1: *Button*

Button: A writing term for a witty or interesting line that tops off a scene.

For longer conversations, the *Conflict* and *Rebuttal, escalation* steps can be repeated as many times as necessary.

Without conflict and escalation, the conversation becomes a boring exercise.

Many game conversations require a high level of exposition, which can be deadly boring without conflict and escalation. People will experience the conversation and say to themselves: "Okay, that made sense, I guess."

BAD EXAMPLE

Jane: It's a full moon tonight.
Frank: So the werewolves will attack the barricades.
Jane: They'll hit the northern side first.
Frank: We'd better reinforce there, then.
Jane: Yes. Then the east side—that's where they'll shift to if we turn them
back in the north.

This may all be important information that the player needs in order to play the level. .. but they won't get the information, because they'll have escaped out of this dreadful exchange.

So, how could conflict and escalation convey a similar exchange?

GOOD EXAMPLE:

Jane: Another full moon. I don't think we can hold them off again.
Frank: We can. But we have to be fast.
Jane: Let's bug out before night falls.
Frank: And leave the wounded? Look, we know they'll hit the northern barricades first, so we reinforce there.
Jane: If we stay, we all die. You know they'll overrun the eastern barricades while we're on the north.
Frank: As soon as they retreat from the north, we run east, and do it all over again. It won't be easy, but we are not leaving our wounded to die.
Jane: You're the boss, Frankie. Right up until a werewolf takes your head off.

Analysis:

The first sentence of the exchange had to do a lot of work—it introduced the context, the problem—and Jane's premise: *We can't hold.*

Frank contradicted Jane and introduced the idea of speed.

Jane contradicted Frank's point and escalated, by introducing a new idea—we can flee.

Frank escalated again, by bringing up the wounded—and used that argument to contradict Jane's point about fleeing.

Jane escalated again: *Stay, and we all die.* Then she contradicted Frank's point: *Reinforce the north, get overrun in the east.*

Frank puts forth the plan and settles the matter: *It won't be easy, but we are not leaving our wounded to die.*

Jane puts the button on the scene—giving in, but mentioning that this way of thinking is going to get Frank killed.

All the same information is conveyed, and more memorably. We also learn that there are wounded to protect.

And we also have a much stronger picture of these characters—we see that Frank is a person of principle, while Jane is more pragmatic. Both are willing to say what they think. And it doesn't seem like this argument is over. If Frank does fall in battle, what do you think Jane would do?

For the cost of two more lines, this conversation is not only richer and more interesting—it actually contributes much more to the game narrative. Yet the conversation does not feel belabored or dense.

We are interested in the conflict between these two characters—who is right? Will it get tense? They're disagreeing! Every time we introduce conflict or a threatening concept, the situation immediately gets worse. And we get more interested.

Always Be Escalating?

You may ask: how can I always be escalating? One key to escalating is choosing your starting point. If you start the conflict and tempo at 11, you have nowhere to go. The first thing to do is to make sure you don't start at the top of the scale.

Example: In Jane's first line, she doesn't "think" we can hold out for another night, but later in the conversation, she becomes more emphatic—to stay is to die.

Escalation can happen in subtle ways too.

Notice that the first time Frank refers to wounded people they are "the wounded." Later in the conversation they are "our wounded." The word choices raise the stakes for us.

Can't You Start with a Bang?

We said you should start at a lower conflict level to give yourself room to escalate. But what happens when you need to start a conversation with a bang? Perhaps you think the narrative needs a jolt of energy, or it's just a rich opportunity to have a character run into a room and yell: "We're all going to die!"

So how do you escalate from there? "We're all going to die!" is pretty much at the top of the spectrum, surpassed only by "We're all going to die, then be resurrected, then killed again!"

In this scenario, the answer is: de-escalate quickly.

DE-ESCALATING EXAMPLE

Lewis: We're all going to die!
Jiro: Calm down, Lewis. Sit, sit.
Lewis: Die, I tell you!
Jiro: Take a deep breath. Good, now explain yourself.

Now you've brought it back down to a point where you can start escalating toward the climax of this conversation.

The Immovable Character

Some characters, by their nature, do not escalate, nor really offer conflict. They are just a blank wall that no other characters hurl themselves against repeatedly.

IMMOVABLE EXAMPLE

Ophelia: We must go rescue the kingdom.
Percy: I'm drinking.
Ophelia: This is more important.
Percy: I have to disagree.
Ophelia: Have you no sense of civic duty?
Percy: Uh ... no.
Ophelia: This is madness! Your people need you!
Percy: Barkeep, I'll have another round. And one for my friend here.

Percy does not offer conflict. Saying "no" is just contradiction, not conflict. And he doesn't escalate.

The key to an exchange like this is that the other character, in this case Ophelia, does all the work, escalating, until Percy can put a button on the scene.

THE AGREEABLE CHARACTER

In a comedic context, you can have a character, usually a sycophant, who will just agree with everything.

EXAMPLE

Knight: We have to go rescue the town!
Squire: Yes indeed!
Knight: I'm going to ride my horse. You run along behind!
Squire: I love running along behind your horse!
Knight: If brigand archers fire from the rooftops, throw yourself in front
      of the arrows!
Squire: I love throwing myself in the path of arro—wait, what?

This scenario is almost identical to the immovable character. One character keeps escalating, and the other doesn't change. But in this case, the one who doesn't escalate is agreeing rather than contradicting. Obviously, this is for comedy, as there's no tension or drama in this exchange.

EXPOSITION

When a character says something to another character that they both already know, it is done solely to communicate to the player; that's exposition. It is honestly the worst.

Exposition is where good writing goes to die. Unfortunately, games have to move fast and with economy, and you will write exposition in your career. Likely quite often.

EXAMPLES

Jimbo, we've been best friends since the second grade. And not once have you ever asked me for money.
   Henrietta, it's your birthday.
   Time to take you to the gallows, Horvald.
   To prevent the core from reaching critical mass, we must locate the four venting latches and open them, in a specific sequence.
   As you know, general, we have been at war for six years.
   You're my sister, and I love you.

There is no reason for a character to say these lines to another character, other than to convey this information to the player.

We discussed earlier how conflict and escalation make a conversation work, and they can indeed help your exposition conversations.

There are two other tactics to consider when writing exposition:

First, does the player need to know this? Sometimes we assume the player needs information that they don't really need. If you're going to write exposition, take a moment to justify its necessity. What happens if you just don't tell the player this? Will their entire experience be ruined? Or will they be just fine? If it's the latter, then you don't need to write the lines.

Second, is now the right time to share this information? If you give the player some information that they don't know is important, the exposition will feel clunky and unwelcome. Instead, allow the player to be confused for a short period, to the point where they're just starting to think "Wait a minute, what is going on here?" If they're already asking that question, and then there is a line or conversation that reveals the answer, it will feel much better.

Earlier we had the exposition line *You're my sister, and I love you.* Usually you'd be tempted to put this line toward the beginning of a scene, just to establish the dynamic right away. But what happens if you don't? What if the two characters have most of their conversation without establishing this baseline. At a certain point, the player will start to wonder: What are they to each other? New friends? Lovers? Colleagues? Old pals from school? And just when the player is starting to wonder this, just when the question is starting to creep into their consciousness, you deliver the line *You're my sister, and I love you.*

Now, because the player was wondering about it, the line feels like a payoff, rather than the awkward exposition it would otherwise be.

CHAPTER SUMMARY

In this chapter, we discussed the following topics:

- Surface, subtext, and character. Conversations must work in three channels at once.
- Structure. A conversation has a structure to it, just like a story.
- Power. In a conversation, one character always has more power than the other. The power dynamic can change during the conversation, but either way, someone has more, and someone has less.
- Flow. Conversations need a well-designed flow. This consists of conflict and escalation.
- Exposition. Sometimes you have to write lines where characters say things they already know, for the benefit of the player. There are a few concepts that may make this slightly less dreadful.

14 Voice Over Sessions

IN THIS CHAPTER

- Overview of directing voice over
- How to conduct a voice over session
- Working with voice actors

As a game narrative person, you will be in and around the voice over process many times. Usually, you will be in the session so that the director and actor can ask you questions and clear up any confusion. VO sessions are expensive, and every second they spend trying to call or email you with a question is a waste of money. So it makes more sense for you to be there, able to answer any questions that arise.

However, on some projects, you may find yourself directing a session. This can happen for a variety of reasons, the most common simply being budget. On a low budget or indie game, there probably is no money available to pay a VO director, or the VO needs are simple enough that a high level of expertise is not required.

So it is wise to understand a bit about VO direction. However, the following cannot be stressed enough: reading this section, and even directing a few times, does not make you an expert on this topic. We are going to summarize a few key points to keep in mind in case you are ever in that situation. But if you find yourself working with an experienced VO director, please understand that this summary is no substitute for their experience. Directing is a deep and wide discipline that could fill a book as long as this one. Approach working with an experienced director with humility and a desire to learn.

OVERVIEW OF DIRECTING VO

The VO director is a person with a deep understanding of the process in the technical and creative arenas. They have a background in directing actors, or even as an actor themselves.

That said, VO directors are expensive, and some productions cannot afford them. It is possible—even likely—that in your career, you will find yourself in a VO studio with an engineer and an actor, with you having to fill the role of director.

This section is to help you with that scenario.

DOI: 10.1201/9781003624882-19

Managing the Process

You, the director, are responsible for driving the whole process. You're the one who says, "We do it this way." For instance, at the start of the session, the director will say something like this:

"Okay actor X, when we get to a new line, I'll give you a little context, then I'll say 'give me 3 when you're ready,' then the engineer will call out a take number, then you give me the 3 reads. I'll call out a select from that, then we move on to the next take. Or, if I have a note and want to try something different, I'll let you know that too."

Some of the above is pretty standard procedure, but it is still imperative that the director establishes this setup and rhythm. Everyone will follow your cue.

You're the one who calls the breaks, calls the return from the break, sets the pace, sets the tone and mood of the entire session. A big part of your job is time management.

Starting the Session

Among the many things you are responsible for is setting the tone and mood of the session. This means connecting with those you'll be working with to put them at ease and let everyone know what will be expected of them. These steps apply if you are working with someone for the first time or the 100th.

Connect with the Engineer

In every area except performance, the engineer can make or break your session. They do far more than just hit "record" and "stop". A good engineer is always listening for any artifact or vocal tic in the line read, and they have better ears than you. While you were listening for performance, they noticed if the actor drifted a little too close to the mic and their "P"s were popping. Or perhaps a helicopter flew overhead, and the microphone faintly picked up the sound.

They will have a huge influence on the pace and tempo of the session by the speed of their fingers. They can save a line that would otherwise need to be re-recorded.

For all these reasons, start the session by connecting with the engineer. Explain to them how you plan to work and what your goals are. Articulate the process you want to use, such as the process laid out above. Emphasize that you trust their technical expertise above your own. This is both nice as a compliment, but is also a way of letting them know they are empowered to speak up the second they detect a problem.

This may feel obvious, but every engineer out there has worked with many overbearing, arrogant clients. They'll take their cues from you. And remember, even if you think your method is "the standard," it is not. There is no standard process.

CONNECT WITH THE ACTOR

Connect with the actor in the same way. Tell them something in their audition that you liked. This will give them a boost of confidence to start, and also an immediate direction to start shaping their performance around. You can also mention any past roles they've done that you enjoyed. While you may be hesitant to come off as fawning, we have never met an actor who did not appreciate sincere flattery.

The actor must perform, which means they must be in the right emotional state and mindset; this is also the moment to start making your actor feel confident in you. Speak calmly and reassuringly, and communicate to them that you know what you want out of this session, and you know they will be able to deliver it. They just need to trust in you, follow your direction, and bring their own creativity to the role.

This is the moment to define their part in the process. We always tell the actor that the lines as written are the starting point, and that as they begin to inhabit the role, they may want to try something different with a line—either different words or even a slightly different intention. We always say that we'd like to get the line as written first, but after that we encourage the actor to improve and contribute creatively.

That's our process, but every project can have its own. On some projects, every syllable of the line has been debated and worked over, and the intention is that everything will be recorded exactly as written. That's okay, just let the actor know that.

Perhaps on some projects, improv is so highly valued that you will want to really get the actor into the mindset that the lines are just a suggestion.

Anything in between those extremes is also possible. It's vital to let the actor know the expectation.

If you do not specify, actors will always default to assuming that you want the line exactly as written, as that is the safest assumption for them to avoid angering the client. This means they will honor every comma in the line, even if that leads to strange reads.

Note: If you do encourage the actor to improvise, we strongly suggest getting at least one read exactly as written. Later, back at your desk, you may realize you needed that line exactly as written for a reason. Since recordings these days are all digital, it costs nothing to get multiple alternates.

SET THE TEMPO

An important part of the VO process is tempo. It is often necessary to get hundreds of lines in a 4-hour session, so you must keep a good pace. Even if that is not the case, most actors do better when they have a clear rhythm in the session.

Read a line, pause for the director to select or redirect, and for the engineer to call the new slate, and then do the next read. This tempo keeps the actor's energy up.

If the actor must pause for a long time while the director drones on and on about a line, they can "go cold." Then their next read won't be very good, which will cause a talkative director to talk even more, creating a spiral.

REPETITION

There's a lot of repetition when directing. If you sit in a session with an experienced director, you may hear them repeat certain phrases each take.

"Okay, moving on to line 32, give us three." This is part of the director setting the tempo and reinforcing the process. It is also a function of the fact that everyone is waiting for the director's cue to move on. They're not going to move on by themselves: the director tells them to.

READING A LINE IN

In some cases, a line is in response to another line, such as follows:

Line A: *What are you doing?*
Line B: *Me? What are YOU doing?*

To get the right read for line B, you'll want the actor to hear line A. If you haven't recorded line A yet, you will have to read the actor in, by reading line A to them right before they give you line B.

In that case, the director must take control of the process to establish how we are all going to accomplish this: "Okay, [Engineer] will call the take number, then I will read you in, and then give us three."

Or in other scenarios:

"Okay, [Engineer] will call the take, then he'll play you the B read from the last set, and then you give us 2 reads."
"We're going to run through the entire scene, and do three takes of each while I read you in."

Again, these folks work with lots of clients who use different processes. You must be clear about the process you want. At times you may seem to be talking more than the actor, or being super controlling, but that's because you're not only explaining/driving the process, but you're also setting the tempo.

TIME MANAGEMENT

Most VO sessions are 4 hours, and you may have hundreds of lines to get recorded during that time. If you don't get the entire script recorded in that 4 hours, and you need 10 more minutes to get three more lines, you'll need to pay for the studio and engineer for another hour, and likely to pay the actor for another 4-hour block.

As the director, you must time manage the session. If you have a good audio producer, you should have enough time to get the required lines in one session. If the total lines needed are too many, the producer should schedule multiple sessions. But everything involved in a VO session is expensive, so even the best audio producers will try to squeeze as much as they can into any given session.

There are hazards. For example, some actors who are not gamers require more explanation for each type of line. Other times, it takes a little longer to "find" the character at the beginning of the session.

VO sessions usually find a good rhythm after the first hour. So you may not get as many lines during that first hour, and so hours 2 and 3 are where the magic must happen. But that's also the time where you have to start monitoring your talent's energy level.

Time Management is another reason you must take control of the process. If you wait for the engineer to realize you're ready for the next read, or for the actor to realize you need something, a few seconds will go by with each read, which adds up. When you take charge and announce that you're ready to do step A, B, or C, you keep things moving.

WORKING WITH VOICE ACTORS

There's a lot that goes into managing the actor's experience so that you get the best performance out of them.

The first is to be generous with your praise. Tell them often that they're doing great, and about every 15–20 lines, call out something special they did in the last read.

This might make them sound needy, but the truth is, doing VO is a deeply isolating experience. They are in a sound-controlled environment, performing for people who have almost no ability to let them know how they're doing. It can get in an actor's head, even a veteran. It costs nothing to tell them they're doing well, even when they are not. Instead of criticizing, you can positively redirect them to the place you want them to get.

If the actor feels safe, and like they are doing well, they have a chance to relax into the role and will give you a better performance. They'll feel safer trying interesting or fun unexpected things that might make it into the game.

LINE READS

A line read is when you read the line aloud to the actor to demonstrate how you want it to sound. Unless an actor specifically invites you to do a line read, don't do it. Not only is it bad form, it can mess up their performance. They are a better actor than you, and if you give them a line read, they'll try to imitate your bad acting, rather than doing their better acting. It's never really a good outcome.

DIRECTING EMOTIONS

Don't direct the actor to act an emotion. Saying "You're afraid" or "You're angry" will not get good results. It's like telling someone how to bake a cake by pointing at a finished cake. There is no context to it.

Instead of "you're angry," give the actor context like "This is the first time you've seen her since she killed your sister!" The actor will do the math.

Sometimes if there's a lot of subtext, you can tell them how they *feel about* what they're saying.

In that case, rather than "You're angry," you can say "You want them to know exactly how badly they've fucked you over."

Overcommunicating

It can be tempting to explain the full context to the actor. Which is how you might find yourself saying things like:

You're talking to an ancient god, long dead, who has recently been reincarnated, and is hungry for new souls. But you're here to tell her that times have changed and you're going to stop her from feeding her evil desires. But she's also the personification of house cats, which you're allergic to, so there's kind of a little danger there too.

We mentioned earlier that a director can kill the tempo by talking too much, and this is one of the main reasons that happens.

To do a great read, the actor really doesn't need this information. The only exception would be if there are many lines later that reference this situation. Barring that, the following direction will achieve the same result more quickly:

You're here to tell this god "I don't think so, not on my watch!" But you also know she's dangerous.

This much shorter direction will give the actor everything they need to give you a great read.

Working Toward Perfection

Rather than try to talk the actor into the perfect read by giving them a bunch of direction before they read the line, let them do three reads of it first, and think of multiple reads of a line as steps on a journey.

Doing multiple takes is not a sign of failure or a problem. It's just part of the process.

If a line is particularly complex—lots of different emotions under the surface— no one is going to get it on the first, second, or third try. So rather than overload the actor with 1,000 instructions for their first read of a 10-word line, try to get them 40% of the way there, then layer on another 15%, and then another 15%. They'll get there, you just have to see it as a process.

Check in on the Actor

Voice acting is a lot of intense work. You'll find that directing a 4-hour session takes a lot out of you … now imagine acting a 4-hour session.

Check in with your actor every now and then. See how they're doing. How's their throat? Do they need a break? Some tea? Are they ready to keep going?

GETTING CLINICAL

There will be times where you will have to get very controlling and tight. This is because some lines are time-locked, or just very specific.

A direction that everyone hates to give and to get is: *Do it faster.*

Yet there are times you will need to do that. When that happens, you can let the actor know that you know it sucks.

GOING TOO BIG

As the session goes on, the actor often settles into the role and wants to experiment a bit more. This can yield great material, but it can be easy for them to start to "go big." This is a default reaction, because as an actor, going big is how you get the laughs and the plaudits.

But you must remember that when the line goes into the game, and all the exuberance and fun of the VO session is gone, and you hear it in a vacuum, the line will sound much bigger than it did in the studio.

As the director, you are the only one who is imagining the future life of this line. Everyone else is in the moment. You must be the buzzkill who brings it down, because you're the one who is imagining it in the game.

EXERTIONS

Many VO sessions include getting "Exertions" or "Efforts." These are the grunts and sounds a character makes.

When they get hit by a club or other blunt object and the wind goes out of their lungs, they make one sound. When they jump in the air and expel breath, they make another sound. When they get shot in the knee, they make yet another sound. There can be dozens of varieties of sounds.

As a writer, you shouldn't need to write exertions, for two reasons. First, there is no writing involved, they're grunts, not words. Second, the audio designer on your project should determine what and how many exertions are needed for a particular character.

For directing a VO session, exertions are very tricky. You want to get enough sounds that your audio team can cut them up and use them. But this part of the session can very easily strain the actor's voice. If that happens, they may be in pain the next day and unable to record another session.

If you have an experienced actor who knows what they are doing, they can probably drive the exertion process. If not, then just work with them carefully. Check in on how their throat is feeling, remind them to take breaks, and assure them that if they feel any soreness, they should tell you immediately.

We mentioned earlier that you should not do line reads for an actor. In the exertion section, if you need the actor to make a specific sound, it's usually okay to just make that sound for them.

VO COMMENTS

When you write a script, you should have a place to add VO comments. These will be included in the script given to the actor. Hopefully, you are present at the session to answer questions, and if you are, then the notes will be helpful for you to remember the context of the line, or if the script was written by another writer, to hint at what that other writer wanted. If you are not at the session, those comments become the only context the actor and director have about the intent of the line.

VO comments are incredibly important, and many writers do a terrible job with them.

Sitting in session, we see a lot of poorly thought out, misleading, even harmful VO comments, and it causes the actors and director to start ignoring the VO comments in general.

Volume. Is the character leaning in to stage whisper? Are they shouting to someone far away, or over the din of battle?

Context. Are we outside? Inside? In a rainstorm? A desert?

Is this line a subtle put-down? Or are we flirting with someone?

Often the actors can pick up on this subtext without the comment, but it's safer to put it because VO sessions often end up being out of order, and so all context is lost.

EXAMPLE

Perhaps in your story, the last time Bertha went to town, she got in a fight with Jubal. So this exchange makes perfect sense:

Bertha: I'm going to town.
Horatio: Be sure to say hi to Jubal.
Bertha: Get stuffed.

But if the actors and director haven't recorded that section yet, and you're not at the session, they'll be puzzled by Bertha's last line. Why the big reaction? They may guess that Horatio is mocking. But they may also guess that Bertha is grumpy about something else. They'll be totally in the dark. So what do you do?

Do you explain the whole context about the last time Bertha was in town? Probably not, because if the VO comments are very long, it can kill the momentum of the session and they may stop looking at them.

It's better to go with a parenthetical like so:

Horatio: (mocking) "Be sure to say hi to Jubal."

Here you are relying upon the skill of the actors. They don't have the full context, but that one word is enough for them to piece together what is going on. Most voice actors are very intuitive about their character and can bring depth to their performance on the slightest of clues.

Subtext. You will need to clue actors in to the subtext of a line.

EXAMPLE: NOT NEEDED VS NEEDED

Jubal: I hate you.
VO Comment: Angry
                This VO comment is not needed. There is no subtext, the line
                is exactly as it appears.
Jubal: I hate you.
VO Comment: "I love you"
                Or
VO Comment: "I forgive you"

This line clearly does need a VO comment. Without your help, the actor will have no way of knowing that the intent is to playfully say "I love you," or meaningfully say "I forgive you."

Word pronunciation. Phonetically spell out complicated names in the VO comment field. This is imperative.

EXAMPLE

Jackson: We must reach the altar before Orzumba awakens!
VO Comment: oRRzoomBAH

The actor for Jackson may say the name Orzumba in one recording session, and then 3 months later be called in for another session where they must say the name again. But the two lines may play moments apart in the game.

If they pronounced the name differently in different sessions, as is entirely possible, it pulls back the curtain: players will be reminded that this is an actor reading a line.

Pronouns. If you are writing a player character that could be any gender, always use "they." This is not simply a matter of courtesy and inclusion, although those are important too. If you are a male actor and the VO comment for your line says "she is stalling," this can cause confusion in the session. Or a dispiriting realization that the writers think of the character as another gender, and you're just "the back up."

"They" is always safer.

Concise and Clear. We have actually seen the following VO comment in a script:

EXAMPLE

VO comment: Funny. But not too funny. Kind of slightly amused.
    This overdirects the actor. Just communicate the intent of the line to them, not the execution.

This would have worked perfectly:
VO comment: Slightly amused.

Don't try to get a specific read. VO comments like "Emphasize 'Never'" is the writer trying to find a way to direct the actor via the VO comments. The writer has a specific read in their head and wants the actor to imitate it.

But the VO comments are not the proper format for this. If you are going to direct the session, then you can try to direct the actor into the read you want. If you are not the director, then you'll have to trust the actor and director to get the best read with the proper context.

Your job in the VO comments is to provide that context.

WHEN A SPECIFIC READ IS NECESSARY

Occasionally you really do need a specific read. You're not being a control freak, there is a pattern in the dialogue that calls for it. We discussed earlier when talking about reading-in a line to the actor. But the VO comment should also call out when there is a specific pattern that is needed.

EXAMPLE

Jane: You are a mystery.
Hoss: Your face is a mystery!

You need the actor for Hoss to understand that he is playing off of the previous line.

So can you just put a comment: *Emphasize the word "face?"*

No. You need the actor to sell the joke with the pacing and tone of the entire line. If you hyperfocus them on the word face, it may derail things.

What you really want is for the actor to understand the intent of the line. They will be able to sell it much better if they understand the intent.

Here is a better VO comment: *Playing off the previous line*, or *Off the previous line*.

It really comes down to this: tell the actor what you need, not how to read the line. Their craft is to get you what you are looking for; let them figure out the whys and wherefores.

Avoid saying what you don't need. This is very similar to a note in the VO direction section. Just avoid saying what you don't need and focus on what you do need.

EXAMPLE

Bad: *Not projected.*
Good: *"Stage whisper" or "Conversational."*

CHAPTER SUMMARY

In this chapter, we discussed the following topics:

- As a narrative person, you will be involved in voice over recording sessions. You may even need to direct one.
- Do not think that reading this chapter makes you a skilled voice over director. This guidance is intended to help you avoid mistakes, but if you are fortunate to work with a real voice director, please listen to them.
- Manage the process. Connect with the engineer and the actor, set the tempo, repeat instructions often, read lines in, and manage the time.
- Working with actors. There is a lot that goes into working with talented actors.
- Exertions. Recording grunts and combat sounds is an art form of its own.
- VO comments. Use these sparingly, only to provide context that is not obvious from the line itself. Is the character outside in a rainstorm? How are certain names pronounced?

Section 5

Cutscenes

Cutscenes seem like a small part of a game's overall narrative, yet they are a huge topic because they are used as marketing, are often the player's first look at the game, characters, and narrative, and are the most expensive narrative asset produced for the game.

DOI: 10.1201/9781003624882-20

15 Before You Write the Cutscene

IN THIS CHAPTER

- Types of cutscene, and how to choose which type a cutscene should be
- The steps necessary to create a compelling cutscene
- Defining the Central Idea
- Working with a team to create the cutscene

Cutscenes have been a part of video games since the earliest days. They've taken many forms and have led to some of the most powerful moments in gaming history, as well as some of the most cringeworthy. Since we'd all rather have more of the former, it's worth exploring the ups and downs of making a cutscene.

In this chapter, we will discuss the many considerations that go into planning a cutscene before you even begin writing.

As the lead writer of *StarCraft II: Heart of the Swarm*, Brian is familiar with the thinking that went into the cutscenes of that game, all the mistakes made, and the lessons learned along the way. So we'll use those cutscenes as examples, but everything here can apply to any sort of game, and most of the points scale from a large development team down to the three-people-in-a-basement team. There may be fewer marketing concerns at that scale, but the craft of creating the narrative for a cutscene remains the same.

TERMS FOR CUTSCENES

Many different terms are used to refer to the game feature "cutscene": cutscene, cinematic, in-game or in-engine cutscene, prerender, scripted scene, interstitial, trailer, and a variety of others. These names are often used interchangeably, even though there are technical differences between them. The difference between Prerender and In-Game cutscenes is significant. The other names, listed here, refer to fairly minor differences.

CUTSCENE

This is the most generic term, and is used here and elsewhere to broadly mean any of the below categories.

DOI: 10.1201/9781003624882-21

CINEMATIC

This typically refers to the opening cutscene of the game and implies a higher level of polish. For the most part, this means a prerender, which is explained elsewhere. The only real takeaway is that when someone says "cinematic," they mean "this is a highly polished, important piece."

TRAILER

This term is also often used to refer to the opening cinematic, although it could also mean a short video edit to be used in advertising. Often trailers do not have full continuity and are not trying to tell a story. Instead they are a series of exciting shots and moments designed to entice people into playing the game.

INTERSTITIAL

This name simply refers to where the cinematic will play. If a cinematic comes between two important moments in a game—say between Act I and Act II of a campaign, then it may be called an interstitial. All this really means is that it is a cinematic—of any quality, scope, and ambition—that plays between two other important elements.

The distinction that matters is between Prerenders and In-Game cutscenes.

PRERENDERS AND IN-GAME CUTSCENES

All cutscenes fit into one of two categories: Prerender and In-Game. These two names describe how a cutscene is made, and both have a significant impact on how it is used and what it can accomplish.

PRERENDERS

Prerenders are produced the same way that animated features, such as Pixar films, are made; characters and locations are modeled, and shots are animated by hand with multiple passes to add in effects and other elements. Each frame is then rendered individually, and when they are assembled in a playback format, they create a high-quality scene of animation. These scenes are then cut together with other scenes to create continuity. A custom-scored soundtrack is often added to accompany specific actions on screen.

The result is a highly polished cinematic, with near limitless potential. Something that can easily be used in marketing and advertising venues to achieve the highest levels of hand-crafted cinema, and is either full of action-packed scenes or touching emotional moments.

But prerenders have drawbacks as well. First, they are expensive. A prerender requires a large crew and expensive technology. Second, they take a long time to create—which contributes to their expense. Narrative often changes quickly in game development, even late in the process, yet prerender cinematics must lock in a particular story long before the game's release. In some cases, several years before. Since game narratives can even be changed by post-release patches, this long timeline is often untenable. The result is a cinematic style that is undeniably impressive, but expensive, slow, and dangerous to use for in-depth storytelling.

Brian has written a fair number of prerender cinematics, and the most successful ones were those which implied deep story, but did not go too far, nor get too explicit, in exploring that story.

PRERENDER EXAMPLE

StarCraft II: Heart of the Swarm, opening cinematic. If you watch this cinematic, you'll see how it is able to show huge armies fighting on a sprawling battlefield. Setting, characters, units, effects—nothing is ignored, in service of the spectacle. But you'll also notice that the story is quite sparse.

The central conflict is simple—two civilizations meet in combat, and one is overwhelming. The only truly narrative moment is at the end. Sarah Kerrigan wakes up on a table in a lab, wondering if she just experienced a memory, a dream, or a prophecy. It's powerful—but also ambiguous and a bit agnostic of the story that is to come in the game. This is what prerenders demand, because if you get too specific, you paint yourself into a corner.

Prerender Strengths

Incredible polish, uses for marketing, powerful moments, impeccable timing.

Prerender Weaknesses

Inflexibility, expense, long schedule.

IN-GAME CINEMATIC

The opposite of the prerender is the in-game cinematic. This can also be called an in-engine cutscene or a scripted scene.

An in-game cutscene is rendered in real time by the game's graphics engine. The engine creates each frame of film just as it's needed, based on code and data. Rather than animating by hand and then rendering, developers write scripts or some other indirect function that creates the appearance of a cutscene through a variety of commands. These are typically done by technical or cinematic designers, rather than animators.

For example, a cinematic designer might write scripting commands that tell a particular character to play a walk animation at double speed. At the same time, another command will tell the character to move from point A to point B. A third command will tell a second character to lock their eye line on the head of the first character.

The result is that one character walks from point A to B, very quickly, while another character watches them. If the distance covered is too great or too little for the amount of time allotted for the double speed walk animation, then the character's feet will appear to slide across the floor, and the tech designer will need to rework their scripts.

Note that there are more direct ways to make in-game cutscenes with some engines, where an animator can work directly on a model. But they are still not so precise as a prerender.

This all sounds like a very complicated way to create a cutscene, and the result will almost always be a bit less impressive than that of a prerender. But the benefits are enormous.

> **Immersion**. The in-game cutscene will look exactly like the rest of the game. While a prerender is beautiful and full of textures and effects, it does look and feel different from the rest of the game, which forces the player to acknowledge that they are seeing a cutscene, rather than something that is happening in the game world. But an in-game cutscene maintains the same textures and feel as the rest of the game, so the transition is seamless. Immersion is not broken.
>
> **Volume**. Designers with the right tools can produce in-game cutscenes faster and in greater volume than prerenders. In some games—such as *Mass Effect*, *Dragon Age*, or *the Witcher*—it's vital to have many smaller but important cutscenes, including interactive conversations. In these types of situations, having a small team of designers dedicated to producing a high volume of cutscenes is vastly preferable to a huge team producing one prerender.
>
> **Flexibility**. In-game cutscenes are also far more flexible. Because they are the product of script commands, rather than custom animations and textures, they are able to change quickly. Taking from our earlier example, if the character's feet are sliding on the floor, the tech designer can simply change a number in a spreadsheet or script and fix the problem. If, very late in the process, it's decided that the NPC should walk slower, a few quick scripting commands can change that element of the cutscene.

Verisimilitude. In RPGs and many other games, the player's appearance may change based on what gear they have equipped, what choices they have made, and where they are in the game's progression. When the cutscene fires, the player will want to see their character featured in it, not just any character, but theirs, the one wearing the silly green hat or wielding the dread axe that they worked so hard to get. If the cutscene fires and the character is wearing some idealized form of their armor, it will destroy the illusion that this cutscene represents the player's character. This may be the most important thing an in-game cutscene does— the seamless transition, the ability to put the character in the action. Only an in-game cutscene can achieve this.

IN-GAME EXAMPLE

An example of an in-game cutscene would be from *Heart of the Swarm*, when Kerrigan confronts a dying General Warfield in his citadel. This cutscene, produced by Blizzard's amazing in-game cutscene team and directed by Ben Dai, looks great, and shows the results of the player's actions. Kerrigan can appear in the cutscene as a human, or as the ZERG queen, depending on the choices the player has made earlier in the game.

Both versions of this cutscene are available for viewing on the internet, and we urge you to watch both and compare.

In-Game Strengths: Flexibility, quick iteration, economy of funding and effort, immersion.

In-Game Weaknesses: Less visual appeal, limited acting/emotional truth.

SIDEBAR: INITIATING A CUTSCENE

Have you ever been playing a game, and when a cutscene started, you found it incredibly jarring? Or even worse, disruptive? This usually occurs when the developers haven't taken the trouble to initiate the cutscene properly.

There are certain times that we expect a cutscene to play, such as when we have just killed a boss, or finished an act or chapter of a game. However, many games require a greater number, and more varied type, of cutscene in the course of play. This is where it becomes important to think about how you're introducing your cutscenes.

If the player is traveling somewhere in the game world and crosses an invisible trigger, which in turn causes a cutscene to begin, this will be disruptive. The player may have been going somewhere with a purpose, or they may have been about to open a menu or their inventory to do something important. They may also have been thinking, "It's late, I need to save and quit." Now they're stuck in a cutscene, and afraid to skip it in case something important happens and they're unable to watch it again later without replaying hours of the game.

The most straightforward solution to this problem is to only ever initiate a cutscene from a specific player action. So if a player runs down a hallway, avoid putting invisible triggers on the floor that start a cutscene, but absolutely launch a cutscene when the player clicks/activates the door at the end of the hall. The subsequent cutscene would begin with the player walking through the door into a new environment. The player may not know that clicking on the door will start a cutscene, but has just taken an action that implies continued engagement and intent to progress.

The key here is to create a shared language with the player about what can initiate a cutscene. Using the same system for initiating cutscenes over and over will communicate to the player, even if subconsciously, that any time they open a door, load into a new area, activate an NPC, etc., a cutscene may happen.

DOES THIS NEED TO BE A CUTSCENE?

Before we talk about the steps involved in creating a cutscene, we must ask: "Should this be a cutscene at all?" To arrive at the answer, here are a few follow-up questions:

IS THE PRIMARY PURPOSE EXPOSITION?

Are you trying to tell the player something they need to know, and this is the only way you can do it? If so, it should not be a cutscene, as there are other ways to deliver exposition. While exposition is necessary, and most cutscenes will have some, it is hardly compelling. Creating a cutscene to deliver exposition will lead to a terrible experience. In turn, this will lose the trust of the player, and they will reach for the escape/skip button as soon as all subsequent cutscenes start.

IS IT VISUAL?

Cutscenes excel at visual storytelling, from a huge space battle, to a subtle expression. However, if your cutscene is going to consist of two characters standing in a hallway having a long conversation, you may be using the wrong tool for this job.

There are almost always better ways to present nonvisual story beats. Quests, journal entries, ambient dialogue, mini-games, and a variety of other game features can all convey narrative and character development, albeit in an inherently less visual manner.

CAN IT BE AMBIENT?

A cutscene interrupts the player's experience and forces them to watch passively. If there is any way to tell the story in the background and let the player choose whether or not to listen, that is preferable.

IS IT EMOTIONAL?

Cutscenes are generally the best way to convey conflicted, complex emotions, due to the extra control of face effects and voice. If you need a scene with that level of emotional depth in your storytelling, it might be a good candidate for a cutscene.

DOES IT HAVE SPECTACLE?

Another good reason to go to a cutscene is that it has a high degree of spectacle or visual drama that would feel underwhelming in the game view. Sometimes a moment needs to have that level of visual excitement to sell an important feeling.

If you have a *StarCraft II* mission set in a base that is being assaulted by Battlecruisers, you could set it up in the game by showing the battlecruisers in standard gameplay. In that case, you would see small Battlecruisers, viewed from above, shooting at even smaller units below them.

Or you could show the attack in a cutscene, using camera angles to drive home the power and terror of such an attack. To get a sense of what that looks like, you can find the *StarCraft II: Heart of the Swarm* cinematic "Get It Together," which is available for viewing on the internet.

However, this cutscene is not simply spectacle for spectacle's sake. Instead, the powerful imagery adds an incredible level of tension to the mission that follows. As the player races their units through the facility, they feel the urgency and danger each time the screen shakes or enemy pods burst through the ceiling. The power of these feelings will be a direct result of the cutscene, which set the tone and pace of the entire mission.

If you're sure that this moment must be a cutscene and that the end result will be a compelling, powerful presentation, then it's time to start the real work, by which I mean … meetings!

SIDEBAR: DOWN WITH CUTSCENES!

Some developers want to avoid cutscenes at all costs. It's an outdated storytelling technique for games. It disrupts gameplay and destroys immersion. They're expensive and unwieldy to make.

These things may all be true, in certain situations, on certain game teams, and if certain mistakes are made. Our philosophy is "the right tool for the job."

Sometimes, a cutscene is exactly the wrong tool for the job, and the resistance to cutscenes likely springs from the many times they were used poorly in the past. They have been misused to deliver exposition that could have been expressed through gameplay, or for frivolous moments, or just because the developers really wanted a cutscene in that spot for no good reason.

However, sometimes a cutscene is exactly the right tool for the job. A cutscene can still do things no other storytelling technique can, and sometimes it can concentrate the drama, and power and danger of a moment into one experience in a way no other technique can.

This chapter is dedicated to all the steps you must take before writing a cutscene. These steps are designed to help you make sure that the cutscene is the right tool for this job.

If you don't need a cutscene, don't use it. But when the moment is right, embrace the power of the cutscene.

KICKOFF MEETING

The next step is to gather all the stakeholders in a room and talk about the cutscene. Even in-game cutscenes require a great deal of work across a wide range of disciplines, and it's important to get everyone on the same page early. This includes the directors, artists, animators, storyboard artists who will work on the cutscene, and the designers who are working on the levels before and after the cutscene. Depending on the studio and the situation, perhaps marketing, community, or public relations people should be present as well. Even on very small teams, it's a good idea to get everyone in a room and talk it over.

The point of the meeting is simply to discuss the high-level goals of the cutscene. What are the important things that must be accomplished here?, not just narratively, but in every way. What is the scope? How much time and money can be devoted to the cutscene, and how does that square with the creative goals? This is also a useful step from a tactical standpoint. Giving the stakeholders a chance to discuss the cutscene will make them much more likely to buy into the final product later.

A checklist for topics at this meeting might look like this:

- Type of Cutscene
- Creative Goals
- Marketing Goals
- Scope
- Runtime
- Timeline
- Potential Blockers or Risks.

SIDEBAR: IN THE SPOTLIGHT

Cutscenes garner a great deal of attention during development. When work begins on a cutscene, people who aren't normally involved in narrative features often attend these meetings. Indeed, sometimes people who are not even directly working on the development of the game will be there, offering many opinions.

There are many reasons for this. For example, cutscenes are among the strongest marketing tools that come out of developing a game, so marketing and public relations professionals may take an interest. At larger studios, high-level franchise development professionals who don't necessarily get into the day-to-day narrative may also wish to be involved, as the cutscene can come to represent an aspect of the entire intellectual property.

Consider the original opening cinematic of World of Warcraft. It was released many years ago and has been followed by many more cinematics from the same game, yet it remains an iconic representation of the World of Warcraft intellectual property.

Another reason for this intense interest, of course, is that telling stories in cutscenes is fun, and seems easy if you don't have to do the actual work. Even so, it's best to approach this intense interest as a helpful tool rather than an annoyance. The differing perspectives that come from multidisciplinary review will make the final product stronger and more compelling. Many of the people in the room will have a fresh eye, and if the cutscene is complex enough to confuse them, it's likely going to do the same thing to the part of your audience who pays closer attention to cutscenes than to the overall game narrative.

PLAY THE LEVELS BEFORE AND AFTER THE CUTSCENE

If the level/mission/quest that precedes the cutscene is in any kind of playable shape, you should run through it several times. Your goal is to understand the momentum, tempo, and emotional energy that the player will be feeling as they cruise into this cutscene. This is the context the cutscene will live in, and if you don't have a firm grasp on it, you'll likely make mistakes in its execution.

Next, you should play the level/mission/quest that immediately follows the cutscene, for the same reason. You want to have a firm grasp on how the player transitions out of the cutscene and back into gameplay. Do the tempo and energy of the two match? Or are they off?

It's vital that you understand this context, as almost nobody else on the project will have this holistic view. The filmmakers working on the cutscene will be looking at it in a vacuum—their job is to make a great cutscene. The designers who do think about the levels before and after are rarely as involved in the development of the cutscene as you. You are the point of continuity, and so it falls to you to research it, understand it, and make it work.

Keywords for this research: Tempo, tone, feel, energy, emotionality.

CHAPTER SUMMARY

In this chapter, we discussed the following topics:

- Prerenders and In-Game cutscenes, the difference between them, and the pros and cons of each.
- Justifying the cutscene. The criteria you should use to determine if a cutscene is the right tool for the job at hand.
- The kickoff meeting. Get the stakeholders together and define the parameters of the cutscene.
- Play the levels before and after the cutscene to understand the emotional state and tempo of the player's experience coming in to, and going out of, the cutscene.

16 Writing the Cutscene

IN THIS CHAPTER

- What elements must be present in a cutscene
- How to handle drafts and revisions
- How to work with stakeholders and the director of the cutscene

FIRST DRAFT

You've committed to making a cutscene. What should you pay attention to in writing the first draft? Hopefully, you have some guidance from that kickoff meeting and some wisdom from your thoughts on whether or not this needs to be a cutscene.

THE CENTRAL IDEA

As you explore the first draft, working on the conflict that is introduced, rises and climaxes, the blocking, and more, there is one question to keep in mind at all times: what is the central idea?

The explanation that follows is the most important concept in this chapter. As a cutscene is developed, various forces will pull and push it—time, money, new ideas, old ideas that rise like zombies, new people, politics, design changes—the list goes on and on. You will fight many battles, and spoiler alert, you won't win all of them. You may not even win most of them. If you're not careful, the cutscene will get away from you. It will turn out to be something which you don't recognize, and you won't even be entirely sure what it's doing here and what it wants.

This is where the central idea comes in. Early on, you must decide what part of this cutscene—what concept, moment, interaction, or beat—is the heart of the matter. Remember when you spent time thinking about why this must be a cutscene? Recall that meeting you had about why everyone cared? Those are part of the equation. Now you need to take a moment and just be a storyteller. Think about what really matters narratively, why you care, and what you (and by extension, the story) need from this cutscene.

This is your central idea. As various pressures exert themselves upon the cutscene, you need to decide where you can compromise, where you can fight back but ultimately retreat, and where you will stand firm, ready to die on the hill of the central idea. As new changes come in, you can evaluate them against your central idea. Does this change or note affect something you like a great deal, but that is not part of the central idea? Then be open to the change.

DOI: 10.1201/9781003624882-22

If that new idea or feedback does affect the central idea, then your obligation is to say no and stand against it. Be sure to explain your reasons. In fact, explain the central idea to other people working on the cutscene until the point where they are sick of hearing about it. You need them to internalize that central idea and focus their thinking around it.

The reason you must define this central idea from the beginning is that your instinct as a creative storyteller will be to fight many of the changes. You will feel that many of them are bad, they damage the original vision, and they are just making the cutscene worse! But it's not true. Some ideas are just as good as your original idea, and you need to find a way to tell the difference. The central idea is the tool that lets you do this. Once you know what the scene is really about, and what it is not really about, everything becomes much simpler.

It is hard to give examples of phrases that represent a central idea, because it can be wildly different for each cutscene. Below are a few from cutscenes We've worked on (with names changed).

CENTRAL IDEA EXAMPLES

- Jane represents embracing hope, Frank represents clinging to hate, and that is their central conflict.
- Dredlord Angura must empty herself of anger before she can see the truth.
- Jane has gained great power, and she is going to use it to get revenge on Frank.
- Even as she dies, Dredlord Angura will protect her soldiers.
- Jane cares only about finding Frank, even as destruction rains down around her.

As you can see, the central idea can feel like a trite summary of the cutscene narrative, and that's okay. This is meant to be so bare bones that it helps make clear which changes damage the cutscene and which support it.

THEME

In defining your central idea, you have likely given some thought to the theme of the cutscene. If you haven't devoted thought to the theme, now would be the time. Take the central idea as your guide, since this theme is a core part of the cutscene.

The theme is not a message like "crime doesn't pay" or "no good deed goes unpunished." Your cutscene does not necessarily need a message or moral. The theme is instead the topic that the cutscene is examining.

EXAMPLE THEMES

- Betrayal
- Who has the power in this relationship?
- Passion vs strategy
- New vs old
- Coming home from a long journey.

As you can see, many of these are related to the central idea. There is a great deal of overlap, but the central idea is a specific component of this cutscene, and is used to keep it on a tight track, while the theme is a statement about the overall feel that the cutscene is examining. The theme can be used to talk to others on the development team and get them thinking about the cutscene creatively.

CONFLICT

The next question is about the central conflict of the scene. Just like any dramatic scene created in theater, film, or any other performance media, conflict is the engine that will drive your scene. This conflict may involve giant, sweaty, armored soldiers swinging axes or elite assassins firing guns. Or it may involve nobles sipping tea and exchanging devastating insults veiled as polite conversation. Maybe it's a raised eyebrow at just the right moment. It could be a family fleeing from a hurricane and a child wanting to go back for the family dog. Conflict can take many forms, but you as the writer must always understand a few things about it:

How is the conflict introduced? Is the conflict already known at the start of the cutscene? Or must it be introduced in the opening moments? If so, how long will it take for the conflict to become clear?

How does it build? Once the conflict is introduced, the stakes must escalate, and the conflict must develop.

How does it turn? Simply introducing a conflict and pumping it up is not enough. Instead, the conflict must turn and evolve.

EXAMPLE CONFLICT

For the first in-game cutscene of *StarCraft II: Heart of the Swarm*, titled "Hopes and Fears," we introduced a basic conflict early on: Jim Raynor is trying to get access to Sarah Kerrigan, the woman he loves. He faces a series of obstacles along the way—people trying to keep him out of the process, and away from her. He overcomes several obstacles, and seems to achieve his goal at last—he gets a few moments alone with Kerrigan. Surely, this is victory?

But then the conflict takes a turn. Jim's vision of a perfect future with Sarah is shattered by an insurmountable problem—Sarah does not share his vision. While he envisions a retreat from the greater conflict of the Koprulu sector, Sarah holds tight to a vision of blood-drenched revenge, and makes it clear to him that they will never have anything of significance until she has achieved that revenge.

This is the classic conflict turn. After telling the audience "Here's what's at stake and here is what the people in this cutscene care about," you can reframe the entire context. Suddenly everything is worse, the stakes are greater, and the apparent solution is clearly inadequate. This is how you turn conflict.

How does it resolve? Naturally, the final question is how the conflict resolves. Is there some sort of closure that leads us to feel like this matter is done? One way in which cutscenes are different from other filmic narratives is that they sometimes must not resolve their conflict. That is to say, if you saw a film where the central conflict was not resolved, you would likely feel cheated. But a game cutscene sometimes must introduce conflict without resolving it because that conflict will very likely be a continuing part of the game and will likely be addressed through player actions.

If the conflict does not resolve, then how does the cutscene come to a natural end? It can be very difficult to end a cutscene that does not have a natural resolution to the conflict. You certainly don't want the cutscene to feel as if it just stops. Therefore, you need to find a way to resolve some other part of the conflict, or end in a cliffhanger fashion that can lead into gameplay, or find some other kind of natural end to the cutscene.

STRUCTURE

The way we've outlined conflict above suggests a tight structure for the cutscene and working through the conflict may be enough. But at this point in your first draft, it is worthwhile to take a step back and consider the entire cutscene holistically. You've already thought about how the player will feel going into the cutscene, so how does the structure work with that?

How quickly do we get to the introduction of conflict? Are we taking the time to establish the setting so that it can have an influence on the rest of the scene? Or are we taking too much time? Where in the flow of the cutscene does the conflict turn? In the first, second, or final third? How close to the climax and/or resolution? How quickly can we get out of the cutscene after the resolution or closure? Is the cutscene setting anything up for future story beats, and if so, where in the flow should that fall? As with all things in game writing, economy and tight pacing are always a requisite part of any solution.

Much of this may shift in subsequent drafts, and so everything you do during this step-back/holistic look, you will need to do again on each draft, as it is easy for the structure to become frayed, or even torn, by multiple rewrites.

DIALOGUE

Once you have the basic structure of your first draft, it's time to go through and polish all the dialogue.

Wait, you ask, why am I polishing dialogue on a first draft? Aren't I going to end up rewriting all of it? The answer is that yes, you will rewrite most or all of it, but you must do this anyway. The reason is that most people, even some writers, are unable to read rough or first pass dialogue without judging it the way they would the final product. And to be fair, that is a hard skill to develop anyway, as it requires reading something that has obvious flaws, but focusing on bigger issues and not letting those obvious flaws affect your feedback about the overall quality of the piece.

If you send out a first draft to people for feedback and it has temp or rough dialogue, your feedback will be contaminated. Even people who don't openly say that they did not like your dialogue will have problems with the characters and their interactions, because they did not like the dialogue.

Even worse, you will likely have this exchange:

Note Giver: I didn't like Dredlord Angura's line in this scene.
Writer: Oh, that dialogue is all temp. Please focus on the structure and themes of the piece. I'll make the dialogue great later, I promise.
Note Giver: Mhm. Well that moment isn't working, and I'd like to fix it now.
Writer: Maybe you feel like that moment isn't working because you didn't like the line?
Note Giver: No, I'm sure it's because the moment is not working.

Now you're way off track, but whomever is critiquing you is focused on that line and there's no way around it.

In the extreme worst-case scenario, someone from marketing who has always believed deep in their heart that they are a great writer will demand that marketing take over the script writing. Sometimes marketing is supplying part of the budget for the cinematic, so this request may have some power behind it.

So you must polish the dialogue, make it as strong, economical, and punchy as you can, so that the feedback you get will focus on the important things—central idea, themes, structure, and conflict.

It is not unusual to become enamored of dialogue after having put a lot of work into it, and that is a good sign, as it shows you care about your work. However, you must be careful at this stage not to become precious or protective of your dialogue, as it has a high likelihood of being changed.

FIRST ROUND OF FEEDBACK

When you're happy with your first draft, or more likely when you've run out of time, send it out for feedback. Once it is out in the wild, find something else to work on, and banish this script from your mind. Don't think about it. This can be hard to do, but is necessary to provide clarity in the upcoming round of feedback. You need some distance.

Only when it is time to start getting feedback from others, should you crack open the script and give it another read. Hopefully, you've been away long enough to see it with a fresh eye. Glaring problems will sometimes jump out at you, and you won't believe that you did not see these earlier.

You'll think: "Did I really send this out for people to read?"

This is good. It means you're already thinking about how to improve the cutscene, and when people start to give you feedback about that very problem, you'll have already had a chance to think about good fixes.

A FEW THOUGHTS ON TAKING FEEDBACK

The proper way to deal with feedback is a much larger topic that we will deal with in a later chapter, but a few thoughts follow:

Be open to all of it, and remember that all of the professionals giving you feedback have their own filter, based on their particular discipline. This means they may see valid problems that you do not.

Your main goal here is to guide the script through the feedback process, using the opinions and insights of others to improve it, to make it stronger and fix its problems. But also to defend that central idea. It is remarkably easy for that central idea to disappear through multiple rounds of feedback. This is another moment at which having a clearly articulated central idea becomes vital. You should test every solution you or anyone else proposes against that central idea. If a proposed change doesn't violate the central idea, it is safe to implement if it makes the script better.

The other high-level concept to keep in mind with feedback is that when people say there is a problem, they are almost always right. Something pinged them as they read the script, and there's a great chance it will ping many other people when they watch the final cutscene.

However, when they define what that problem is, or even when they pinpoint the spot where the problem exists, they are often wrong. Oftentimes people will say that a beat feels inauthentic, and suggest many changes for that beat. But the reality is that this beat feels inauthentic because the beat that preceded it did not set it up well, or flow into it well.

When people give feedback, suggesting a fix for the problem they've articulated, they are even more likely to be wrong. This is not because they are untalented. Instead, as we discussed in the previous paragraph, they likely have not identified the true source of the problem, and so their intended solution won't work.

As the storyteller, it is your job to talk to them about their concern, and try to decode what is actually wrong. It's a good idea to let people know you'll be asking them about their feedback to better understand, so they don't interpret your barrage of questions as skeptical defensiveness.

SECOND DRAFT

The second draft is your attempt to revise the script in order to address all the feedback that seems relevant. It may end up being incremental changes, or it may be a page one rewrite. The notes and feedback will determine that. So long as you keep that central idea in mind, and keep that pure, the scale of the rewrite is irrelevant—aside from the amount of work you must put into it.

The second draft also brings a few new concerns to the process.

PACING

Now that the overall shape of the cutscene is becoming clear, you should consider its speed. How fast does it move? Is there fat you can cut? Does every character need to be present? Do you need all these locations?

Brian once had a producer cut two of the three proposed locations in a cutscene, for logistical reasons. He had to revise the script heavily to deal with this new reality of having one location. As a result, the script got significantly stronger, particularly the pacing.

DIALOGUE

Yes, once again you must create polished, sparkling dialogue. This draft, and every draft. However, now that you've got a clear sense of the conflict, you can also take a second look at the dialogue with an eye toward character and subtext.

CHARACTER

This is just a simple matter of reading the lines out loud a few times and thinking about how this character expresses themselves. Are there ways that Dredlord Angura would say this line that no one else would? If the current construction of the line feels like it could be said by any character, you can probably do something to make it more specific to the character who actually does say it.

SUBTEXT

Characters are often driven by a deeper emotion or intention than their words would suggest.

EXAMPLE

Jane comes home to discover that her roommate, Frank, has not done the dishes when it was his turn. So Jane tears into Frank. In detail, when he shrugs an apology, she thinks it's not enough and attacks again.

From this, you may think that Jane takes dish hygiene very seriously. But there are a variety of other things that could be going on under the surface.

Perhaps Jane feels that Frank does not pull his weight around the house in general, and the dishes are simply the straw that broke the camel's back. Or perhaps Jane is regretting her decision to let Frank stay at her apartment, and so is starting to attack him at every opportunity, in hopes that he'll leave. Perhaps Jane is deeply angry about something else entirely and Frank just happened to be the first target.

For any of those to be clear, the player would need to have further context outside of the cutscene, and they often will. This is why cutscenes are great opportunities to write dialogue with subtext.

In fact, much of the dialogue in your first pass may actually be the subtext. That is to say, in your quest to be economical and clear, you may have written a scene in which all your characters say exactly what they mean. The second draft is your chance to revise the scene so that the things the characters said so bluntly in the first draft are revised to feel more natural, with the original meaning still layered in.

Taking from our previous example:

In the first draft, Jane, looking at the dirty dishes, said:

You're a useless roommate, and I regret letting you move in. I want you gone! Get out!

In the second draft, Jane, looking at the dirty dishes, could say:

When you moved in, I didn't know it was going to be like this. How hard is it to do the dishes? Are you even trying?

The first line is the subtext of the second. Jane wants him gone, but she says it in a way that is far more natural and entertaining. The "Are you even trying" is the telling part, because this is a question that is usually only asked by someone at the end of their rope. This also lets the conflict build a bit more as Frank has a chance to defend himself.

Seek Help from the Art and Audio Teams

This is a visual medium, and if you didn't get much feedback from the art team about the visual excitement and visual aesthetic of the script, something is wrong. During the second draft, it is incumbent upon you to seek out some of the artists and discuss how or if the cutscene could be more visual.

The same applies to the audio team. These are people who can make the cutscene support your central idea in a much stronger way, and it's a good idea to get them involved and activated as soon as possible.

Subsequent Drafts

When the second draft is ready, send it out as you did the first, and once again, put it from your mind. From this point on, you will be repeating most of the steps of the second draft: incorporate feedback, stick to the central idea, see what you can polish.

ANIMATIC

The final part of making the cutscene that we will take a look at is the animatic. This is a rough version of the film made with hand-drawn storyboards and cut together to simulate the final film. Not all cutscenes get one. Scripted scenes tend to simply have a rough cut of the cutscene itself. But if you are fortunate enough to work on a cutscene with a storyboard team who will create an animatic for it, there are a few things to keep in mind:

THE DIRECTOR

At this point in the process, you and the director should feel like collaborators. But this is the step where the director begins to take more control of the cutscene, and your involvement diminishes. This is perfectly normal, as they have many skills and concerns about how to actually make the cutscene, which have little or nothing to do with narrative.

Hopefully, you have developed a good relationship with the director, so they know that if a major narrative change comes up after you've stepped out of the process, they should loop you back in.

UNEXPECTED CHANGES

As the storyboard artists and director start to flex their creative muscles, they may add new ideas or render an idea in a way you did not expect. At this point in the process, you've lived with the cutscene for a while and have had many discussions about it, and it may feel like people are just changing it with no regard to all the thinking and planning that went into it. This is a good moment to sit back and take a deep breath. See where these changes go.

And remember, the director has been along for this ride with you, and so they will also know the areas where it may need to be pulled back. The basic takeaway is to make sure you and the director have a strong bond of trust and mutual respect. That will go a long way toward keeping the cutscene in good shape as it moves through production.

CONCLUSION

Writing a cutscene can be a quick and simple matter of jotting a few words down, or a herculean task that, off-and-on, takes several months. It may be entirely your vision, or you may spend much of your time in meetings, wrangling diverse opinions.

The key to navigating the process, no matter how vast it becomes, is to take each step by itself, and define those key principles that guide you through each of those steps. It is helpful to articulate them to yourself along the way.

The result is going to be exciting!

CHAPTER SUMMARY

In this chapter, we discussed the following topics:

- First draft. There is a lot to accomplish in this draft.
  - The central idea, the theme, the conflict, the structure, and the dialogue. All of these must attain some degree of solidity and polish in the first draft.
- First round of feedback. Be open to everything, but remember your job is to keep the central idea intact as you guide the script through the feedback rounds.
- Second draft. Work on pacing, dialogue, character, and subtext. Seek help from the art and audio teams to ensure the cutscene is working on the visual and auditory levels.
- Subsequent drafts. Repeat the feedback and revision steps from earlier.
- Animatic. Make the director your best friend. Be ready for unexpected changes.
- One step at a time. Cutscenes have a lot of moving parts. Just take one step at a time and keep moving forward.

Section 6

Intellectual Property

Making a story that can become an Intellectual Property is one of the most important parts of game narrative. Having a cohesive universe that can spawn an array of stories means that you have made something that can touch multiple generations over the years.

DOI: 10.1201/9781003624882-23

17 Now You're Thinking with IP

A quick reminder from our World Building chapter: IP technically means something much bigger than how we're using it here. For the purposes of this book, when we say IP, we're referring to the creative parts of a game universe that players experience.

So, we're not talking about logos or matchmaking code. But we are talking about sound effects, music, color palettes, environment and character art, gameplay, voice over, characters, stories, UI—basically, anything the player encounters while playing the game.

Believe it or not, even in this day and age, you will sometimes be asked to justify the added effort and expense of developing the IP in the game.

THE IMPORTANCE OF IP

A great game needs great gameplay and stunning graphics. For some games, it also needs a tense, engaging story filled with fascinating, appealing characters.

But none of that is enough without a deep, compelling world. A fully realized world is the secret ingredient, so many games promise but often fail to deliver. How many times have we seen *Fully Realized World!* slapped on the game description, only for the actual game to fall short?

World building sounds fantastic in kickoff meetings. It's inspiring. But in practice, it's hard, time-consuming, and expensive. As development ramps up, team leaders inevitably ask: *How many more copies will we sell if we put extra time and money into building out this world?* It's a fair question—every decision in game development is a balancing act between resources and returns.

The problem is, the answer isn't simple, and that often leads to poor decisions. Sure, good world building improves the game and how it's received. Players who immerse themselves in a rich world become your most passionate advocates, and reviewers love to praise well-crafted worlds.

But if you put "World Building" head-to-head with "Giant Robot with Lasers" in a battle-of-the-features, the robot always wins. And you can't really name a hard figure on how many more copies the game will sell, or users it will retain, from having a richly rendered universe.

However, the value IP provides is critical.

THE TWO CRUCIAL ROLES AN IP PLAYS

First, it's a *baseline requirement*. Players won't rave about good IP development as much as they'll notice its absence. They will say things like, *It just felt empty* or *I couldn't bring myself to care*. Those are project killers. Unless you're making a puzzle game, you need solid world building to avoid a hollow experience. Without it, your game is crippled.

Second, a successful game with little IP development has a hard time passing the threshold to the next level. A successful game with a strong IP comes out of the gate roaring, lending itself to community participation, transmedia, other game genres, and more.

If players love spending time in your universe, they'll want to return to it—in books, comics, shows, and future games. Even if one game underperforms, players will still believe in the universe and come back for the next entry. Build a world people believe in, and you'll earn a long-term, loyal audience.

SIDEBAR: TOO COOL TO FAIL?

A very successful IP achieves escape velocity. This means that it has such deep roots in the culture that it can no longer fail. If it has a series of bad releases, people will grow tired of it, but it has not died. Rather, the IP holder needs to just give it a break, let it rest for a while. After a few years, when a new release is ready to come out, people will have started to develop nostalgia for the IP, and realize they've been missing it.

A classic example of this comes from one of the most durable IPs in history: Batman.

Tim Burton directed the first two modern Batman films, *Batman* (1989) and *Batman Returns* (1992). These combined the enormous power of the Batman IP with Burton's signature style, and the result was a success, both financially and in the hearts of fans.

Joel Schumacher directed the next two films, *Batman Forever* (1995) and *Batman & Robin* (1997). These films were a complete mismatch for what people wanted from Batman at the time, and they were also just not very good films in their own right.

Batman Forever made a great deal of money, building off the success of the Burton movies. But *Batman & Robin* saw a steep decline. After watching *Batman Forever*, most viewers did not want to come back.

Warner Bros. had lost the trust of moviegoers. Not just Batman fans, the wider audience. Doesn't it seem like that should have been the end for Batman? Not so with an IP that has achieved escape velocity.

First, there was an extremely successful Batman animated show going on at the same time, along with the eternal comic book itself. More importantly, Warner Bros. knew they had time on their side. They just let Batman lie fallow for a time.

Eight years later, Christopher Nolan's *Batman Begins* (2005) came out, and was a huge hit, relaunching the franchise.

Think of your own experience, after the second or third bad release in an IP you love, you may swear off of it. *Mutant Knights of Mars is dead!* But 5 years go by, and you hear a rumor that a different studio under the same publisher is starting work on a new MKoM title. You may be cautiously hopeful, but honestly you probably also have a little jolt of nostalgia. You'll definitely try *Mutant Knights of Mars: Attack of the Plutonians!* When it comes out.

An IP can reach a point where it can't fail. It can suffer setbacks, but in time, it will return.

A Case Study: *Overwatch*

Blizzard's *Overwatch* illustrates the power of world building perfectly. As Blizzard's first new IP in 17 years, the stakes were sky-high. Would it be a hit? Could it become a true franchise with transmedia appeal? Would players rally around its world and characters?

At launch, the gameplay was highly polished, as you'd expect from Blizzard. The character designs, maps, names, voice lines, and UI hinted at the kind of world *Overwatch* wanted to be. These elements offered a thin layer of implied world building and IP, and implied world building can be powerful. It invites players to imagine and fill in the blanks themselves.

But that wasn't enough. To establish *Overwatch* as a vibrant, believable world with room to grow, Blizzard invested heavily in another avenue to share the IP with players.

The studio produced cinematic shorts—high-budget, glossy mini-films that introduced key heroes and expanded the world's lore. The announcement cinematic was a given for a game of this caliber, but Blizzard followed up with more shorts, each one giving players a deeper look at the characters and the world's history. Webcomics told smaller stories that added texture and context.

This wasn't cheap. These resources could have gone into gameplay features or other development priorities. But Blizzard was not launching a game. It was launching an IP. Its reputation is built on crafting worlds that fans want to live in, and it understood that *Overwatch* needed that investment to succeed as an IP.

THE PAYOFF

The result speaks for itself. *Overwatch* became more than a game—it became a cultural phenomenon. Players didn't just love playing it; they loved the world and the characters within it. They created fan art, cosplay, and endless stories of their own. And they stuck with it, ensuring the game's long-term success.

If you build a rich, enticing universe around your game, you don't just create a great experience. You create a world that players want to return to, share with friends, and stay loyal to for years to come.

Now *Overwatch 2* is being met with mixed reactions, and it may ultimately be considered a disappointment. But we'd argue that while *Overwatch* hasn't yet achieved escape velocity as an IP, it can definitely come back from a bad release, due to the power of its IP engine.

Not all game developers truly understand the importance of IP, not when it's adding extra days and dollars to the budget. But it is vital.

HOW DO YOU EVEN WORK ON AN IP?

As you work on the game, particularly in world building, you'll be creating IP. But that doesn't mean you don't have to think about it. IP that happens by default is bad.

A number of games came on to the scene as a huge hit, and developed global communities very quickly. But because they had given no thought to the IP, and perhaps passing attention to world building, when making the game, they were unable to capitalize on the success to spin the game into an IP.

Case Study: *League of Legends*

League of Legends is a worldwide blockbuster of a game. Yet Riot was not able to release related titles or games for many years.

This was not due to a lack of skill on the part of Riot's developers—many talented people work there. But League had been developed without much thought about how to incorporate IP into the game. In fact, Riot actually ruled the game's internal narrative and worldbuilding non-canon several years after its release.

Today, of course, *League* has vaulted off the success of the animated show *Arcane* to take its placc as a global IP. But it took more than a decade, and the success of a very expensive animated show, to accomplish this.

A DIFFERENT CASE STUDY: *FORTNITE*

Fortnite was an overnight success, is one of the biggest games in the world, and has been for years. Yet it is not a strong IP in the sense that we mean the term in this book. In this case, it was not due to a lack of foresight so much as a different strategy.

Epic took a more business and tech approach to their game. They doubled down on licensing skins, with the result that there was no IP cohesion to the game. You could see Darth Vader and a man dressed as a banana fighting against Iron Man and Catwoman during a *Fortnite* match. That's a chaotically compelling image, but it doesn't leave any room for *Fortnite* as an IP.

Epic had a different plan: they didn't want *Fortnite* to be an IP. Rather, they wanted to make it a platform. Many of the benefits we listed of having a successful IP apply to being a platform as well, just in different ways. It's a less creative but more tech-savvy approach, and it seems to be working quite well for Epic.

But we cannot imagine a Fortnite movie or novel. And if there is ever a *Fortnite 2*, it will most likely be a massive technology reset or update. In fact, since it is a platform, it seems unlikely they would ever want to make a *Fortnite 2*, just as there is no Facebook 2 or Instagram 2.

Unless you are making a game that will serve as a high-tech platform, you need to actively focus on making the IP for your game great.

As mentioned in Chapter 7, most of this applies to world building as well, but world building is focused on the moment: what do I need to do now to ship this game? IP is focused on the long term: Where does this IP need to grow into? How do I keep room for it to grow? How do I keep it fresh? How do I keep it consistent?

TWO WAYS TO WORK ON IP

As a narrative developer, there are two main ways you'll work with IP.

DEVELOPING A NEW IP FROM SCRATCH

This is the tougher and rarer job. Why? Because you're starting with a blank slate. Nothing exists yet, so anything can mean anything—and that usually means everyone on the team has a different vision of what you're making. It's hard to get aligned when there's no shared foundation. There are other challenges too, but this is the big one.

WORKING ON AN EXISTING IP

This is also challenging, but at least you're not starting from scratch. There are already some stakes in the ground—something you can point to and say, "This is the IP! See?" You've got a framework, but you'll still need to navigate how to build on it while staying true to the established identity.

The following two chapters cover these two paths. However, there is a lot of complementary information in each, so it is a good idea to read both.

CHAPTER SUMMARY

In this chapter,, we discussed the following topics:

- The importance of IP. Not everybody understands how important IP is to the long-term success of a project, a team, and a studio.
  - When Blizzard shipped the original *Overwatch*, they knew they needed to launch more than a game. They took the time and expense to launch an IP, and it was a huge success.
- How to work on an IP. The simplest way to think of working on an IP while working on a game is to plan ahead and consider how to grow the IP in the future, then plant the seeds of that growth in the game.

18 Creating a New IP

IN THIS CHAPTER

- Essential questions when starting out in a new IP
- Defining and creating the core philosophies to make an IP
- Defining the Pillars of an IP

In this chapter, we'll focus on the first scenario: building an IP from the ground up. It's a big, messy process and there is no perfect way to start, so we'll cover the most important concepts for you to consider in what feels like the most natural order.

Unless you are a one-person indie dev, all the steps in this chapter will likely need to be done with other stakeholders. The IP of the game is everybody's business, so it will require a lot of debate and discussion to arrive at answers that everyone loves.

ASK YOURSELF: WHAT KIND OF IP IS THIS?

Creating an IP involves tackling a wide range of questions about the game's nature. The most important one is defining: *What kind of IP is this?* and a corollary of that: *How should this IP make people feel?*

Case Studies: *Mass Effect* vs *StarCraft*

Both are science fiction games with interstellar travel and humans interacting with a variety of alien species—some peaceful, some not. Both rely on futuristic technologies as core elements of their worlds. Yet, these two game universes couldn't feel more different, and that difference shapes how players experience them.

Note: We are huge fans of both IPs, and Brian worked on both. This is about understanding how their distinct IP choices shape their identities; it is not a qualitative or merit comparison.

Mass Effect is fundamentally optimistic. Despite tensions and even wars between alien species, the overarching narrative is one of cooperation. The majority of species have come together to form a political structure aimed at mutual benefit. Diplomacy and trade are the norm, and while the threats faced by humanity and its allies are deadly, there's always the sense that everyone will band together to meet them.

StarCraft, on the other hand, is grim to its core. War, betrayal, and internal conflict are constants. The various races—terrans, zerg, and protoss—are perpetually at war, not just with each other but often within their own factions.

Even temporary alliances forged to fight greater threats inevitably collapse into treachery and chaos.

The worlds themselves reflect these tonal differences. *Mass Effect* dives deep into detail. Each planet you visit has a sense of governance, infrastructure, and public sentiment. You get a feel for how these worlds operate—the bureaucrats, police, and surveillance systems that keep them running.

In *StarCraft*, the approach is broader. Locations are painted in bold strokes: the ice planet, the lava planet. The focus is on which faction occupies the area and whether they're friend or foe, with the answer almost always being foe. The smaller details of daily life don't matter as much. That's not to say *StarCraft* feels less compelling—its focus is simply different.

Even humor highlights these contrasts. In *Mass Effect*, humor is character-driven. Quirks and habits, like Mordin Solus's rapid-fire babbling, bring levity while staying grounded in the narrative. There's also situational humor, such as Shepard's habit of hanging up on the Council. But it all feels natural—fitting within the world's rules.

StarCraft, the darker of the two, leans into sillier humor. The "pissed lines" (dialogue triggered by repeatedly clicking on a unit) often break the fourth wall, with characters delivering over-the-top or self-aware remarks. Scenes like Tosh accidentally cursing the wrong person with a voodoo doll or a Marine's "I love you, Sarge" moment add an absurd charm. Yet even *StarCraft* sets boundaries—pop culture references, for instance, are rare, as they'd break immersion entirely.

Character relationships reflect these contrasts too. In *Mass Effect*, bonds grow over time. Characters share secrets, build trust, and develop meaningful, sustained connections. *StarCraft* takes a more operatic approach: love, betrayal, and animosity are dramatic and absolute, with less focus on the journey to those emotions and more on the actions they drive.

The treatment of death and violence also highlights the difference. In *Mass Effect*, death exists, but it's not omnipresent. Many people live normal lives, untouched by violence. Large-scale tragedies, like the attack on the Citadel, are rare and underscore the stakes. This aligns with the third-person RPG format, where combat is frequent but not overwhelming.

In *StarCraft*, death is a constant companion. Entire planets are wiped out, and the game doesn't shy away from it. But there's a sense that this is just how life is in this universe—a brutal, unrelenting fight for survival. As an RTS, *StarCraft* asks players to send hundreds of units into battle, knowing many won't make it back. The message? Everyone's going to die someday, so fight hard and save what you can.

These are just a few of the countless ways these two IPs diverge. Despite their shared core—humanity traveling the stars, interacting with aliens, and facing catastrophic threats—they feel worlds apart. That's the power of an IP. It's the sum of all the tiny decisions about how the game experience operates, what it values, and how it makes players feel.

QUICK COMPARISON: *GAME OF THRONES* VS *LORD OF THE RINGS*

Both are Medieval fantasy.

If we asked you which IP would you be more likely to witness someone get their finger cut off? How about a scene in which everyone sits down to a rich meal and eats to their stomach's content?

The chances are very strong that you instantly identified each of those moments with one IP or the other, just based on how it felt.

The answer to *What kind of IP is this?* is: what kind of things can and cannot happen in this IP? And, as always: how does this IP make you feel? That's what kind of IP it is.

TONE, AND HOW IT MAKES YOU FEEL

As always, everything discussed here for tone applies to world building. During development, a game develops its sense of tone through world building on that game. Over time, an IP also develops a tone, and we will elaborate on that in the next chapter.

But for now, we do need to understand what tone is and how it works, so that in developing a new IP, you can at least set a goal for what the tone will be, even if it may change a bit across multiple releases.

MATERIAL AND TREATMENT

Tone is defined by two elements: Material and Treatment. Most people think of the material when they consider tone, but they forget that the treatment of it is the biggest influence.

Material is the content of the IP. It consists of stuff like the history of the world, the events of the plot, the backstories of characters, and what the characters do.

The treatment is how you present the material. You can present light material in a dark way, or present dark material in a light way.

Material and treatment both influence the tone, but the treatment is the dominant part of the pair. A key part of the treatment is how the characters in the story feel about what is happening to them.

If the characters are going through a rough patch in their relationship, but it feels to them like a profound and agonizing moment, the tone will be reflected in their feelings. If the characters are going through terrifying experiences, but they're having a good time, or at least don't take it too seriously, the tone will reflect that.

Case Study: *Borderlands*

Borderlands. The material in this game is dark. A remote planet with a posta-pocalyptic vibe, a wasteland filled with gangs and psychos. Death is a common experience. In the wider world, everything is run by soulless mega-corporations. It's the tale of a group of treasure hunters looking for an ancient vault, but competing with various factions of insane and evil corporate stooges.

The game ends with the vault being resealed without the heroes getting their due. It is strongly implied that something in the vault transmitted a code to a robot on Pandora who may lead a robot uprising in the future.

Based on the material, *Borderlands* sound pretty dark, or at least bleak.

Yet the treatment of the material is light and fun. The characters, despite the horror around them, are having a good time. The exaggerated shapes of the visual design give a sense of fun as well.

Everything about the treatment of the material helps us see it in a different way, creating a unique tone and feel.

Consider how the tone of the four projects below would feel very different. In some cases, the difference would be subtle, but still meaningful. In others, the tone would vary widely.

EXAMPLE

- An exciting action story with exciting treatment of the material
- An exciting action story with understated treatment of the material
- An understated action story with understated treatment of the material
- An understated action story with exciting treatment of the material.

A WAR OF PHILOSOPHIES

At its core, an IP is a war of two philosophies. They cannot co-exist, so while both are present, there will always be strife between them. But neither can ever really be defeated either.

If one philosophy destroys the other on all fronts, its adherents may enjoy a brief golden age, where nothing much happens. But over time, that other philosophy will come back into existence, operate in secret, gather its strength, and strike, toppling the existing order.

This unending war between two philosophies is the engine of an IP. It is the conflict that drives every story in the IP. It scales infinitely—it will influence sweeping, epic tales of war, and fuel the bitter feud between a father and son.

This is a vital step not only to understand how to fuel content in your IP, but also to determine what is a critical element at the heart of the IP, and what is not.

EXAMPLE

We're going to look at all this in the context of *Star Wars*, which is an overused IP in analysis in general. However, *Star Wars* represents the clearest and cleanest example of this, and it is one of the most durable, successful IPs in history.

There are many strong associations with the *Star Wars* IP: Darth Vader, Jedi, Sith, Lightsabers, and more. It can be easy to mistake all of these as "must haves" for something to feel like *Star Wars*.

Yet none of them are critical. You can tell a *Star Wars* story that feels like *Star Wars*, and fits in the IP, with none of those.

Take for example Andor, a recent Star Wars show, and probably one of the more successful *Star Wars* shows in history. We do see a few things coded as *Star Wars* throughout the first season: Imperial uniforms, Storm Troopers, and the occasional Tie Fighter. Yet none of those are really a core part of the show.

Critically, there are no Sith, no Jedi, and no lightsabers. There is no use of the force—light side or dark.

None of those elements represent the war at the heart of *Star Wars*.

THE HEART OF THE IP

At the heart of the *Star Wars* IP are the philosophies of the light and dark side of the force. Not the force itself, however. The philosophies represent a much greater school of thought.

The philosophy of the light side of the force is a loss of self. Yoda says "You will know when you are calm, at peace. Passive." It represents putting the good of others, or community, or the greater whole, before yourself. It involves pushing away your emotions and drives, finding collective strength with others.

The philosophy of the dark side of the force is the supremacy of self, drawing on your emotions to harness great power, embracing your own inner strength to impose your will on a chaotic universe. Not relying upon others, when you have yourself. Darth Vader says, "Your anger gives you great strength."

You can see how these two philosophies could never coexist. You cannot simultaneously surrender your own identity to the greater good and put yourself on a pedestal. Eternal strife is inevitable.

Neither Philosophy Can Be Forever Defeated

Star Wars is full of stories about how one or the other philosophy was dominant— the Old Republic, the Republic, the Empire, etc. And then avatars of the other Philosophy come roaring back onto the stage. From a secretive Sith lord plotting his ascendancy, to a plucky band of rebels trying to destroy an Imperial super weapon, the defeated side is always fighting back.

This is not simply done for the sake of fueling more conflict. It's an inherent part of the philosophical heart of an IP. Both philosophies represent something that can reset with each generation, that is inside all of us.

In *The Empire Strikes Back*, the Jedi master Yoda tells Luke to enter a cave that is strong with the dark side of the force. Luke asks "What's in there?" and Yoda replies, "Only what you bring with you."

This makes clear that the philosophies of the light and dark side are present in everyone, and that is why neither one can triumph "for all time." It's a war that renews itself each generation.

What about Andor?

Andor is about Cassian Andor, a small-time thief with a talent for stealing from the powerful. He does this for himself and the small circle of people he cares about. Although he robs those who follow the philosophy of the dark side, he himself also follows this philosophy, even though he would not describe himself that way.

The show opens with a scene where two Imperial guards harass Andor. He accidentally kills one, then realizes he must kill the other, since the other has seen his face. The other guard is no threat, and begs for his life, but Andor murders him. He's not bloodthirsty or cruel. The guard's continued existence was potentially harmful to Andor, and by extension, his loved ones.

At the time of this writing, only the first season is out. But that season tells the story of how this small-time thief grows to care about something bigger than himself, even at the risk of his life. He begins to see the damage the Empire is inflicting on individuals and on societies as a whole. He starts to care, and to believe he can make a difference, and that it is worthwhile for him to make a difference.

There are other characters on the show who either reinforce Andor's journey or inhibit it. One who reinforces it makes the dramatic statement: "I burn my life to make a sunrise that I know I'll never see," which is a very lightside thought. Others represent the opposite path: putting their own needs and well-being above everyone else.

Part of the power of understanding the two philosophies at the heart of an IP is that it doesn't just fuel the main story and protagonist/antagonist. All the subplots, all the side characters, and all the incidentals represent a different view or angle on these two philosophies.

And when you map out the influence a side character may have on the protagonist, you can basically think of them as leading the protagonist toward one philosophy or the other.

As with all tools, this should not be a limiting way to think about your IP. There are a million variations and flavors within any given philosophy. You should think of it as more of a filter that you run ideas through, rather than a template that you mold ideas around.

Is It Good vs Evil?

The two philosophies can certainly be coded to look like good and evil. In fact, that is often the case. Our protagonist(s) either follow the "good" coded philosophy, or the story is them learning to follow that one. Their opponents follow the "evil"-coded philosophy, and that is usually part of their downfall.

That is certainly true in *Star Wars*. The Sith like black clothes, and enjoy betraying each other, and have a host of other signs pointing to being evil.

But if you look under the surface, the philosophy of the dark side is not inherently evil. It's just the application of it that is evil or wrong.

You could also understand the philosophy of the dark side as standing up for yourself. Protecting those you care about. Being in touch with your emotions rather than suppressing them. Indeed, creativity and advancement are generally associated with some form of destruction, and even egomania.

And you can understand the light side to be about letting go of everything that makes you human, and seeking the consensus answer, rather than the right one. The jedi are amazing, versatile fighters. But when you give them power, they suddenly seem like a bunch of useless incompetents.

In the *Star Wars Prequels*, the Jedi Council comes off as ineffective and caught in endless debate. Meanwhile, the Sith seem forceful and direct and energized.

A great example from another IP is *The Good Place*. In that show, the leaders of the good place are ineffective wimps, too busy criticizing each other and themselves over minor infractions to actually do any good at all.

Both Philosophies Are Strong

Don't be distracted at first by how the philosophies are coded. It's vital to understand each philosophy at its highest aspiration.

Let's look at how the light and dark side philosophies can be coded in the opposite direction from *Star Wars*.

Example: The Dead Poet's Society

A group of young men are being educated in a strict environment, and are taught to repress their feelings, to be of service, to be obedient. The four pillars of the school are Tradition, Honor, Discipline, and Excellence.

Yet a teacher shows up, who strives to teach them a different philosophy: Carpe Diem, or seize the day. He teaches them not to conform, but to examine themselves to see who they really are. To experiment and grow as individuals.

There are a few differences, but the underlying philosophy here is essentially the light and dark sides of the force. However, the way they are coded is reversed: elevation of the self is the "good" path, loss of self is the "bad."

Even if your IP will code the philosophies very strongly on a moral basis, you must grapple with the appeal and power of both philosophies. You must consider each at their highest aspiration.

That is the only way you'll be able to construct an IP around both.

PILLARS

Once you've done all the previous steps, it's time to create some pillars for the IP. Other stakeholders who have been too busy or uninterested for the previous steps must come into the mix at this stage.

Defining the pillars is still a creative step, where you refine everything from the previous steps into a tight phrase. And because the whole process is organic, defining the pillars may also change the underlying philosophies, the tone, and even the answer to "what kind of IP is this?" After boiling complex ideas down to a few pillars, you may find that you need to go back and adjust or rethink the previous steps.

However, Pillars are also the final step. This is where it all comes together in a tidy package.

So ... What Are Pillars Then?

Pillars are three to five statements that capture the experience of playing a game, seeing a movie, or reading a book in that IP.

Here are some sample phrases:

Victory comes at Great Cost.
Magic is Rare and Terrifying.
Friendship is True Strength.
Free Will is Worth Dying For.

There are thousands of phrases that could be used for IP pillars.

Sometimes, the pillars each stand on their own, but more often they are meant to work together to convey the breadth and depth of an IP. In these cases, they can also be a bit more mechanical and less aspirational than the examples above.

Ubisoft has said these are the IP pillars for *Assassin's Creed*:

Historical Settings: Each game immerses players in meticulously recreated historical periods.

Parkour and Free-Running: Seamless navigation through complex environments.

Assassination Gameplay: Strategic elimination of targets.

Modern-Day Narrative: A storyline connecting past and present.

And Square Enix has said these are the IP pillars of *Final Fantasy*:

Epic Storytelling: Complex narratives with deep character development.

Innovative Combat Systems: Evolving battle mechanics across titles.

Fantasy Worlds: Diverse and richly detailed universes.

Musical Excellence: Memorable and emotive soundtracks.

EXTERNAL FACING

All the work you've done on the IP helped define and refine it. But when trying to define an IP to a dev team, or to outside contractors, you can certainly talk about the overall feel of the IP and the tone. If you're greatly daring, you may even try to describe the underlying philosophies. But all of that is hard to communicate well. It can sound vague or pretentious.

Imagine hiring an art outsource company to work on your IP, and you're talking about loss of self vs elevation of ego. You would likely get some blank looks.

Pillars are clear and well-delineated. People trying to understand the IP so that they can work on it will read these and return to them again and again.

This is another reason why Pillars are the final step, and why all stakeholders must be involved. The pillars will be shared with the wider dev team, the publishing team, marketing, PR, and with outside contractors.

The Pillars are everyone's best bet for getting on-board with this new, fledgling IP.

ALL THE ELEMENTS

Once you've gone through all the steps to map out the boundaries and pillars of your IP, you've done the foundational work that will let you actually start working on it!

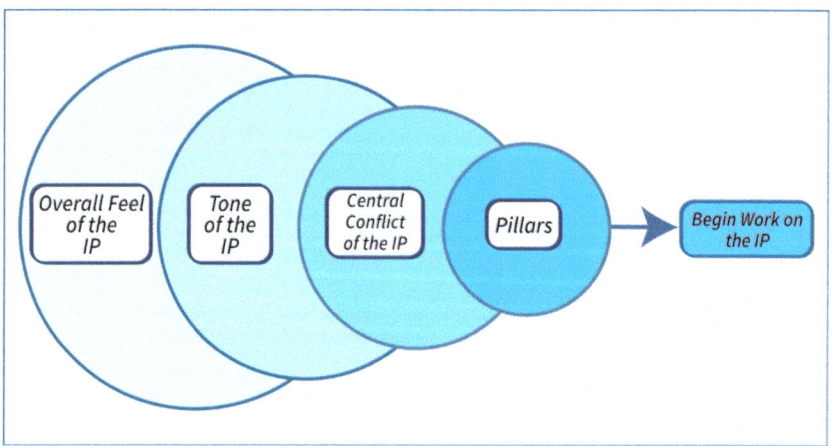

CHAPTER SUMMARY

In this chapter, we discussed the following topics:

- What kind of IP is this? What sorts of things can or cannot happen in this world? Just as important: how should this IP make people feel?
- Tone. It is a product of the material and the treatment of the material. It's important to understand both parts of the equation in order to craft a strong tone.
- A war of philosophies. At its core, an IP is fueled by two philosophies that cannot coexist and must always be at war. But neither one can ever truly be defeated by the other.
  - The two philosophies can be coded as good or evil, but they don't have to be inherently so. As the storyteller, you must find the appeal of each.
  - Both philosophies must be strong and have some appeal.
- Pillars. Take everything else you've done so far in developing the IP, and boil it down to a few key pillars. Be sure to include all the IP stakeholders in that discussion, because these pillars will be your roadmap moving forward.
- All the elements. When you combine all the steps together, you should have a clean, clear, strong IP.

19 Developing an Existing IP

- How to get started working in an existing IP
- Finding or defining the Pillars in an existing IP
- Building new content in an existing IP

World building for a game that is part of an existing IP is by far the more common experience for a narrative game developer. There are many existing IPs in the games industry, most with an array of titles.

When approaching an existing IP, the obvious first step is to get a strong grasp of that universe. Even if you're a huge fan of an IP, creating stories and expanding the IP in that universe is a different experience from consuming content in that IP.

IMMERSE YOURSELF

When you start work on a game that is set in an existing IP, immerse yourself in it. Read any transmedia associated with it, and find out what (if any) internal resources your studio has available. Speak to anyone on the team who has worked on prior titles in the IP. Look up old interviews with creative directors and others from previous titles to see what wisdom can be gleaned. Find out if anyone ever generated pillars for the IP.

Spend some time lurking in online communities to learn what the IP's fans think the IP is really about. These online communities may be filled with speculation, and so not a true reflection of what the IP is about, but learning what they believe is really going on is instructive, and it is a good idea to take their opinions very seriously.

CORE FANTASY

Ask yourself: what is the core fantasy of this IP? A game has a core fantasy, usually centered around gameplay. When you sit down to play a Sid Meier's Civilization game, your core fantasy for that play session involves exploring and expanding your empire, taming nature, going to war, and discovering technologies. It does not involve getting a really cool gun, or meeting interesting characters.

DOI: 10.1201/9781003624882-26

In the same way, an IP has a core fantasy. This can be a bit vague because it must transcend a single title. It is the essential expectation of the player when they sit down to play any game in the IP. As always, it is: *how will this experience make me feel?*

The answer to that question is the core fantasy of this IP.

We didn't bring this up in the previous chapter because when you are starting to develop an IP, you often don't yet know what the core fantasy is. It's rarely the case that you can just set the intention of having a core fantasy for your IP and then execute on that. Rather, it normally emerges over the course of the first few titles. Certain concepts, story beats, and yes, feelings keep arising until a pattern comes clear.

When you are working on an existing IP, you will be able to identify the core fantasy, and you should keep it in mind at all times.

TONE

In Chapter 18, we went into detail about tone. Everything said there applies to understanding the tone for an existing IP.

For this chapter, there is just one illustrative example to add to the discussion of how a massive IP works.

Case Study: Marvel Cinematic Universe

The Marvel Cinematic Universe (MCU) has an overall tone, feel, and aesthetic. Every movie or TV show that is a part of that universe must give off that tone. But each individual title has its own feel and tone. This is why an Iron Man film will feel very different from a Guardians of the Galaxy film, which will feel very different from the Loki television show. But they all share some quality or feeling that makes them noticeably part of the MCU.

An easy way to track this difference is to watch older Marvel efforts and notice how they feel different. The first Iron Man movie, which kicked off the MCU, has some notes that would grow to become trademarks of the MCU, but it also feels less like a part of the MCU than any of the marvel movies released 4 or 5 years later.

This is because as more MCU movies came out, they began to be able to refine the IP pillars more fully.

WHERE DOES IT FIT IN THE GRAND SCHEME?

The next step in working on an existing IP is to think holistically. You are adding new content, and how does that fit with the existing content? Not just temporally, but how all the pieces fit together. This may seem obvious, but it can be easy to let details fool your analysis.

EXAMPLE: *STARCRAFT*

There are three playable races in *StarCraft*. Imagine a scenario where you must add a fourth. The designers and artists are working on what makes them unique in terms of gameplay and visually.

But you are responsible for coming up with their lore and overall vibe.

You may start by thinking about what would be fun or exciting about a new race. But pretty soon, you'll have to start thinking how they fit in the bigger picture of the other races.

The terrans are a plucky, rowdy race of highly individualistic types. Low on class or sophistication, they can be counted on to take the initiative— and likely to screw each other over. If there were a single word for terrans, it would be: resilient.

The zerg are a slimy, sinister bunch of adaptable creatures with no free will. Each zerg is part of a greater whole, guided by an overarching intellect. Life does not matter to the zerg, their own or anyone else's. A single word for the zerg would be: endless.

The protoss are an ancient race, full of sophistication. They have a long memory and hold honor as among the most important attributes. They swear powerful oaths and live by them. Most protoss have a shared consciousness called the Khala, which allows them to keep their individuality, but still be a part of the greater whole. A single word for the protoss would be: powerful.

When you step back and regard the races from that perspective, you see why each is distinct and how a fourth race must find its own place in the lineup, distinct in every way from the other three.

If you don't think holistically about this in short order, you'll come up with an idea that you love, but muddies the water in the *StarCraft* universe.

If you think systemically in terms of the IP, you can fit new pieces into the mosaic in a way that adds to the canon and improves the overall picture.

FIND OR DEFINE PILLARS

From the previous chapter, you know the importance of pillars. Often a dev team that's worked on an IP for a few releases doesn't talk about the pillars, nor have them available. In a few cases, they may not have pillars at all and just got lucky.

When you join the team, you should try to find the original pillars, or pull the stakeholders together to define pillars, working from what has already been released. Some on the team may grumble at this, but once you have IP pillars in place, you'll start to hear people quoting them in meetings, to reinforce certain ideas.

SIDEBAR: NEW INFORMATION VS RETCON

New information vs retcon. Fans of an IP sometimes refer to "retconning" or retro-continuity. This refers to the situation where narrative developers decide to tell a story or make a change that directly contradicts something that has gone before.

Fans get understandably upset by retcons. It devalues the emotional experience they had from prior moments. Continuity is a difficult beast: an inconsequential choice made by a story team a decade earlier can become binding in very restrictive ways as an IP ages. But talented storytellers can usually find ways to tell their story without changing what has come before.

However, they often do this by adding new information to the backstory. If the evil overlord can only be killed by a blade forged in the fires of hell, players may assume that the special blade they acquired in game one was the only such blade. But there could certainly be multiple blades forged in the fires of hell. Or there could be a quest in game 3 to actually go forge a new blade in the fire of hell.

Players often perceive new information as retcons, even though they are not. To be fair, there are cheap, shallow ways to add new information that can feel like a retcon. For example, if the player witnessed the Emperor get assassinated in game one, but in game 2 the emperor turns up alive and well, and it is revealed that it was actually the emperor's body double who was assassinated, that will feel like a cheap way to reverse an earlier decision.

The key to knowing how and when to use new information to change the player's understanding of past events is to ask if it adds to the player's understanding of what happened, or denies it?

In the case of the sword, it presented a limitation the player labored under in game 1, but the story never promised that the sword in question was the only one—it merely stated that this was the only sword available to the player at this time. Learning that there is another sword out there, or that the player can make a new sword, is simply new information. It should not invalidate the player's previous experiences, unless it is handled badly.

In the case of the body double, the player had a strong emotional reaction to the emperor being assassinated, and it seemed to send the story in a new direction, and because the storytellers seemed to say "this happened" it had the voice of authority. To later say "Just kidding!" does indeed deny the player's experience.

It is important to honor the player's previous experience. A new wrinkle in the retcon discussion is the more recent advent of canon and non-canon categorization, but that will be discussed elsewhere.

DON'T MAKE THE IP LIMITING

One of the hardest parts of working on an existing IP is the competing priorities of moving an IP forward and protecting what is vital to the IP.

An IP needs to keep moving. If it's particularly old, it must modernize, although you should be careful not to add anything that is too "of the moment," as it will age rapidly. But sensibilities change over time, and the IP will seem out of date unless you can modernize it.

It also needs to add new, accessible content. New characters, new factions, new locations. These not only keep the IP fresh, but they also give new players a chance to access the IP. If there's a new region or faction in the game, the new player can experience it for the first time along with the rest of the community.

Otherwise, if everything in the IP is solely descended from something else in the IP, a player trying to get into it may feel like they have to go back in time and do a lot of homework, read wiki pages, and ask questions of hostile redditors. They're not going to do any of that. If your IP is inaccessible, they'll move on and find a different one.

At any given point, your IP should have some kind of access point that new players can use to get into the IP, i.e., somewhere to start that will grab them, and get them interested enough to go on the ride.

At the same time, there is a natural resistance to change. Existing fans of the IP will be upset if you seem to be ignoring existing elements of the IP that they love. They will often complain that the devs "don't even like or know the IP!". And the Korbins on the team will definitely let you know that you are not honoring the IP enough.

Even if they are being dramatic, they are not wrong. You can't just do what you want and expect fans of the IP to go along with it. The IP must make them feel the core fantasy of the IP.

Case Study: Liara, *Mass Effect*

In *Mass Effect*, Liara was presented as an awkward, naive scientist, fairly nerdy, but also cute. In *Mass Effect 2,* when we first meet her, she is threatening someone on a call. She seems to be a fixer or information broker now, rather than a scientist.

Many fans were understandably upset. It was too far, and seemed to ignore everything that made Liara who she was in the first game. The dev team had definitely not ignored that. Instead, they'd plotted out how she went from point A to point B, and presented her at point B, with the intent of filling in the details later. But if you are changing something in a major way in the IP, you should probably avoid that kind of in medias res approach. You've got to walk players the first few steps down the path, with foreshadowing and setups, so when they see the end result, they understand how it happened.

COMPETING PRIORITIES

Those are your competing priorities: move the IP along and potentially alienate the existing fans, or let it become static and inward looking, so that it becomes inaccessible to new players.

Defined in that way, either path leads to doom.

This is why you had to do all that work of defining the overall feel, tone, core philosophies, and pillars of your IP. With all those at hand, you have guideposts to brainstorm, discuss, debate, and implement new IP concepts.

If a new concept matches all those tools, then it's safe and will likely add some great excitement to the IP.

HATERS

Some IPs (but not all) have communities that are very closed off to new ideas. They feel threatened that the devs are trying to make it more accessible to others, which is true. But they also fear that this will somehow make it less "theirs," or somehow take something away from them, which is not true.

It can be overwhelming to see the cascade of negative reactions. If you have a good community team, they should shield you from this. Just be aware that, as we mentioned earlier in this book, 300 people complaining on a subreddit is not a statistically relevant sampling, so don't feel defeated. (Again, because 300 self-selected opinions are not a valid sample.) It bears repeating from earlier as well though: people on the subreddit are superfans, and you shouldn't ignore what they're saying. But you should try to analyze it absent any vitriol they may have added.

You should also be aware that the negative feelings will pass in time. The stronger the reaction, the more the individual loves the game. And after their initial reaction to change, most community members settle in and experience the change, and come to value it. It's true, there may be a few who feel so alienated that they leave, but most fans of the IP really want it to be good, so you have to be patient while they adjust to the change.

CHAPTER SUMMARY

In this chapter, we discussed the following topics:

- Immerse yourself. Become a subject matter expert on this IP.
- Core Fantasy. Understand and define the core fantasy of this IP. How will this experience make me feel?
- Tone. Understand the tone of this IP, using the tools and insight from the tone discussion in the previous chapter.
- Think holistically. Everything you add to an existing IP affects everything else that is already a part of it.

- Find or define pillars. Shockingly, some existing IPs do not have pillars, or the original pillars were lost. For you to do effective work on the IP, you must understand the pillars.
- Don't make the IP limiting. Developing an existing IP often means balancing the priorities of adding new flavors and concepts to the IP against protecting the ingredients that make the IP what it is. All the steps you took in this and the previous chapter should give you the tools to navigate this tricky path.

Section 7

Game Narrative Professional

The final section is about being a game narrative professional. Perhaps the most unique part of being a storyteller in games is that you work as part of a team, whether you are Indie or AAA. That changes how you tell stories. This section covers the collaborative nature of a game narrative person. It also touches on a subject aimed more at beginners and students: being a professional in a creative field.

DOI: 10.1201/9781003624882-27

20 Being a Professional

IN THIS CHAPTER

- Pinpointing your strengths and weaknesses
- Being a good collaborator
- How to give and receive feedback

We've seen lots of promising young developers make dumb mistakes because they simply didn't know how to operate in a creative environment. It's not usually fatal to their career, but it can certainly set them back by some time, and absolutely lead to a few burnt bridges.

There is no natural structure to this topic. The chapter is more of a collection of vaguely related topics. Rest assured that each is important, and the common thread is: you need to know this as a creative professional.

KNOW THYSELF

A professional knows their personal strengths and weaknesses. Learning these requires diligence and reflection, but it is vital for your long-term success. You can lean on your strengths to earn trust and get a few wins on the project, but more importantly, once you identify areas where you are weaker, you can start focusing on those.

FEAR OF LOOKING BAD

Few people enjoy failing, and fewer still enjoy doing it in front of their colleagues. Who wants to work long hours on something that will cause your teammates to scratch their heads and argue with each other about why it doesn't work?

You can become especially susceptible to this feeling a year or two into your career. After all, now you're a professional, and you've passed a certain threshold. You're not allowed to be bad at anything or to fail now. You're not even allowed to be mediocre.

On a big enough team, it becomes easy to hide weakness. You can angle to get assigned tasks you know you'll do well at, and avoid those at which you suck. Are you good at writing bombastic types, but bad at emotionally subtle characters? If you can fill your calendar up with bombastic archetypes, you'll "never have time" for emotionally subtle work.

DOI: 10.1201/9781003624882-28

Your boss and the team can be enablers. They will want you to focus on the things at which you excel. You're delivering high-quality work, and they want more of that. But this process will turn you into an unbalanced professional. When this project is done and you go on to another team, your shortcomings will quickly become apparent.

Really, a senior narrative designer who sucks at X or Y? Did we make a mistake hiring them?

The Trap

Fear of looking bad will keep you bad. You must constantly lean into the things you do poorly. It is true, your job is not school: they're not paying you to create student-level work because you want to develop yourself. So you'll need to ensure that you are still delivering good work.

If you look around your team, you will very likely see professionals with 10 or 20 years of experience who have weak spots that they are obviously hiding, using a crutch similar to the one we described. Know that such professionals live every day with fear. They stand at the foot of a mountain they believe they cannot climb, and so they must do everything in their power to avoid that mountain. They're in too deep, too scared to start at square one in some part of their craft. Terrified that others will see their weakness.

In truth it's never too late. If the previous paragraph described you, there is nothing besides fear that can prevent you from improving in those areas in which you are weakest. You can start focusing on your weaknesses tomorrow. Unless tomorrow is the weekend, then give yourself until Monday.

Be Fearless

Embrace the things you cannot do well, charge them head-on, and never let your ego make you weak. In this way, you will become a well-rounded professional, incredibly strong in some areas, merely competent in others, but weak in none. That is the gold standard.

A professional who can announce "I suck at this kind of thing. Let me take a shot at it!" actually sounds stronger and more confident than one who hides their weakness.

TALK TO EVERYBODY

Imagine a character introduction. The player sees the character and immediately gets a sense of them from their appearance. Then they start walking toward the player, and their walk tells the player about them. At this point, the player will surely notice the interesting props the character has: a whip, or a harp, or a six-shooter. Then the character starts speaking, and two or three words into the line, the player gets a sense of the character's voice.

This means that before the player hears one full line you've written, they'll have already formed a strong impression of the character from the visual design, the animation, the props, and the voice over.

The main tool writers use to convey character and story is dialogue, yet it's one of the last game elements to hit the player.

The truth is, dialogue is not the main tool for a game writer. It's a last resort. Your main tool is communication. By enlisting the concept artist, the animator, the prop designer, and the casting director to your vision of the character, you've already conveyed everything you need.

SIDEBAR: EQUIVALENT EXPERIENCE

You may be coming to games with creative experience in another medium. Perhaps you are an accomplished fantasy author or talented screenwriter. Many of the concepts we discuss here are already well known to you.

Great! However, you should be aware that you will face different challenges. We have both worked with a number of professionals who transferred from other media and were simply terrible. They may have been talented in their field, but they arrived in games with a defensive or arrogant attitude and an unwillingness to learn.

If you've worked hard in another field, it can be unpleasant and humbling to make a change that sees you being treated like a wet-behind-the-ears kid. Brian went through this very process switching from film, where he'd directed a TV show, to games, where he was essentially starting from scratch again.

The key thing to remember is that you really are ignorant of many things you need to know. We don't say this to diminish you, but to drive home the attitude you need: intellectual curiosity, humility, and a desire to learn.

There is so much about games that is different from your prior experience. This is true in the creative arena, the technical arena, and even in the procedural arena. Game production can look a lot like film or TV production, but it is fundamentally different. You've got a lot to learn, and you'll only do that by keeping your eyes and ears open.

Are we saying that your prior experience is irrelevant? Absolutely not. First of all, it likely got you the job you have now. More importantly, once you've learned the key things you need to master, you'll progress much faster than the recent college grad sitting next to you. All the struggle and learning you did in your previous industry is still in that kid's future. That becomes a hugely important part of your skill, achievement, and progression … as soon as you learn the game-specific lessons.

So be humble, avoid insecurity or entitlement, and start learning what makes games different!

Talk to everybody. Gain trust with everybody. Make sure everybody knows what the narrative goal is. Most writers are more comfortable at a keyboard, but this is a critical part of the job.

RECEIVING FEEDBACK

Games are a collaborative medium, and giving and receiving feedback is one of the most frequent and important parts of the job. Early in your career, you'll spend more time receiving feedback than giving it, so let's start there.

We all want to believe people love everything we do. Of course, that's not true, and confronting criticism can be tough. To make matters worse, many professionals in the game industry aren't great at giving feedback. This can tempt you to dismiss badly delivered feedback or misunderstand it entirely. But feedback is critical. Listening to criticism is the best way to improve, and taking it well is a great way to advance in your job.

If someone says:

I played your level. It sucks, like it reminds me of my friend Nord, and he sucks too. Like one time he put his shoes on the wrong foot and stole my lunch. So ... that's your level.

It will be easy to think:

This person has some problems, and there was nothing useful in that mess.

On paper, you're correct. But if someone is expressing, however badly, that they had a problem with the narrative of your level, you need to take that feedback seriously.

Note that as a writer, you will often receive feedback from people who are vastly more senior to you on the org chart, and are very bad at giving feedback. You're going to have to learn how to deal with this problem, as it never goes away.

CONCEPT VS EXECUTION

When receiving feedback, the first step is to understand what's being critiqued: concept or execution? Every piece of work—whether a sweeping game pitch or a single line of dialogue—contains both.

The concept of a line of dialogue is its purpose: what the character is revealing about themselves, their thoughts, or the story. What are you, the writer, hoping to achieve with this line? Where is it taking the conversation?

The execution is how it's written: the voice, rhythm, timing, and interplay with other dialogue.

Often, feedback will be vague, like "I don't like this line." "I thought what he said was dumb." Does that mean the idea behind it doesn't work? Or just the phrasing? Without clarity, improving the line is a shot in the dark.

If you and the person critiquing your work differ on the character's priorities, the issue is conceptual and will create persistent problems until you resolve it. But if the disagreement is purely about execution, the fix may be straightforward.

Misdiagnosing these issues can lead to unnecessary rewrites or even derail a character. You might make three or four changes to a line, altering the concept each time, when in fact your teammates just didn't like a particular word choice. Now the intent of the line and the flow of the dialogue have been deeply altered, for no good reason.

THE FIRST QUESTION

When receiving feedback, ask "What are you trying to fix?" Often your teammates haven't really thought through why they're offering feedback. Their thinking has gone as far as "I don't like this." Try to engage with them and get to specifics.

If you know what they are trying to fix, you'll already have an idea of whether or not they're talking about concept or execution. But if you are having trouble boiling their feedback down to fixing a specific problem, the second question to ask is more blunt: "Are you concerned about the concept? Or the execution?"

Asking this can be a good way to focus their feedback. However, many Critiquers will say "both." If that happens, start with concept. Aligning on the concept first ensures discussions of execution don't go in circles.

THE DANGER OF ASKING QUESTIONS

Some Critiquers perceive too many questions from you as a sign of resistance or protectiveness. If the Critiquer becomes impatient when you ask questions, acknowledge this up front: "I'm asking these questions to understand your feedback better—not to resist it."

As you build trust and the rest of the team gets used to the pattern of you asking questions, this problem will recede.

FEEDBACK AND TRUST

Feedback is relational and built on trust. The person receiving feedback must trust the Critiquer's intentions: that they're trying to make the work better, not just exert control or boost their ego. If you don't trust someone's judgment, they'll sense it, and the working relationship will erode.

Set parameters early, especially the right to ask clarifying questions. This prevents miscommunication and ensures the feedback process is collaborative. For example, you might say, "I'm going to ask some questions to make sure I fully understand your feedback." This clears the air and avoids tension. If that doesn't clear the air, then you definitely have a trust problem in the relationship, which will require time and repeated engagement to build.

ANOTHER SOURCE OF FEEDBACK

Another common origin point for feedback is that someone on the team has a preconceived vision for the story, character, or scene. They think it should just go another way, and their feedback is essentially "You didn't do it like I saw it in my head."

If you receive this kind of feedback from a peer, and you like their suggested direction, great. If you don't like it, you can try explaining to them that you appreciate their direction, but in the end, someone has to make the creative call, and in this instance it is you.

If the person giving this kind of feedback is your lead or someone else on the upper end of the team's org chart, then you're in a more difficult situation.

You can try negotiating with them, engaging in a discussion about why they like this direction so much. But as always, there are many hills and only one of you, so you must choose which hill to die on, and you should consider just taking the feedback and moving on.

EMBRACING FEEDBACK WITHOUT OVERDOING IT

Some juniors overcompensate on the feedback, rewriting entire scenes when only minor adjustments were requested. This wastes time and effort, and the rewrite often loses some element that everyone liked. Unless explicitly told to do a page-one rewrite, stick to the notes provided.

We give feedback in passes, going from broad to specific. The first round of notes on a piece of work may comprise three or four big notes that can change the direction of the scene or will require revisions to most of the lines. There's no point in getting specific at this stage. Each subsequent round will have more notes and more specific notes. By the time we are giving many nitpicky notes, it's a sign that the work is near completion.

If your lead or director has a similar pattern, it's better to address their specific notes rather than revise the whole thing.

The exception to this is that occasionally feedback can spark an exciting new idea that addresses the note and improves the writing as a whole. When this happens, consider still addressing the specific feedback, and then create a second version with the shiny new idea.

MANDATORY CHANGES VS SUGGESTIONS

Feedback often includes both mandatory changes and optional suggestions. For example, your lead might say, "This scene is boring and must be fixed. Here's one way to do it."

Mandatory feedback: The boringness of the scene must be fixed.

Suggestion: Here is a good way to do it.

If you bring the scene back to your lead and you've completely ignored their proposed solution, but the scene is no longer boring, the lead should be happy. If they are not, it's a communication issue. When they said "Here's one way to do it," what they must have meant was "Do it this way." That's good information to have, and probably a good discussion topic to have with your lead, in order to clarify moving forward.

As leads and directors, we often provide a suggestion as a way to give our individual contributors an idea of what we are looking for. It's meant to be helpful, a time-saver, and a way for the team members to understand our tastes.

If you like the idea, feel free to use it. Your lead will likely be happy. If you think the idea addresses the lead's concern but loses something you care about, then you must try to come up with a new fix that still addresses the concern.

EXAMPLE

On one project, a young video editor came back after working on a revision, having completely ignored a note from one of us. The young editor said the suggested line was too long to fit in the space allotted, since the video was very tightly edited.

We had to have a conversation similar to the points above:

You don't have to take the suggestion, and saying that the suggestion doesn't fit with the rhythm and pacing of the video is a very strong point. But that does not mean you can say "so I will do nothing." What it means is that you must find a solution that addresses the underlying note, while keeping the rhythm you have established.

Fortunately, when the feedback was laid out clearly and simply like that, the editor was able to quickly put in a great fix.

Never ignore mandatory feedback. If you disagree with the concept of the mandatory feedback, discuss it with the Critiquer rather than bypassing the note.

SAY YES TO EARN YOUR NO

A tricky part of being a writer is knowing when to push back on feedback and when to accept it. Early in your career, it's often best to accept most feedback from an experienced lead. Ask questions, learn, and see where their guidance takes you.

As you gain experience, you'll encounter moments where you genuinely believe feedback is wrong or harmful. The key is to choose your battles. You earn the right to say no by consistently saying yes. If you've embraced feedback three times this week and then pushed back once, your lead is more likely to respect your stance because they know you're not being defensive or contrary.

Conversely, if you push back on everything, you'll gain a reputation for being difficult. People will stop taking your concerns seriously. It becomes the boy-who-cried-wolf scenario. When it really matters, you will not have the trust of the team.

On the third hand, if you never push back, you risk will be perceived as a pushover or someone without strong opinions. This is probably the most irrational part of the feedback loop. If you've simply said yes month after month, people mentally put you in a category of worker-bee. When you finally push back on something important, rather than being open, some people will be furious: *how dare you?*

There is a balance out there, and you must find it. But as a starting point: say yes to feedback whenever you can.

In fact, we often hear feedback from colleagues that we refer to as "Six of one, half dozen of another." That is to say, feedback that does not materially improve the game. But it also does not really harm the game. It's just a different idea that this colleague came up with and is very proud of. In those situations, we always accept the feedback and implement it. It's a continual demonstration of open-mindedness and collaboration. The key ingredient there is: it does not harm the game. If you think a new idea harms the game, then you must not put it in for the sake of appearing collaborative. Of course, if your lead demands you put it in, then put it in. We're not trying to get you fired.

IT'S A NUMBERS GAME

If you are getting lots of notes about a particular element, say a beat or a character interaction, that is a sign that something is not working in that element. That seems obvious, but it can sometimes be easy to miss because when you have a lot of feedback on one thing, it will often be contradictory.

You may get the following notes on one dialogue exchange:

It was too intense for the moment.
It was boring.
I didn't think it was funny. Isn't it supposed to be funny?
It was hilarious, but I think that's the wrong vibe.
It was totally unbelievable that someone would say that.
Super predictable that she'd say that.

Given that range and incoherence of notes, it can be easy to dismiss each individually. Surely if there was a huge problem there, everyone would be giving the same note? You can't assume that at all. Remember, most people critiquing your narrative element are not narrative professionals.

So you can ignore their diagnosis about what is wrong, but if they're all aggroing the same element, there is definitely a problem there. Or, per the next section, somewhere near there.

As a corollary of the above, you should know that when people tell you there is a problem, they are usually correct. But when they tell you the nature of the problem, they are often wrong. Hear them out, but think broadly about the note.

THE PROBLEM MAY BE ELSEWHERE

In narrative feedback, people will always tell you exactly where the problem is, but are often wrong. We cover this in more detail later in a section called "Getting Blocked." But it's worth mentioning here that people are actually telling you where they noticed the problem, not where the problem actually is. Sometimes it's exactly where it appears to be, but many times the place where people notice it is when the symptoms of the problem emerge, but the roots of it lie earlier in the story.

Perhaps there was a faulty setup? Or a badly defined character arc? Now, later in the story, people are confused, or don't buy it.

GIVING FEEDBACK

As you advance in your career, you'll find yourself giving feedback more often. Even junior writers may critique peers in a healthy writer's room. The dynamics depend on experience levels, but the principles remain the same.

You'll see some repetition in this section; everything that we said about receiving feedback applies to giving it as well.

ORDER YOUR THOUGHTS

In the section on receiving feedback, we pointed out that many professionals are bad at giving feedback, because they haven't taken the time to establish what they are trying to solve, or even why they don't like something. Don't be that professional.

Try to answer these questions before you deliver feedback to someone:

1. What am I trying to fix?
2. Is it concept or execution?
3. Is it possible that there is nothing wrong here, and I just have a different take that I like better?
   a. If the answer to this is "yes," that is totally okay! Maybe the person you're critiquing will like your idea better. Just be clear with them that this is an alternate idea, not an attempt to resolve a problem.
4. What kind of changes are necessary to address the problem?
5. Will fixing this problem have a ripple effect elsewhere, and if so, do I have any insights on how to handle that?

a. Example: This NPC party member is immune to poison and having them in the party means the entire anti-poison branch of the healing talent tree is pointless. We could take away the NPC's immunity, but that will have a broad impact on system and combat design throughout the game.

6. Any proposed solutions to address the feedback?
7. If you have authority over the work or person being critiqued, consider which parts of your feedback are optional? Which are mandatory?

If you have good answers to these questions, it's time to go give your feedback!

Proposed Solutions

On some teams, you're not allowed to bring up problems unless you have a proposed solution. Other teams think it's better to raise problems even when you don't have an immediate solution at hand.

We are in the latter group, but it's good to find out what the culture on your team is!

The Shit Sandwich

When giving feedback, especially to juniors, balance critique with encouragement. Start by highlighting things that worked. Then get to the meat of your critique: what does not work and why. At that point, close with a positive note, something to the effect that you think this piece could be really great with some iteration.

Some people would characterize this as "beating around the bush," but unless you know the temperament and experience of the person you are critiquing, the shit sandwich is the most effective way to make sure your feedback is heard. And getting your feedback heard is the whole ballgame.

Avoid harsh language or jokes that could be misinterpreted. Instead of saying, "This sucks," say, "This could be stronger." Be honest but constructive.

You know you're in a great place with a team or colleague when you can just tell it straight. But you rarely start there.

Unsolicited Feedback

Do not, and we cannot stress this enough; give unsolicited feedback. If you are on good terms with a teammate, you can say something to them like this: *I played your level, and I had some thoughts. Just my opinion—did you want to hear it? Totally fine if not.*

Only at the most advanced stages of trust, where you've gone skydiving or defused a bomb together, will you be at the point where you can casually give unsolicited feedback to a peer.

Don't approach the Art Director on your third day with your revolutionary art ideas.

WHAT ARE YOU BEING ASKED TO CRITIQUE?

When you are asked to give feedback, try to clarify where the subject matter is in its development life cycle, and what kind of critique the creator is looking for.

As a junior or mid-level narrative developer, you will often be invited to give feedback as a courtesy. People will ask for your thoughts on something when it is in the right stage for team-wide feedback. This means it is well realized enough that people's feedback can be targeted, but that it is almost too late to make big changes.

At that stage, the creator has likely revised the work several times to the specifications of their lead or director. The overall shape of the thing is pretty well established.

Don't misunderstand: this courtesy feedback is not a meaningless step. Your fresh eye may turn up a big problem everyone else has overlooked. Or your particular tastes in dialogue may lead you to suggest a witty line that no one else would have thought of.

Giving feedback well is a great chance to impress your colleagues and boss with your insight and professionalism. Just make sure you define the scope and scale of feedback they are seeking.

Case Study: *Diablo III: Reaper of Souls*

Late in the development of *Reaper of Souls*, Brian gathered a group of QA analysts from another team who weren't familiar with the project, and had them do an all-day playtest, under observation. Many valuable lessons were learned.

But late in the day, one of the analysts asked:

So wait, what happens if Malthael gets the Black Soulstone? I know there was some dialogue about it earlier, but I forget.

This was a facepalm moment. We'd established the stakes in dialogue earlier in the game, but as we discussed in the Narrative Concepts chapter, if players don't see the consequences in the game, it's not real.

The team had to pull together a 2D cinematic very quickly, showing the consequences of Malthael controlling the Black Soulstone. That simple question by a Blizzard analyst not even working on the project saved us from an oversight.

MULTIPLE ROUNDS

If you're going to give multiple rounds of feedback, it is useful to think about the pace and type of feedback that is useful. If your first round of feedback on a conversation contains big, structural, or character notes that would mean rewriting a large portion of the conversation, it's pointless and wasteful to give feedback on a particular line that will likely be rewritten.

On the first big round of feedback, we often just give three or four macro notes, rather than weighing the IC down with dozens of notes, many of which won't matter when the big notes get addressed. As the narrative feature gets closer to being done, our notes get more specific, smaller, and more numerous.

Obviously, this approach only works if you know you will be giving multiple rounds of feedback.

COMPROMISE

Whether giving or receiving feedback, a key ingredient to the process is to understand that most of the time, nobody gets everything they want. If the discussion comes down to the binary of "Make this change, or leave it as is," it's a sign that something has gone off the rails.

The reality is that Critiquer and Critiqued often have asymmetrical goals.

Case Study: *Robo Recall*

On *Robo Recall*, Brian had structured a scene to open with a humorous moment. A peer from another department was adamant that this was a terrible idea, and kept trying to find ways to kill the moment. Normally, Brian would be accommodating, but this moment came early in the game, and was important for establishing the overall tone, so Brian resisted.

It took a lot of discussion to get to the heart of the matter: the colleague wasn't necessarily against having a humorous moment. Rather, he thought the temp joke Brian had put in as a placeholder was not funny, and in fact didn't really understand it, which made him feel stupid.

Once the asymmetry of his and Brian's viewpoints was clear, it became a simple matter to fix. Brian simply asked him to supply a temporary placeholder joke that we could come back to later. The colleague suggested something, and Brian put that in as a placeholder.

Brian got what he wanted: a humorous moment early in the game, and the colleague got what he wanted: something he found amusing. In the end, the temp joke was replaced with something else, but the key point is that through discussion they discovered that their opinions were not in direct opposition to each other. There was a way for both of them to get what they wanted, but they had to do the work to arrive at that realization.

Note that the only way to reach this ideal is to have clear and constant communication.

GETTING BLOCKED

Sometimes it feels impossible to move forward. There is a famous condition called Writer's Block, which is either a deeply psychological scourge, or a completely made-up excuse, depending on who you ask.

This section is not about Writer's Block. Here we are simply discussing those moments when there doesn't seem to be a natural way forward in the story, and nothing seems to break the logjam.

Sometimes this can manifest as avoidance, which looks a lot like procrastination; you're not sure what to do or which way to go, so you find lots of excuses to do other things. It's an old joke among writers that you can tell when they're trying to write, because their apartment is suddenly very clean.

It can also manifest in the opposite way: you work long hours, writing thousands of words, and putting index cards up all over your office, but somehow, the story doesn't move forward, and you keep throwing your work out.

There may be a wide variety of reasons for this condition, but in our experience, it usually comes about from one of two mistakes:

OVERTHINKING

Stories have lots of moving parts. And each change or new idea, or new scene, or new word seems to have a huge ripple effect, which in turn changes everything else.

Perhaps you've realized that your character really should get mad at her friends. If she doesn't, it will feel fake. But if she does, it throws the rest of the story into chaos. This is not a story about a woman who is mad at her friends. And how will the friends react? Won't that throw things even farther off the rails? But you can't not have her get mad, right? You don't want to write a fake story. But what about –

The first step, as with so many things in life, is to take a deep breath. It's going to be okay.

You're trying to solve one hundred problems at once, and the human mind simply cannot do that. It can't even do a good job of solving two problems at once.

So focus on the problem in front of you, and treat it like a logic flowchart. Should she get mad? Yes or no? If yes, then what happens next? Don't worry about

EXAMPLE: A MOMENT THAT DOESN'T FEEL RIGHT

Moira and Mustafa see each other again after years apart when they attend the funeral of their mutual best friend. Soon after, a surprise romance sparks between them. What kind of monsters find romance from their best friend's funeral?

EXAMPLE: A SOLUTION THAT FEELS CHEAP

Your characters have been locked in a cell and you need them to get out quickly. But how? If they find a tunnel dug by another prisoner, it's clearly a bad, cheap solution.

chaos further down the road, just map out what is happening now, and then what happens next.

Even more important than the flowchart, is the promise to yourself. Right now you are creating and mapping. Promise yourself that you'll come back later and edit. Conforming the story to new changes is a problem for future you. Present you simply must dive in, put one foot in front of the other, and slog through the change.

Future you will come back with a fresh eye, see what disasters you've wrought, and figure out how to fix them. While future you will be burdened by needing to clean up the mess you've created, they will be unburdened by the need to map out the changes—that was your task, and you did it.

One side benefit of this process is that oftentimes you see new and interesting opportunities for the characters or plots, based on this new and unexpected mapping.

You're Looking in the Wrong Place

Often when we are stuck, it's because a scene or moment just doesn't work. It doesn't feel right. Or the characters have a problem and require a solution that would feel cheap or fake.

In the overthinking section, the way forward was too complicated and confusing. In this section, the way forward just seems untenable. It's not complexity holding you back: there just isn't a clear, strong way to proceed. There are thousands of variations of this scenario, in all genres of story.

The trick to dealing with this problem is to realize that you've become hyperfocused on the moment where the problem appears—at the funeral or in the jail cell. But that is just the moment the problem makes its presence known. The actual problem lies earlier in the story.

You might think of it like the common cold. You wake up with the sniffles one day, but you caught the cold two days earlier when you touched that doorknob. The sniffles are just the symptom showing up.

We tend to focus on the moment the problem appears because that's human nature, and because we tend to think of our stories as operating in a single direction. The story starts, it develops, and then it ends. Even if time within the story moves in strange ways, the experience of the story unfolding is still unidirectional. That is how we experience stories.

But as the storyteller, you are perfectly capable of moving bidirectionally as you work on the story: forward and back. Fix a problem in Act II by changing something back in Act I. This may seem obvious, but it is incredibly easy to forget in the moment.

For our Funeral problem, perhaps earlier in the story we learn the soon-to-be-deceased best friend always thought Moira and Mustafa should have been together. Or perhaps it's not even that heavy-handed. Maybe the dead friend simply loved love, and wanted everyone to find happiness. Or perhaps they just had a wild sense of humor. Any of these will add context to Moira and Mustafa's budding romance.

It is important to note that whatever change you make to the dead friend, players must learn it before the funeral scene. There can be powerful drama in having people learn something new about a dead character, but in this case, it would be correctly perceived by the audience as trying to justify the relationship, whereas if they learned it earlier in the story, it's just accepted fact. In this way, you're harnessing the fact that your players can only experience the story in one direction, while you can move forward and back.

In the case of the jail cell, the possibilities are endless. We could learn earlier in the story that one of our companions is a master lock picker. Then in another scene before the jail cell moment, another companion could have suffered a setback where the hinge of their beloved locket is damaged, and now we have a subplot where they must find a silversmith to fix it. But here in the jail cell, our master lockpick can use the sliver of metal from the bent hinge to pick the lock.

This could lead to some fun interaction, where the character with the locket is outraged that the lockpick wants to use their precious locket for a nefarious purpose. This bit of flavor will take some of the heat and scrutiny off of the solution.

More importantly: the unexpected combination of two previously established elements makes the solution feel earned. If our lockpick character just had a lockpick on them and the guards didn't take it away, then it would feel cheap. Instead, things happened earlier in the story that seemed unrelated. We learned our companion was a strong lockpick, and our other companion's locket broke. This second event feels like the setup to another quest or plot, and very well could be. Thus, the combination of the two is surprising.

The key element though is that you've set these things up earlier in the story, so that when our characters need to escape, the solution is still surprising, but believable.

CHAPTER SUMMARY

In this chapter, we discussed the following topics:

- Know thyself. Be aware of your own strengths and weaknesses. Lean on the strengths to earn praise and trust from the team. But lean even harder on the weaknesses to improve yourself. The most successful game professionals are those who have an all-around level of competence and a few strengths.
- Talk to everyone. Narrative is conveyed across a range of disciplines. The dialogue you write is among the least impactful. If you enlist the help of art, animation, design, and audio, you've elevated the narrative.
- Receiving feedback. Learn the ins and outs of getting feedback. Understand the distinction between concept and execution, and the difference between mandatory notes and suggestions. Say yes whenever you can, and pay attention to what part of the story draws the most feedback. Remember that the problem may lie earlier in the story than the scene that drew the criticism.
- Giving feedback. Order your thoughts, and layer your criticism between compliments. Do not give unsolicited feedback. Define what you are being asked to critique. When you can, give your feedback in multiple rounds, each more focused than the last.
- Compromise. The person giving feedback and the person receiving it often have asymmetrical goals. This means the critique should rarely come down to: either my way or your way. There is often a compromise where both parties get something they want, but not everything.
- Getting blocked. This can be due to overthinking or from looking in the wrong place. Either way, there are strategies to unblock yourself.

21 Navigating the Creative Workplace

IN THIS CHAPTER

- How to brainstorm with others
- Keeping good work boundaries
- Building trust in the workplace

Game studios often have casual atmospheres, but they are still workplaces. Misreading casualness can lead to mistakes. Many game developers are bad at reading social cues, a problem compounded by the seemingly freewheeling, fun atmosphere of most game teams.

HALLWAY CONVERSATIONS

Don't interrupt hallway conversations without knowing their context—they could be serious discussions.

We have seen a junior developer walking down a hallway, and encounter the creative director and the production director having a quiet conversation. Having interacted with both of them in the past, and observing that they're both cool, chill people, the junior smiles and joins their circle.

This is a mistake. They may be discussing something important. You may ask why they would have such a conversation in a hallway. There are many reasons. They may have ducked out of a meeting to have an especially discrete exchange. They may both be incredibly busy and just ran into each other. Regardless of why, they are relying upon the common sense of their team members. Even if they're in public, it's not a public conversation. Imagine a bubble of privacy around them.

When you first join a team, observe how the more experienced veterans act, to try and learn the unspoken rules. Even then, know that the rules are slightly different for them than for you. The senior texture artist who has shipped four games with the creative director has a more intimate relationship than you do.

The key point here is to understand that no matter how a team looks on the surface, there are unspoken rules, and when you're new, you don't know them. There is no handbook that will explain them to you. So you must keep your eyes open. Pay attention, learn, and most of all, know that there is something you don't know.

If you're unsure about anything, ask your lead or a senior team member, it is better to clarify than to risk causing issues.

DOI: 10.1201/9781003624882-29

BRAINSTORMING WITH THE TEAM

Brainstorming ideas is a crazy, dynamic process. When you participate in, or lead, brainstorming with other developers who are not primarily narrative professionals, there are specific problems you may run into.

We don't always have easy solutions for these problems, but at least it is useful to identify them.

ORIGIN-POINT BIAS

People often think that the work of fiction where they encountered an idea is the first time that idea has ever come into existence.

EXAMPLE: POWERED ARMOR

Many gamers first encountered the idea of powered armor for space soldiers in the *Warhammer 40k* universe. Whenever they see a similar concept elsewhere, they are sure it's been stolen from *Warhammer.* Yet the concept clearly appears in Robert Heinlein's novel *Starship Troopers* released in 1959. The idea likely predates that work as well.

It is important to understand this bias because the person declaring an idea to be a "rip-off" of some work they love is reacting emotionally and is unable to see that the idea is ubiquitous enough to be a convention, or at least a common ingredient, rather than a rip-off. If it's a common ingredient, it's fine to use in your particular recipe, flavored as it is by other unique ingredients, or a unique mix of them. If it's a rip-off, it needs to be avoided entirely.

Perhaps if you identify this bias in someone's feedback, you can try to educate them on the many times this concept was used before the particular work where they encountered it. Just please don't educate them with the phrase "Well, actually…"

Please note that Origin-Point Bias is not a defined, accepted cognitive bias; it is a term we've invented here to define a bias we see in creative endeavors.

CREATOR VS CONSUMER

Many developers you work with in games are experts in their own discipline, such as game design, art, or programming. But in many cases, they have little experience being on the creation-side of narrative, world building, and characters. This does not invalidate their opinions on these subjects, but it means they can easily fall prey to another area of subjective bias.

When you experience a powerful moment in a story, whether game, film, book, or other, there are a host of factors that influence how you experience that.

The music, performance, emotional stakes, momentum, context, or any other of a hundred factors feeds into the moment. Critically, as a consumer, you are absorbing what happens, and will only analyze or question if the moment is so badly done that it breaks through all those other factors.

When you are on the creator-side of that equation, you experience the moment very differently. You just read a summary in text, or perhaps someone mentioned it in a meeting. And because you are building something, you tend to analyze it much more rigorously than you would something you were consuming.

The result is that quite often a non-narrative team member will declare something impossible because "no rational character would do something so self-destructive!" or "This has no emotional resonance!" They will react this way to a moment that, if they saw it in a movie, they would easily accept.

Narrative people who create worlds, narratives, and characters for a living are presumably (but not absolutely) immune to this bias. However, if you work with a wider game team, you will certainly run into this bias, and perhaps being aware of it will give you some tools to try to persuade your teammates away from it.

Other Factors

Another factor is conflict aversion. Some people hate to see characters make destructive choices or create needless conflict—even though that is the heart of most storytelling, they will sometimes argue against the most acute such moments. There are many other factors as well that lead someone's subjective judgment to differ from your own, too many to list here.

It is useful to be aware of why people come to different conclusions. We have witnessed many creative disagreements where the participants struggle to convince each other, fumbling through lines of attack with vague, almost meaningless terms like "cool," "original," and "exciting." Cool, original and exciting to whom? What do those words even mean?

When a debate stumbles into areas that are purely subjective, there are only two ways to anchor the discussion, and they both must happen:

First, establish objective standards. You can't establish objective standards about what makes something funny. But you can establish whether or not the goal is to be funny at this moment.

Second, figure out who makes the final call for subjective elements. This is one reason that most films are a benevolent dictatorship rather than consensus-based. Some things just require a single sensibility to declare it funny, or scary, or thought-provoking, even if others disagree. Games are a more consensus-based medium, but in those key moments, there will still have to be a decision-maker. Hopefully, that individual hears everyone's feedback and takes it into account, but in the end, they must decide. Then the matter must be put to bed, and everyone moves on.

It can be helpful to have a RACI chart for some features that are subjective. This chart lists the stakeholders for a particular feature, breaking them down by:

- Responsible
- Accountable
- Consulted
- Informed.

Whoever is listed as responsible must make the final decision. Those who are accountable must make it happen. Those who are consulted will give advice, and it should be taken seriously. Those who are informed can also offer feedback, but they must understand from the outset that their place on the RACI chart means that their ideas will only get as much attention as they deserve.

KEEP TO THE STANDARDS OF YOUR TEAM

Every team has their own culture around attendance, output, and the appearance of work. Our approach has always been to treat people like adults. They know what they must produce, and how much time they have to produce it. If they want to come in late, leave early, or spend most of the day watching Twitch, who cares, so long as they are producing quality work at the right pace, and showing up to their meetings prepared? We don't confuse the appearance of working with actually working.

We've both worked at organizations where the appearance of working was paramount. We've seen developers work from 10 in the morning to 8 at night several nights a week, yet produce less work than a focused developer who comes in at 9:30 and leaves at 5.

Other studios are stricter about matters such as arrival and departure time, which can be annoying, but at least makes it easy to understand the rules. Because there are always rules, spoken or not.

In the more relaxed atmosphere we described, it falls to you to be aware of the rules. You have a right to expect your employer to treat you like an adult. But remember, that also obligates you to act like an adult. If you are producing at a lower rate than you should, or show up to meetings unprepared, you have demonstrated that you are unworthy of the trust your lead placed in you. No matter how casual the atmosphere, it will be noticed.

Some studios have alcohol readily available everywhere. This has declined in recent years, but it is still something to be aware of. Just because the break room has beer in the fridge, and an old veteran has a half full bottle of Jack Daniels at their desk, you still must demonstrate common sense about when, where, and how much to drink.

As always, pay attention to how others on the team behave and take your cues from them.

Note: If your studio has a culture of drinking onsite during the workday, and this for whatever reason makes you feel unsafe, you have every right to discuss this with Human Resources.

CRUNCH

Crunch, or prolonged overtime near the end of development, used to be the norm in game development. In recent years, it has become less common, as studios have started to realize several things:

1. It is less productive. When people work long hours for extended periods, the amount of work they produce per hour starts to drop. They're tired and they lose focus. They know they'll be here until 10 tonight, so if it's 4:30, why not watch another 30 minutes of TikTok videos?
2. It has bad long-term effects on a team. After a period of crunch, much of the team gets sick. We don't know the medical reasons behind this phenomenon, but "crunch flu" is real. In the end, it costs the studio more in lost productivity than was ever gained by the crunch.
3. Even if the studio does not care about your mental and physical well-being, extended crunch periods end up being a public relations hit. Word gets out in the industry, and talent won't join the studio. Sometimes it even reaches the player community.

Hopefully, you are never asked to crunch, and if you are, you must decide on your own boundaries. Be aware that in some work cultures, refusing to crunch when asked can bring penalties like a bad review, or even dismissal disguised as a layoff. Nonetheless, whatever boundaries you need are the boundaries you should enforce.

For us, we both are open to some limited overtime, if there is a clearly defined goal and the team or project really needs it. If we are asked to crunch due to scheduling incompetence, we are far less likely to do it. Any project that regularly requires crunch to meet its basic operational goals is actually factoring crunch into the schedule, and that is unhealthy and exploitive.

Again, it's something for you to decide, if faced with the request.

If you are ever a manager who must ask someone on your team to crunch, make sure that you stay late when they do, even if you don't have any need to be there. Never ask someone to stay late and then go home yourself. It's just bad form, and you will lose a great deal of trust from that developer.

STAYING LATE ON YOUR OWN

If you're an excited junior just starting out, you may be tempted to work late quite often, because you just love the work so much. Don't do this. Even though you're young and energetic enough to proceed this way for some time, you are actually teaching yourself a very bad habit.

If you come in to work with this mindset:

I have X amount of work to do today, and Y amount of time. I am leaving at 6 o'clock, no matter what. If I mess around all day and don't accomplish what I need to, I'm screwed, because I'll be behind. I'll have to make up for it tomorrow—or even hand my work in late. So, knowing that I will leave at 6 no matter what, I'd better focus up!

You will find that before long you are accomplishing everything you need each day. It's liberating!

However, if you have this mindset:

I'll stay as late as I need to, in order to finish this work! I don't care, midnight, 1 am, whatever! I love my craft and I love this job!

You will quickly find that you've barely started your work by 6 pm. The day zips by. You watched some great videos on the internet, had a fascinating conversation with Joane in the break room or on a Zoom call, enjoyed an extended lunch … and the day got away from you. Every day will get away from you because you've released a pressure valve in your head by not having a hard out at the end of the day.

Learn the path of discipline and focus by creating a negative consequence for yourself: *If I don't get my work done by 6, I'm screwed!*

The Early Crunch of Writing

Note: In this section, we talk about crunch as if it is inevitable. It is not, but in this case "crunch" is a convenient word to mean either working long hours, or simply intense work done during normal business hours, which is still demanding both physically and mentally.

Being a writer in video games means your deadlines often come much earlier than everyone else's. It looks like this:

- Writing must be delivered so that we can start…
- Voice Over Recording, which must be delivered so we can start…
- Localization, which must be delivered so that we can start…
- Localization VO Recording, which must be delivered so that we can have…
- All VO implemented, all other disciplines must be delivered as well for the…
- Final Build.

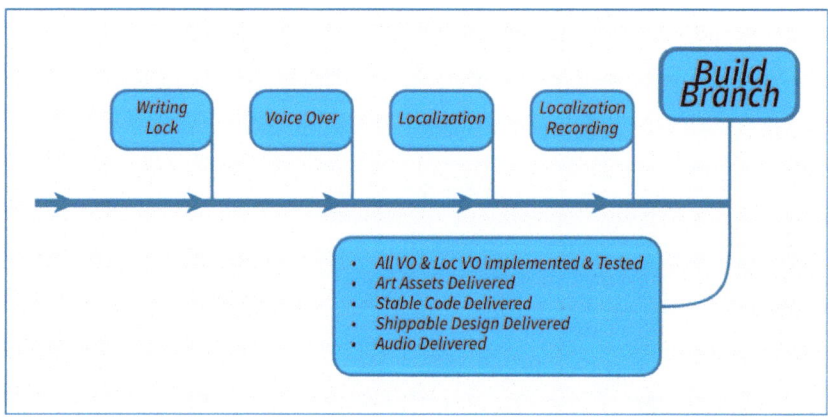

You can see how writing may need to be finished months ahead of all the other disciplines.

There are, of course, other types of writing that can continue until the end of development, such as text entries. But once dialogue has been localized and recorded in 12 languages, it's almost impossible to change without incurring massive costs. For example, rerecording a single line of dialogue in multiple languages can become prohibitively expensive.

The practical effect of this is that the writing team often crunches months, or even a year earlier than the rest of the team.

This can lead to odd dynamics. If the rest of the team begins to crunch toward the end of development, writers may leave at 6 pm, while others stay late. This can create resentment or misunderstandings. It's essential for leads and writers to communicate clearly, reminding the team that earlier in development, the writers went through their own crunch.

There's also the concept of "sympathy crunch," where writers might feel pressure to stay late simply because the rest of the team is crunching. While the sentiment is understandable, it's worth pointing out that no one volunteers to sympathy crunch alongside writers during their earlier stressful periods.

BUILDING TRUST AND PROFESSIONALISM

Building trust takes time. You don't get that level of confidence from your team or lead immediately—it must be earned. Sometimes it takes shipping a game or consistently delivering excellent work over several months. People need to see you're reliable, that your head and heart are in the right place.

Humility also plays a key role. Many young creatives start with a humble mindset, eager to learn and grow. But occasionally, someone enters the field with the belief they've "arrived" and now deserve recognition. While it's natural to feel proud that you made it into the industry, it's crucial to remember that reaching this point was just the beginning. All your achievements got you here, now you're at the starting line of the race. Go!

REPUTATION AND PRECONCEPTIONS

The games industry is a beehive of gossip and rumor. Unless you're on a one-person indie team, you'll have a reputation, one way or another.

Your reputation often precedes you. Before you meet someone, you may hear, "Oh, Janet from the UI team is great!" or "Janet is a nightmare to work with." While it's good to take note of others' experiences, it's even more important to form your own judgments. People's opinions are often colored by single experiences or personal biases.

Twice in his career, Brian has had a colleague tell him: *I heard you could be difficult to work with, but you're actually very easy going!*

It was unsettling to hear the first part of that statement, and reassuring to hear the second part. But it makes one wonder if there were others who might have been influenced by those negative preconceptions and missed the chance to build a good working relationship.

There are three key parts to this point:

- First, be aware that you have a reputation. It may be good or bad, and it may be accurate or completely false. Either way, you must be aware of it, and do what you can to make sure your reputation is both good and accurate.
- Second, think of the harm that you can do to someone by spreading false, misleading, or even just negative rumors. You should resolve never to do this. If you think someone is a nightmare to work with, and they are joining a team of people, there is no need to try and poison the team against them. If they are the nightmare you think they are, they'll make themselves known quite quickly.
- The exception to that rule is when you are asked about your opinion of someone during the hiring process. Obviously, if you think someone is toxic and you don't say anything, then that person joins the team and is toxic, and you'll be partially responsible. Be honest in those situations, but word your critique carefully so it doesn't sound personal.
- Third, resolve to make up your own mind about people. When someone tries to warn you that so-and-so is terrible, or great, or anything, thank them politely, and then forget about it. You'll be working with that person soon enough, and you can form your own impressions. Letting others prejudice you in any direction is a trap. Don't fall into it.

YOU'RE PART OF A TEAM

Narrative doesn't exist in isolation. Other developers—artists, UI designers, and level designers—contribute to the narrative through their decisions, even if it's not their primary focus.

Art: The visual design of levels, characters, and props can either support the story or undermine it.

UI: Buttons, menus, and HUD elements impact storytelling. If they're out of sync with the game's tone, they can detract from immersion.

Design: Level flow and pacing affect how players experience the story. A good-level designer is a narrative developer's key collaborator.

EXAMPLE

Part of your narrative is that the player character is a wizard cursed to carry a demonic spellbook, which lends them great power, but comes at great cost. A UI artist could make a creepy, demonic-looking spellbook for the inventory icon … or a standard spellbook. Their creative choice either enhances the narrative or undermines it.

Collaboration and communication are essential. Harnessing the power of your team elevates the narrative.

PART OF A TEAM: COMMUNICATION

A subset of being part of a team is that communication is not only necessary, but it is the most powerful tool at your disposal. If you had to choose between good communication with the team or your keyboard, you'd be a more effective narrative developer by choosing communication, and having no keyboard.

GET THE TEAM ONBOARD

Building off of the previous note, one of the most important goals of a narrative developer should be to get the rest of the team onboard with the story. Superficially, this is vital because if they don't believe in your story, they'll fight you every step of the way, and the result will be ugly, for everyone.

But there is a deeper reason as well: if they really understand what you're going for, and you've addressed their notes and incorporated some of their changes, you will have activated another part of their brain.

Instead of coming to you with ideas that run counter to what you're trying to accomplish, they'll start coming to you with ideas that plus up and enhance what you're trying to do. Even better, they'll incorporate ideas into their own work that enhance the story, ideas that you would have never thought of!

DEFENDING THE WORK

In the crunch section, we discussed how narrative is on a different schedule than the rest of the team, due to VO, localization, and other factors. This presents a unique challenge to narrative.

The other major creative disciplines working on the game, such as design, art, audio, and animation, are able to iterate much later into the process. Design in particular values flexibility, and can patch system changes to an already-released game.

Late in development, these other disciplines will encounter problems that seem important to solve. But these changes will affect the story. The same story that's already been recorded in 12 languages. From their perspective, there's a problem in the game, and they want to solve it. They have the ability to fix it. And you're there waving your arms saying they can't.

EXAMPLE: THE STRAWBERRY POTION QUEST

Your game's story establishes that the Evil Dreadlord is allergic to strawberries. Midway through the game, the player collects strawberries and distills them into a potion to make the Dreadlord vulnerable during a boss fight. The cutscene, VO, and translations for this sequence are complete.

But late in development, the art director decides strawberries don't fit the game's aesthetic. This is not an impulsive change. Earlier in development, the look for the game was still coming together. Now, many art assets are in, and the overall aesthetic is much clearer … and strawberries don't fit. He replaces them with bananas. The prop artist has already modeled bananas, and no strawberry was ever created.

Meanwhile, designers, reacting to playtest feedback, change the gameplay from collecting something to smashing something. They don't care if it's strawberries or bananas, but now you smash, not collect.

Now, the narrative is in ruins. The cinematic references strawberries. VO in 12 languages references strawberries. The quest requires gathering, not smashing. Yet bananas are the only visible fruit in the game. Art and design insist you "make it work." Perhaps bananas weaken the Dreadlord spiritually? Maybe the cinematic is discarded altogether? Both solutions harm the narrative.

SOLVING THE STRAWBERRY POTION QUEST

In this example, is there any solution that will address art and design's concerns without ruining the story? What would that look like?

You can add a quest before the boss fight where the player helps a strawberry farmer clear his field of invasive bananas. You run through the fields, smashing X numbers of bananas. As a reward, the farmer provides strawberries for the potion from his warehouse. We will see the strawberries as an icon in your inventory, but we never see them in the world—the farmer drops them into your bag via the reward screen.

From that point, everything proceeds as it did in the original plan. The cinematic and VO remain intact, and design gets its smashing mechanic. Everyone wins.

Design may not want to implement another quest before the boss fight, and art may not want to add a warehouse to the farmer's level. But you can remind them that you're helping them fix the problems they have, and this is the cost. Compromise works in several directions.

Finding Solutions

You've probably played games where the story made no sense, and you wondered if the storytellers had lost their minds. In almost every case where a game story seemed nonsensical, it was due to the forces at work in the Strawberry example.

What steps can you use to find a solution similar to the one we've listed above?

Empathy and collaboration are your best tools. Understand that your teammates want to improve the game, even if their changes create problems for you. Rather than digging in your heels, look for creative compromises.

Clearly communicate to them why their changes are harmful, and try to get everyone into a meeting where you can collectively brainstorm a solution.

Finally, remember that "because it costs money" is one of the most powerful phrases in game development. You may not have the power to shut down the art and design directors, but the executive producer does. And the EP will be very concerned about expensive changes.

You always want to be careful about seeking help from a higher power. But if the stakes are high enough, you may want to schedule a meeting with the relevant directors, and the EP. You can bring up the amount of money being thrown away if you cut out the narrative content, and the amount of money it would cost to redo it.

JOB TITLES AND ORG CHARTS

Don't get hung up on titles. It's easy to feel annoyed when someone outside your field, like an associate prop artist, offers unsolicited advice on storytelling. Often, their feedback may seem unhelpful or patronizing.

But the quality of the feedback—not the source—matters most. Even poorly delivered notes can contain valuable insights. Separate the feedback from the person delivering it and evaluate it on its merits.

Obviously, when feedback is coming down from a source much higher on the team, then the org chart does matter. But you should still try to get to a place where you can push back on feedback you disagree with. If you approach it rationally and professionally, most developers are open to a discussion.

Turnabout Is Fair Play

Just as you should remain open to feedback from others, you should feel comfortable offering your thoughts on aspects outside your expertise.

When critiquing art or design, approach it respectfully. Start with something like, "I'm not an artist, so take this with a grain of salt, but here's what stood out to me." Frame your feedback as opinion, not absolute judgment.

CHAPTER SUMMARY

In this chapter, we discussed the following topics:

- Brainstorming with the team. This is a very vibe-oriented experience, so you must pay attention to the unspoken rules in the room. Be aware that many other developers don't have a lot of experience with brainstorming and may themselves fall into certain traps that we discussed.
  - RACI charts are very helpful when dealing with subjective standards, such as humor, appeal, coolness, and other such elements.
- Keep to the standards of your team. The casual atmosphere of most game teams disguises the fact that there are many unspoken rules and

standards. Make it your business to find out what they are. Step one is: keep your eyes open and observe how others behave.

- Crunch. It is generally a bad policy, and most studios are trying to do away with it. But making games is a long, complicated process, and sometimes there are periods of intense output toward the end of the project. Learn about crunch, and define your own boundaries. Do not stay late on your own. It teaches you bad habits.
- Build trust and professionalism over time, through actions large and small.
- Be aware that you will soon have a reputation. It may be accurate, or slanderous, but it exists. You will meet people who've heard about you before they met you. Try to cultivate a good and accurate reputation, and avoid spreading unfair or untrue gossip about others.
- You're part of a team. Remember that many other people contribute to the narrative, and you need their help to do a good job. Communication is your strongest tool.
- Defending the work. Narrative locks earlier than other features. This means you will enter a strange period near the end of development where you may have to prevent other parts of the team from making changes that will harm the narrative. Try to find a way to help them make the change they need, but in a way that does not damage the narrative.
- Job titles and org charts. It can be easy to get misled by someone's title, or where they live on an org chart. Try to pay attention to the quality of their feedback, and how invested they are in the game. Of course, anyone that wants to give you feedback should be open to feedback from you.

22 Addenda

There are a few discussion topics that do not fit neatly in our section-and-chapter structure, so we have added them here.

ARTIFICIAL INTELLIGENCE

We would be remiss if we did not discuss artificial intelligence (AI) and its current and future impact on storytelling. However, there is not too much to be said because AI is still in its infancy, and there are many ways it could go from here.

AI TODAY

We've discussed the difference between Love, Hate, and Like. Like is the bland, tepid feeling that doesn't offend anyone, but also does not really appeal to anyone.

That's where AI is today, creatively. You can think of a Large Language Model (LLM) AI as an averaging machine. It doesn't create anything new, but it can take in huge swaths of data and create something like an average.

You can ask a LLM AI to create a Shakespearean Sonnet, and it might give you something that seems appealing. But you will have trouble remembering that Sonnet tomorrow, whereas an original Sonnet you read years ago may stick with you. It may also have been terrible and forgettable; human creative endeavors are wildly uneven. But each has the potential to also be great.

AI has a higher floor than human work. That is to say, at its worst, it's still better than the worst work a human can turn out. But at its very highest quality level, AI work is not even close to what a human can achieve. And in its current LLM incarnation, it has no path to reach human levels of greatness.

It looks something like this:

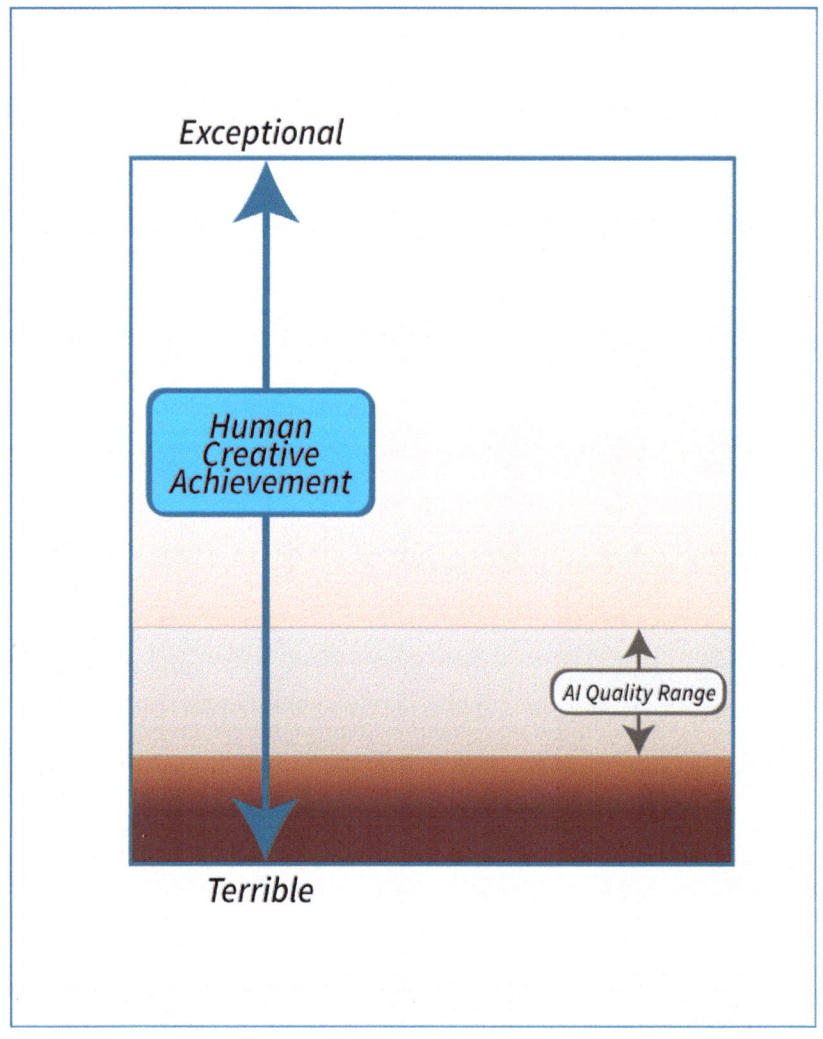

In the case where we asked it to create a Shakespearean Sonnet, we narrowed the field of what is being averaged, so that rather than using all human poetry, the AI used Shakespeare's sonnets. But it still created an average.

The Practical Result

With this approach, AI is able to create inoffensive, not-bad, forgettable work. As a narrative developer, you have the potential to create far better stories and characters. But as is true in any capitalist system, you must always be mindful that you are competing against the lowest bidder. Studios inevitably see AI as a huge time- and money-saving device.

You can't be cheaper or faster than AI, so you will have to be better than it can ever be.

Ethics Concerns

AI has no concept of intellectual property. The companies that make different AI platforms certainly do, but if any human creative work is available as digital data, it will be swept up into the vacuum cleaner of every AI platform out there. Including any work of yours on the internet!

Therefore, you must be careful when using AI, from both a legal and ethical standpoint. You wouldn't put your name on someone else's work, but if you use AI, you are very likely building upon the work of others. We all learn from our creative heroes, so being influenced by another's work is understandable and okay. But you must define the line in your own mind between inspiration and copying.

In an earlier section, we talked about how your work is not derivative when you are inspired by the works of others, because you take that inspiration and mix in your own tastes and choices, making something unique. AI does not do that, but it merely copies.

THE FUTURE

The AI models we are familiar with have the severe limitation that they cannot create anything new. Given a large enough data set, they can become better and better at disguising the sources that they are averaging, and so appear original. But they are not.

However, we are not technology futurists, and have no idea if there are other models or paradigms that are being developed elsewhere that could lead to different outcomes. We are not predicting the future of AI.

You will have to accept a hard truth about the future of AI: it is here to stay. You cannot unring a bell, and humanity has created AI, and will continue to develop it. Ignoring it or fighting against it is pointless. If you were a scribe when the printing press was invented, you would have many opinions about the mechanization of your craft, but none of those opinions was going to make printing presses be uninvented.

So the only option left to you is to try and understand AI as well as you can. For now, you still have a choice about whether or not to use it, although that may change in the future. But if you do use it, you have an obligation to use it in the most ethical, pro-human way possible.

EXAMPLE DOCUMENTS

There are certain kinds of documents that are commonly created in the course of making a game. This is another area where it is difficult to provide guidance because every team, studio, or project uses different formats and includes different content.

As a narrative developer, one of your most important and common tasks is getting the rest of the team on board with your plans. If you or the narrative team want something presented a certain way in the game, you'll need to get artists, designers, QA analysts, and many others onboard with your vision.

This is not a question of authority. Perhaps the art director makes the final decisions, or perhaps the executive producer has granted you the power to make the final call on this concept. Regardless, your idea won't turn out the way you'd hoped if the other professionals involved are just trying to realize your vision without a deeper understanding.

You must find a way to convey everything important in a simple, direct format. Hopefully, there're also ideas in that format which will excite your teammates. But the bare minimum is clear and direct.

Two of the most common document types are the character one pager, and the zone or region one pager.

ONE PAGERS

Many types of narrative documentation in games must be limited to one page. Most of your colleagues will not read anything long or laborious. We are generalizing here, but it is a safe bet that a meticulous, thoughtful 10-page biography of your character will go unread.

Limiting yourself to one page is a promise to your teammates: you're not going to waste their time. You've thought about what you want to say and you're going to say it in the most concise way possible. Every word is necessary.

There are a number of reasons your teammates will refuse to read anything long. They are busy with their own tasks and are just looking for the most relevant information that will inform their work.

Many, particularly artists, do not absorb information the same way you do. They can look at a painting and gather hundreds of cogent data points, while you'd just look at it and say "cool." In the same manner, your detailed document doesn't convey much to them.

Finally, many of your teammates have been burned by other narrative folks in the past. These other narrative developers demanded that everyone take the time to read their extensive documents, only for the documents to be self-indulgent, bloated works with little real value, which were soon abandoned in any case. You may be innocent of these crimes, but you are still dealing with the fallout of them.

Working in a one-page format is also a great restriction to put on yourself. If you need to cut something to make your overview fit on one page, you'll naturally find the least important thing to cut. In narrative documentation, just as in most storytelling, limitations make you better.

You will often be asked to create documents like this. Again, the specifics of format and content will vary by team, so trust your lead's guidance over what you see here. But it is still useful to understand the main purposes of such documents.

One Pager Style

It should go without saying, yet it somehow does need to be said, that the only style consideration for documentation is clear and concise. This is not the place to show off your clever turn of phrase or power-similes. Just say the thing in the tightest, clearest, most unambiguous way possible.

THE CHARACTER ONE PAGER

Here is a sample character one pager:

Uncle Fimbul

Class: Ice Conjurer

Keywords: Warm, Talkative, Learned, Optimistic, Avuncular, People-pleaser, Casual, Homicidal.

Attitude: Accommodating and friendly, until he needs to kill you.

Overview: Despite his harsh childhood, Fimbul displays an unshakable friendliness and optimism. He's genuinely interested in those around him. Yet all of that can fall away instantly if needed, and he will kill anyone if he believes it is necessary. Yet his upbeat manner will remain. It's never personal with Fimbul. Just the rules.
One of the most powerful ice mages in the Known Lands.

Biography: A foundling, Fimbul was raised by the Order of the Wastes at the bottom of the world. The harsh ice mages of the Order gave him a childhood marked by beatings and a perpetual state of cold and hunger.

When Fimbul reached adulthood, the Order sent him out to explore the world, to gather knowledge and complete missions. In the meantime, he is free to wander and do as he pleases. He quickly made friends everywhere. At first, he got into trouble because he would casually kill when it seemed convenient. But over time he learned that you are not supposed to do that, so instead he seeks other ways to resolve conflict and only engages in murder when necessary. If he had his way, he'd be friends with everyone.

Lines:

Hey, look at you! Need anything? I'm Uncle Fimbul, by the by!

A round for the house!

If you need someone to talk to, I'm always here.

The Order has spoken. Sorry! Oops, sorry!

Battle cry: The Ice take your heart!

Character One Pager Review

You'll want to start with clear categories of text; don't just start writing.

If the character's class is defined, list that. Or if they have a role, such as "Capital city merchant," you can put that. Basically, any information that will ground this character for the team, so they understand how, why, and where they will appear in the game, is useful.

Next, keywords are incredibly useful. You don't need to explain them, just share what they are. These words should capture something about the character, and it is perfectly fine if they contradict each other. Many colleagues are far less concerned with the "why" than you as a narrative person are. They just care more about the "what." "Oh, she's a jerk? But also a fiercely loyal friend? Got it!"

In fact, some of your colleagues will stop reading at the keywords, so make sure they'll have already learned the most important stuff!

Next, include some character art. If the concept team has created a character design, use that. If there's a 3D model, use that. If there is no art done at all yet, you can find something on the internet to use temporarily. It's important to have some kind of visual accompaniment. Let the art team know that this is just your attempt at capturing something about the character, but that they should bring their own skills and judgment to bear in creating the character's look.

Very important note: If you do download an image from the internet, make sure everyone knows this is for internal use only, just a temporary placeholder. The art must never find its way into the game, or it could get your company, and you, in a great deal of trouble.

The next section is attitude. This is most useful for the concept team and the animators. As with so much documentation, the key here is to tell, 'don't show.' You don't have the space to be clever; just tell us directly what the character's attitude is.

Next is the overview. A brief one or two paragraph block of text where you tell us what is most important about this character. As you can see from the example, some biography might creep into this section, but most of it can be saved for the next. Decide what the most important thing to know about this character is, and share that. If there are some contradictions in the keywords that readers might be wondering about, this is where you can elaborate on why this character is described as both "kind" and "mean."

The next section is the biography. Many narrative people think this is the most relevant part of a character, but as you can see from this format, it is not. And some of your colleagues will skip this part. Make it short, snappy, and as telling as you can.

Finally, you can include a few lines of dialogue, as this helps some teammates better imagine the character. As you can see from the example, these lines are not shippable. As you develop the character further, you'll create much more nuanced and flavorful dialogue for them. The purpose here is just to help colleagues imagine the character speaking.

ZONE ONE PAGER

Just as with the character one pager, you must sometimes convey the most important information about a zone or region of the game in very few words. All the rules about not wasting your colleague's time apply here just as well.

Thicket of the Nagala

Theme: Forest primeval. Wild, untamed, and overgrown.

Keywords: Ancient, Overgrown, Dark, Mysterious, Dangerous, Alien.

Biome: Northern European Old-growth forests. Coniferous and deciduous trees.

Features: Massive Lake in the center of the forest, with impenetrable mountains to the southwest, and water on all sides. Red Basilisks roam the northeastern part of the forest, and many of the trees in that region are dead or dying, but the cause is unknown. An ancient, ruined castle of mysterious origin lies in the northwest.

Vibe: Ancient trees tower above, with a thick canopy that keeps the forest in a perpetual state of twilight. The canopy keeps new growth from surviving, and recent fires have burned away most of the brush, leaving the forest floor clear. Trees show scars of past fires, and some fallen trees cross the  ground, covered in moss. The forest is creepy, and there always appears to be motion out of the corner of one's eye. Sound travels easily, creating a chilling hum of animal activity. Occasionally, the forest falls into total silence, and that is scariest of all.

Enemy Types: Red Basilisks, Bears, Wolves, Forest Trolls, Goblin Tribes, Forest Spirits, and Boss: Heart of the Forest.

Settlements: None. The player may encounter Charcoaler Camps, but these are nomadic, maddened people who will warn the player not to go deeper.The ancient castle ruins are deserted.

Overview: The oldest forest on the continent, it has defied all attempts to exploit or settle it. Several times through the centuries, large parties of humans have entered the forest or attempted to build settlements on its outskirts. All disappeared mysteriously. The forest is under the protection of an entity called Heart of the Forest (temp name) that can control all the flora and fauna to coordinate attacks against intruders.

However, the Heart of the Forest is dying, and there may be an opportunity to either kill it, or save it, with very different outcomes.

Zone One Pager Review

You'll notice that the basic format of the zone one pager is similar to the character one pager. It's small sections of text broken up by category. As before, everything is on-topic and to-the-point.

However, the categories are different, and for good reason. A character's description leans heavily on who they are in the world, and what they are likely to do. A region's description is more focused on how the place feels, and the sorts of things that would or would not happen here.

The first category is theme, although in some cases you'd want to start with terrain type. In this example, we don't need to, because the theme is Forest Primeval, which tells us the terrain type.

The Definitive Game Narrative Guide

As with characters, keywords are a vital and direct thing to convey.

Biome is really a comparison to familiar environments on earth, so that the concept team can go looking for reference.

Features list the most prominent landmarks in the region. Each of these may inspire teammates to have new ideas for the area. Unless there is a very good reason to stick to your initial ideas, be open to changes suggested by your teammates. An environment artist or level designer will think about regions in a different way than you do, and that's valuable.

Enemy Types is a straightforward category: what sorts of enemies will the player face here?

Settlements is also straightforward: are there cities? Towns? Any human-made structures or population centers?

Overview: Coming this late in the document, the overview is really a chance to tie all the things listed earlier together into one coherent package.

What about Wikis?

Wikis are simultaneously a great and terrible idea.

Pros:

Concise and On-Topic. With the ability to hyperlink, you can make each entry on-point. If you bring up another concept in your description, you don't need to briefly explain it—just hyperlink to it and get back to the topic at hand.

One-Stop Shopping. You can link the team to the wiki and tell them that all their questions will be answered here, and they are expected to know the contents of the wiki. While you should encourage teammates to come to the narrative team with questions, as opposed to just doing whatever, it's also acceptable to ask your colleagues to review short, concise documentation. Since the wiki experience is self-directed, they can poke around and follow whatever thread interests them.

Cons:

Maintenance. The moment you finish the wiki, it will be out-of-date. Narrative and world building change quickly. Having built it, you will now need to devote at least a few hours a week to updating it and keeping it relevant … for the rest of the project.

Bad Info. Even if you update the wiki, it will likely end up with out-of-date information on it. Bad information is worse than no information. If someone looks up a concept on the wiki and begins creating work based on that, only to later find out that the information was not correct, the entire team will refuse to use the wiki ever again. We have seen teams that do not use their wiki because they don't know if they can trust it.

Conclusion about Wikis

Wikis are useful for mature IPs with several released games. Any information about released content is pretty safe. But any entries about concepts that are still in development are too volatile.

Use the wiki to help the rest of the team get up to speed on what has come before. Documentation, update meetings, and lots of one-on-one interactions are the best way to handle a story and world that are still in motion.

GLOSSARY

General Game Development Terms

Agile Development: An iterative, flexible approach to development, focused on short sprints to achieve specific goals. There are a lot of opinions out there about what specifically makes something agile, and we are not going to wade into that, so we'll stop here.

Build: When all of the assets in development are committed and combined into a playable package, that is called a build. For most of development, builds are unstable and buggy, since new assets are being added every day.

Developer: An individual who works directly making a game. For example, a texture artist is a developer, while a marketing executive is not.

Development Studio: A game studio that works directly on a game. This is in contrast to a publisher, which provides a number of services that are tied to the game but do not directly go into the game.

Flat Structure: A company that does not have levels. Instead, everyone works according to their passion and expertise. In our experience, no company is truly flat. Instead, it just means the hierarchy is obscured but still present.

Found Work: Games are a young medium, and with the pace of technological change, every game involves some reinvention of the wheel. A byproduct of this is that in any schedule there will be "found work," meaning tasks or complications that arise and cause delays in the delivery of work. Narrative tends to have more found work than many other disciplines.

Franchise: A gameworld that exists in multiple instances. It could be a game with one or many sequels, or a game that also has a novelization or webcomic. If there is a persistent universe that stretches across multiple titles, platforms, and products, then it is a franchise.

Game Engine: A software package that interprets all of the input from the dev team and outputs a playable build. The foundation of the engine is displaying graphics and setting the frame rate. When a game looks outdated, it is likely because the team was using an older engine.

IC: Individual Contributor. This is a way to describe a developer that focuses on their output. Leads and directors manage groups of people and are responsible for entire features, team coordination, etc. Producers are likewise responsible for communication and scheduling. An IC can be any level from associate to principal, so the label doesn't indicate anything about their seniority or experience. It simply means that their primary responsibility is to produce the work for their discipline. If they are a designer, they create designs, get them approved, and put them in the build. If they are a modeler, they work from approved concept art to create a 3D model and perhaps coordinate with the rigging department.

IP: Intellectual Property. Section 6 of this book delivers a detailed explanation of what IP means. It is anything that is not physical, but is still owned. A logo, computer code, a musical score, a character, a storyline, are all IP. In the games industry it generally refers to the parts of the world, story, and characters that persist across multiple titles. It is used interchangeably with the term "Franchise."

NPC: A Nonplayer Character.

PC: The Player Character.

Pods: A multidisciplinary group assembled to explore or develop something over the long term. For example, a character artist, designer, narrative designer, and programmer might be put into a pod to explore a future title, start thinking about an expansion, or even just develop a new zone in a game. Everyone in the pod likely has duties outside the pod as well. Differs from "Strike Teams" in that strike teams are formed for a specific, targeted goal and dissolve when that goal is achieved.

Publisher: A bigger company that provides a wide range of support for a game. It includes marketing and public relations, legal services, distribution (both physical and electronic), platform services, web hosting services, and more. Many publishers own the IP and games they publish. Others have a contract with independent game development studios. The latter case has become rare in recent years.

RTS: Real-Time Strategy.

Sprint: A short period of time that different disciplines within a game team use to accomplish a dedicated set of goals that work toward building the game as a whole.

Strike Team: This term changes at different studios, but the most general definition is a group of subject matter experts from different disciplines who are assembled temporarily to achieve a specific goal. A strike team might be put together to deliver a specific feature or critique a part of the game. When the goal is accomplished, the strike team dissolves. This differs from "Pods" in that pods are a multidisciplinary group put together to explore or develop something over the long term.

Timebox: The practice of containing a series of tasks inside firm timelines. "We need three new buttons, and we've timeboxed the task to be one day." This sounds like a basic description of deadlines in general, but many deadlines are elastic in games due to the amount of found work. Timebox strongly implies that there is no elasticity.

Waterfall Development: A linear production process that is very close to the way humans think. First, step A. Then, step B. In a complex development cycle, which games always are, it may cascade outward, so that A leads to B and C. And B leads to D, E, and F. But it is still a linear process with one stage's origin point coming at the end of another.

Voice Over Glossary
The Voice Over process has many different terms and it's a good idea to be familiar with them.

Actor: The talent who comes in and reads the dialogue lines. They must be able to quickly inhabit the character from very few context clues, be consistent, have strong breath control, microphone discipline, and be very focused and ready to perform for up to four hours.

Alt: When the director makes a select, but thinks that another line may have some value and wants that line to also go through post-production, they can ask to have it as an alt. This should not be overused, as it defeats the purpose of selects. But occasionally, it is a good way to try something new and different.

Bottom: The end of a line. While "end" is a loosely defined concept, you and the engineer will always know what it means in context. If the director says, "Bring it down at the bottom of the line," this means to bring it down at the end.

Director: The person responsible for running the session. Schedule, pace, and tone all come from the director. The director is also responsible for helping the actor get the correct read and the engineer to get all the audio files the way the director wants. The single individual who is ultimately responsible for the quality of the session.

Engineer: The skilled professional who controls the recording equipment during the voice over session. They must be highly technical, creatively talented, and have fast fingers.

Exertions/Efforts: The sounds a character makes when they are hit, hurt, or do something with effort. The grunt they make when they jump or land, for example.

Frankenstein: Engineers can usually cut parts of two different reads together. So the director might say, "Can I have the top of read A with the bottom of read B?"

and the engineer will stitch them together seamlessly. "Top" means the beginning of the line and "bottom" means the end of the line. This process is also sometimes called "Stitching Together."

Green Apple: If an actor has a lot of saliva in their mouth, it will make small clicking sounds, which a good microphone will pick up. A few bites of a green apple will help tighten up the vocal chords and salivary glands.

Off-Mic: Refers to when an actor has turned their head, or moved while gesturing, and their voice is no longer properly captured by the microphone, resulting in lower or inconsistent sound quality.

On-Mic: Speaking into the microphone, or near enough to it that it sounds good.

Pre-Life: The thing some actors say before a line. For example, if the line is "I can't believe it!" and the actor says "Holy shit! I can't believe it!" the "holy shit" is pre-life. By default, expect that the engineer will edit this out. If you want to keep the pre-life, specifically ask the engineer to keep it. (Occasionally, if unsure, the engineer will ask—but 90% of the time, they'll just cut it.) This also applies to vocalizations. If the actor adds a "Haha" or "Whoa!" to the top of the line, assume it will be cut unless you ask to keep it. (90% of the time, you'll want to cut it.)

Projection: This is not quite volume. It's like a weird combination of volume and energy. You'll know it as soon as you hear an actor do a second read with "more projection" or "less projection." For multiplayer PvP games, projection is incredibly important to keep in mind.

Read: When the actor says the line one time, that is a read. An actor may do one set of three reads. Each read should offer something different from the others. It's useful to be able to label the action so that the director can say something like "Give me two more reads."

Read-In: When the director reads the line that comes before the actors line, just before the actor reads the line. This conveys the momentum or feel of the moment in which the character says the line.

Redirect: After the actor has done a read of a line, or a set of reads, the director either makes the select or redirects. This means asking the actor to read the line again, with some new information or guidance from the director.

Run/Run Lines: When the actor "runs" lines, they read them all in sequence, without stopping to get direction or take numbers. Do this when you want the lines to build on each other and gain momentum, or if it will help the actor's performance.

Select: When an actor does multiple reads of a line, the director will select one to be saved. In reality, all the reads will be saved in memory, but it would be time-consuming and costly to do post-production on the entire session, so the director calls out one select for each line. Later, if that select doesn't work as well as hoped, the team can go back to the session recording and find another read to use.

Stitch Together: Engineers can usually cut parts of two different reads together. So the director might say, "Can I have the top of read A with the bottom of read B?" and the engineer will stitch them together seamlessly. "Top" means the beginning of the line and "bottom" means the end of the line. This process is also sometimes called "Frankensteining."

Take: When the engineer begins to record and then stops, everything that was recorded during that period is all part of one take. In the digital age, engineers record the entire session, but it is still useful to break it up into takes as a way to categorize and manage the vast amount of content in a single session.

Throat Coat: A type of tea that is good to have on-hand when the actor is recording. If their throat begins to hurt, a cup of this tea will help.

Top: The beginning of a line. While "beginning" is a loosely defined concept, you and the engineer will always know what it means in context. If the director says "Go big at the top of the line," this means to go big at the start of the line.

There are many other more amorphous terms in Voice Over, like "bring it down," "flatten it out," etc. But these are contextual, so you'll have to pay attention to how they are used.

CONCLUSION

We hope this book has been useful. As you develop your skill and talent, you may find that you disagree with some of the lessons we've discussed here. This is perfectly normal—we each develop our own rules and best practices.

The fundamentals remain the same, but how you use them will vary with each person. That's what makes every narrative developer special in their own unique way.

Index